COYOTE NATION

WORLDS Of DESIRE
THE CHICAGO SERIES ON SEXUALITY, GENDER, AND CULTURE
A Series Edited by Gilbert Herdt

Also in the series:

COYOTE NATION

SEXUALITY, RACE, AND
CONQUEST IN MODERNIZING
NEW MEXICO

1880–1920

PABLO MITCHELL

THE UNIVERSITY OF CHICAGO PRESS
Chicago & London

PABLO MITCHELL is an assistant professor of history at Oberlin College.

The University of Chicago Press, Chicago 60637
The University of Chicago Press, Ltd., London
© 2005 by The University of Chicago
All rights reserved. Published 2005
Printed in the United States of America

14 13 12 11 10 09 08 07 06 05   1 2 3 4 5

ISBN: 0-226-53242-9 (cloth)
ISBN: 0-226-53243-7 (paper)

Library of Congress Cataloging-in-Publication Data

Mitchell, Pablo.
    Coyote nation : sexuality, race, and conquest in modernizing New Mexico, 1880–1920 /
    Pablo Mitchell.
        p. cm. — (Worlds of desire)
    Includes bibliographical references and index.
    ISBN 0-226-53242-9 (alk. paper) — ISBN 0-226-53243-7 (pbk. : alk. paper)
    1. New Mexico—Race relations. 2. New Mexico—Social conditions—19th century.
    3. New Mexico—Social conditions—20th century. 4. Racism—New Mexico—History.
    5. Imperialism—Social aspects—New Mexico—History. 6. Body, Human—Social
    aspects—New Mexico—History. 7. Mind and body—New Mexico—History.
    8. Sex—Social aspects—New Mexico—History. 9. Sex customs—New
    Mexico—History. I. Title. II. Series.
    F805.A1M58 2004
    978.9'04—dc22

                                                        2004007885

⊗ The paper used in this publication meets the minimum requirements
of the American National Standard for Information Sciences—Permanence
of Paper for Printed Library Materials, ANSI z39.48–1992.

TO BETH AND TO BEN

CONTENTS

ILLUSTRATIONS

PREFACE

A NOTE ON *COYOTES*

One of the most familiar images associated with New Mexico is the howling coyote. Dear to the heart of gallery owners and state tourism officials, the coyote wailing into the lonely night promises that newcomers will experience an adventure filled with both excitement and comfort (the coyote, after all, is only howling, not prowling, in the night).

New Mexico has a long history of coyotes who are far rangier and wilier than the reassuring tourist image would suggest. In southwestern folklore, the coyote is a trickster figure, a shifty being bent on unsettling the familiar and the known. Presently, the term is used to describe the guides who, honorably or not, smuggle clients into the United States from Mexico. Under the Spanish system of racial classification in New Mexico, a *coyote* was the child of a Spaniard and an Indian slave. This last definition was the meaning of *coyote* that I came to know when I moved to New Mexico from Michigan as a child in 1979. With an Anglo father and a Latina mother, I found in *coyote* an acknowledgment, despite its derogatory nature, of a more nuanced set of racial and ethnic identities, ones less beholden to stark racial dichotomies or based, like the "mulatto," on black/white race relations. From tricksters to smugglers to mixed bloods, *coyotes* are thus for me intimately linked to New Mexico.

A century ago New Mexico, was, like the coyote, an eccentric figure within the American nation. Commonplace, even seemingly natural notions of racial and sexual order proved too blunt and clumsy to function effectively in polyglot, plural New Mexico. Remarkable innovations followed, most notably in the increased emphasis placed on bodily comportment in determining social status. New Mexico was, and is, *coyote*-like, a troubled and troubling member of the American polity.

ACKNOWLEDGMENTS

I am delighted to be able to thank the many people and institutions who have provided such generous support to this book. This research was greatly assisted by a fellowship from the Sexuality Research Fellowship Program, under the inspired leadership of Diana di Mauro, of the Social Science Research Council, with funds provided by the Ford Foundation. I have also been the fortunate recipient of assistance from the Mellon Minority Undergraduate Fellowship Program, the Rackham Graduate School at the University of Michigan, and from Oberlin College. Sandra Jaramillo, Stan Hordes, Al Regensberg, Nancy Brown, and the staffs of the New Mexico State Records Center and Archives, the Center for Southwest Research at the University of New Mexico, and the National Archives Regional Office in Denver, Colorado, were gracious, patient, and eminently knowledgeable guides through the archives. The members of the Department of History and the Comparative American Studies Program at Oberlin College have been outstanding colleagues and friends. Likewise, the students at Oberlin College have been an inspiration to me in their intellectual drive, their political commitments, and their ferocity. I cannot think of a better place to teach.

I am eternally grateful to the following friends and colleagues who have offered so willingly of their valuable time and resources throughout this process: Ernesto Chávez, Chuck James, Kevin Murphy, Celine Parrenas, Susana Peña, and Johanna Schoen; in Albuquerque, John Herron, Elizabeth Jameson, David Simmons, Marian Simmons, and Jane Slaughter; in Ann Arbor, Tomás Almaguer, Barbara Berglund, Adrian Burgos, Dorothy Marschke, April Mayes, Kate Mazur, John McKiernan-González, Ed Miller, Natalia Molina, Estévan Rael-Gálvez, Tom Romero, David Salmanson, and David Scobey; in Pittsburgh, Randy Keech, Aarti Malik,

Tom Shuttlesworth, and Kate Trapp; at Oberlin College, Lisa Abend, the late Rachel Beverly, Pam Brooks, Anna Gade, Meredith Gadsby, Frances Hasso, Heather Hogan, Moon-Ho Jung, Peter Kalliney, David Kamitsuka, Clayton Koppes, Wendy Kozol, Haipeng Li, Daryl Maeda, Isaac Miller, Charles Peterson, Rafael Reyes-Ruiz, Karen Rignall, Debbie Schildkraut, Andy Shanken, Brenda Snell, and Ellen Stroud.

I have had the great honor to work with the legendary Douglas Mitchell at the University of Chicago Press. His enthusiasm and faith in this project have been a sustaining force throughout, and I am grateful to him for his patience, good cheer, and humor. Thanks also to Timothy McGovern, Erin DeWitt, and the rest of the staff at the Press. I would also like to thank Gilbert Herdt and an anonymous reviewer of the manuscript for their deft and insightful comments.

I am indebted to a terrific set of advisers. Virginia Scharff has been unsurpassed as a teacher, an editor, a cajoler, and a friend. She welcomed me into the history profession and taught me that historians are writers and that writers are finishers. At the University of Michigan, George Sánchez was a model adviser and department chair, creating a thrilling, truly interdisciplinary intellectual environment. María Montoya, a wonderful adviser and role model, has been tireless in her support, from letters of reference to keen editorial advice to solid counsel, and is an exemplary teacher, scholar, and friend. Carroll Smith-Rosenberg has been wonderfully generous with her time and intellectual energy. Her support and enthusiasm for this project has been a source of great sustenance. Finally, for years, Ramón Gutiérrez has served as a most gracious and generous mentor. I am most appreciative of his commitment to rigorous scholarship and clear prose. His careful and diligent reading of various versions of the manuscript has led to dramatic and significant improvements.

My family and loved ones have been constant and true in a way that only a ragtag collection of transplants, migrants, easy readers, and mixed bloods can be. With love and admiration, I thank the following: Sharon Braman, the Butkevich family, the Cadavid and Parr family, Fran Cornell, the deObaldía family, the late Domingo and Ester Maria deObaldía, Julianne Gallegos, Oliver, and Estella, and the Mitchell family, especially the late Herman and Marianne Mitchell. The McLaughlin/Orr family has welcomed me into their home on countless occasions and has nourished me intellectually and otherwise for years now. Alexander McLaughlin has given me much appreciated words of encouragement and I am lucky to have him as a brother-in-law. The late Helen Garrison and Mildred Garrison have endowed this project with their love, their resilience, and their tenacity, and I am forever in their debt.

My parents, Beatriz and Philip Mitchell, have given me and this project unswerving love and support. They have offered me, through their example, the courage to take risks and the strength to resist the urges of self-absorption. They believe in justice and because of them, I do too.

My brother, Ben Mitchell, has inspired me for as long as I can remember. Over the course of countless conversations and adventures, he has been a bottomless source of wisdom, humor, outrage, good cheer, affection, and tenderness. He has infused this project with his love and spirit.

It is only on the brightest of days, in the warmest of seasons, when gloom and doom are safely tucked away, that I dare to imagine my life without Beth McLaughlin. She works harder than anyone I know, is even-tempered, easily amused (in a good way), and is a perfect combination of high-end intellect and lo-fi grit. Living with her makes me happy when skies are sunny, and gray. I'd like to go on but she says it's bad luck (she's like that), so I'll stop there and thank her for everything.

INTRODUCTION

BODIES ON BORDERS

In steps both utterly familiar and strangely new, several thousand travelers climbed off the train into the strong sun and thin air and strange accents of New Mexico between 1880 and 1920. At the railroad depot, such settlers—immigrants from Europe and Asia, African Americans from the North and South, and native American white, almost white, and never to be white—met the settled of New Mexico for the first time. Undoubtedly there was much mulling about and mutual gawking and misfired queries. Undoubtedly some Iowans saw their first Indians, and some Indians their first Iowans, and some Iowans their first Hispanos who looked like Indians but were actually Hispanos, and so on.

After days aboard the transcontinental railroad, what else did these travelers discover? What did they see? What did they smell? *How* did they smell? What prompted these travelers to unload their bags in turn-of-the-twentieth-century New Mexico? What vistas did they leave behind and what dreads and delights did they encounter upon arrival? And what of the settled in New Mexico: the Hispanos and Pueblos and Navajo and Zuni and Apache, the African Americans and Asian Americans and Anglos? What fits and starts shook *them* when the train whistle blew?

Such were the questions that emerged when the railroad arrived in 1880. New Mexicans, new and old, converged at a time and place of great upheaval. It was in New Mexico where the forces of modernity and imperialism met with a special intensity. The arrival of the railroad in New Mexico brought increased integration into national markets and an unprecedented flow of mostly Anglo immigrants to the territory from throughout the United States and Europe.[1] New Mexico's population jumped from 120,000 in 1880 to nearly 200,000 in 1900 and 360,000 in 1920.[2] While Hispano leading families scrambled to maintain their status, new elites rose to prominence in the growing towns of Albuquerque, Las Vegas, and Santa Fe. These emergent elites, mostly Anglo but with a sprinkling of Hispanos, utilized new techniques and strategies in the consolidation of power. Increasingly, the informal, mostly Hispano-Indian traditions governing interpersonal relationships, land use, and the transfer of property gave way to more formal, rationalized methods of interaction and control. This transition, actually the emergence of a modern New Mexico, appeared in countless guises, from the meticulous surveying and distribution of the land and legal realms, to the explicit regulation of personal behavior through science and medicine, mass consumer culture, gender patterns, and education.

The American railroad and railroad systems also brought together Indian, Hispano, and Anglo peoples for the first time in a modern and modernizing setting. Contemporary accounts echo this unprecedented convergence in New Mexico. Imagine Hopi Indian Polingaysi Qoya-wayma's first encounter with a railroad in the early twentieth century. "Trains rumbled and screeched along the rails that bisected the town," she remembered, "accompanied by a clickety-clacking sound, unfamiliar yet interesting." Charles Brown recalled that the train ride into Rincon, in northern New Mexico, inspired flights of "myth and folklore," with images of "tall, spare crosses" and the "ruins of an old church." Ernest Peixotto writes of his first visit to Albuquerque, "The Isleta women sit by the station, and are familiar figures to all transcontinental travelers. And, indeed, they make a brilliant group against the well-planned background of the great depot, whose long procession of grey arcades with their pottery roofs and bell-towers tell vividly against the turquoise sky."[3]

Like Brown and Peixotto, Americans throughout the period disembarked in newly conquered lands in the nineteenth and early twentieth centuries. After all, the most precious cargo upon the trains heading westward were the soldiers and military personnel who also entered the West aboard the nation's railways. Between 1848 and 1898, American military victories led to the annexation of 1,274,187 square miles of territory. The United States ballooned in size, from 2,463,603 square miles to 3,737,790 square miles.[4] In 1848, in the aftermath of the Mexican-American War, the United States annexed 530,000 square miles of Mexican land, territory that would eventually become the states of California, Arizona, Nevada, Utah, New Mexico, and part of Colorado. After 1848, Americans flooded into the formerly Mexican land. In the next half century, the region was steadily incorporated into developing U.S. political, economic, and legal systems.

Between 1850 and 1900, those of Mexican origin (either born in Mexico or American born of Mexican descent) suffered great losses: in land, in wealth, in status, in political power, even in percentage of the population. By one estimate, in 1900 the Mexican-origin population in California, which had been predominant in the state prior to the Mexican-American War, was 48,579, or 3.2 percent of the state's population. Texas was similar, with Mexican-origin peoples accounting for 198,841, or about 6.5 percent of the total state population. Native Americans throughout the West suffered similar losses. In California the devastation was especially horrific as the Indian population plummeted from approximately 150,000 in 1845 to 16,000 in 1880. By 1910 over 60 percent of the original indigenous tribes had disappeared.[5]

Unkempt and volatile, the American railroad was none other than the ultimate agent of American modernity and imperialism. Modernity is, at its most basic, a collapsing of time and space into new sets of measurable relationships. Modernity differs from earlier periods in several important respects. In a major break from previous eras, the time required to manufacture a broad array of products was dramatically shortened. To take one of a great many available examples, a new cigarette-making machine in the 1880s produced seven thousand cigarettes per hour. Human workers could at the time produce far less, only three thousand cigarettes in a full day. The time required to "disassemble" products was similarly slashed, as meat producers developed new, far more efficient production lines devoted to the processing and packaging of goods. According to one account, the annual production of goods jumped by $2 billon in 1865 to $13 billion in 1900 as the United States came to lead the world in productivity. In modernity, spatial divides proved as outdated as previous notions of time. With the railroad, the local became national, with newly elaborate timetables, schedules, and maps that brought Americans within hours and days rather than weeks and months of each other. Railroads also carried to new lands a stunning variety of consumer goods. Stoves, pianos, watches, and fashionable clothing poured into region after region as railroads incorporated broad swaths of the country into an expanding national market.[6]

In this modern eclipsing of time and space, new relationships emerged between individuals, communities, and institutions. At the forefront were changing gender roles and transforming relationships between men and women, husbands and wives. Suffrage movements, increasing educational opportunities for young women, and widespread female criticism of male behavior ranging from alcohol consumption to sexual promiscuity to political corruption led to new "modern" forms of appropriate femininity and masculinity. New relationships between professionals also emerged as professional organizations of lawyers, doctors, and university professors—complete with bylaws, licensing, and standards of conduct—formed in the modern era. These new affiliations, often national and regional, replaced older local relationships between townspeople. A lawyer from Albany increasingly had more in common with attorneys in Albuquerque than with fellow Albanyites. New modern measurement techniques, based on developing sciences, sought to categorize and classify many of these relationships and were especially noticeable in the new racial and sexual sciences that created elaborate scientific hierarchies of racial groups and sexual types.

The rise of modernity was not alone in transforming the American nation. From the end of the Mexican-American War in 1848 to the aftermath of the Spanish-American War in 1898 (where the United States seized the previously Spanish colonies of Puerto Rico, Cuba, Guam, and the Philippines), Americans followed military conquest with the establishment of U.S. political and economic institutions. While scholars have traditionally reserved the term "imperialism"—the attempted extension of rule or influence by one government, nation, or society over another—to describe post-1898 American intervention in foreign countries, the notion, as I will demonstrate in the following chapters, applies to the American Southwest as well. So, too, is colonialism, the always-contested political and economic control over an area by an occupying force, an apt description of the American domination of both New Mexico and Cuba, Puerto Rico, and the Philippines.

Indeed, the similarities between New Mexico and other colonial regimes like Puerto Rico are striking. Native New Mexicans proved especially resilient in the face of Anglo incursions. In 1900 New Mexicans of Mexican origin constituted nearly 50 percent of the population (93,356 of 195,310).[7] Moreover, despite the substantial influx of Anglo-Americans, Hispanos continued to hold considerable political power, wealth, and status, and Hispano culture still persisted, if not flourished, in New Mexico as a great many New Mexicans continued to speak Spanish and identify proudly with their Hispano heritage. Indians (Pueblo, Navajo, Ute, and Apache) similarly retained relative power and numbers in New Mexico. More than fifteen thousand Indians lived in New Mexico in 1880, comprising almost 10 percent of the population. By 1920 almost twenty thousand lived in the state. In light of such imposing demographics, the establishment of racial order in New Mexico presented challenges that American colonizers in Puerto Rico and throughout imperial America would have found most familiar. As the subsequent chapters will make clear, the roots of American imperialism are deep in New Mexico.[8]

In this exceptional land, where modernity and imperialism met in an unprecedented manner, Anglo newcomers faced a peculiar dilemma. In order to achieve statehood and the rights of full citizenship (until 1912, when New Mexico became a state, even the most elite Anglo man in New Mexico, no matter the purity of his lineage or the excellence of his ability, was barred from voting for president or running for governor), Anglos would have to prove to the rest of the country that New Mexico was worthy of full membership in the American political system. Principally, Anglos would have to demonstrate that social order in New Mexico had been established, and that New Mexicans, especially Hispanos and Indians, could be transformed into Americans. This, of course, was a demanding task, turning what a great many outside New Mexico considered "mongrel land" into a true American state. I will argue that central to this project of re-creating New Mexico's social structure, and transforming New Mexicans into Americans, was the human body. As I will demonstrate, the human body's entrances and exits, protrusions and blemishes, incapacities, shames, triumphs, failures, and desires together constituted an overlooked, yet absolutely critical, component of the creation of American colonial order in New Mexico.

Bodily comportment was an integral piece of Anglo efforts to claim that Indians and Hispanos were socially inferior and not white. This racialization process (which I will describe more precisely later in the chapter) proceeded along many fronts. In chapters 2 and 3, I will concentrate on two sites of particular interest, U.S. Indian schools and trials for sexual assault, where the racially different status of Indians and Hispanos was articulated. Wealthy Hispanos, like colonial elites throughout the world, however, posed a significant challenge to this racialization project. As chapters 4 and 5 will explain, the continuing political and economic power of Hispanos forced Anglos to abandon wholesale denunciations of "native" New Mexicans and focus instead on bodily comportment as an index of social status. To claim whiteness, however, Anglos in New Mexico could not simply racialize Indians and Hispanos as nonwhite; they would have to assert their own whiteness as well, in effect racialize themselves as white. Chapters 6 and 7 will describe precisely this process of the creation of whiteness, focusing on the bodily comportment of Anglos in medicine and consumer space.

Before elaborating on my argument, two terms deserve some clarification: whiteness and citizenship. Far more than light skin or blue eyes, whiteness is the historically specific melding of physical characteristics (which could include, based on historical context, hair length, body composition—as in fatness or skinniness—skin tone and texture, volume and quality of speech, practices of consumption of food and liquid, and elimination, as well as light skin) with economic and political power.

David Roediger and George Lipsitz have described the economic benefits accruing to those managing to claim whiteness. The "cash value" (Lipsitz) or "wages" (Roediger) of whiteness vary based on historical context, but are nonetheless substantial. The political power of whiteness similarly shifts depending on context, but generally equates the physical characteristics of being "white" with voting rights, civic leadership, and legal protections.[9]

While citizenship is similarly complicated, it is, at its base, about belonging. National citizenship designates citizens in a political sense, as those individuals who have rights, like voting, and obligations, like jury duty or military service. Other definitions of citizenship, beyond a strictly legalistic interpretation, are broader, encompassing a more full membership in a society. This understanding of citizenship can vary based on the setting and historical context, but at its core views citizens as those members of a society who command respectful and dignified treatment in the most basic aspects of their lives: choice of occupation, residence, choice of spouse or sexual partner, style of noncoercive personal pleasure. Those with power and authority in certain settings—like police officers, school principals, government officials, store clerks, and librarians—treat such individuals, such citizens, with care, rather than suspicion and alarm. Citizenship, according to this broader understanding, describes those individuals that society values and protects. Citizenship, to offer some specific examples, includes those who control material resources; whose ideas receive attention and respect; who walk the streets and enter businesses without special scrutiny; whose economic and political activities find favor in the courts, banks, and newspapers; whose births, marriages, and deaths are reported in the press; whose ailments find speedy and dignified treatment; whose children's peccadilloes amuse rather than enrage the judiciary; whose labor is acknowledged and well rewarded; whose tragedies are made not the stuff of jokes, but of sympathy; whose sex lives remain discreetly hidden. In this book, I will rely upon this latter, broader definition of citizenship.

In the national context, problems of whiteness and citizenship have plagued America from the colonial era to the present, but achieved a special intensity in the late nineteenth century as the aftermath of the Civil War coincided with the advent of widespread immigration from Europe. Among its many consequences, the end of Reconstruction in America ultimately fortified white supremacy in both the North and the South. As state after state in the 1880s and 1890s actively denied African Americans basic rights as citizens, the link between whiteness and American citizenship achieved newfound clarity and vigor. At the same time, in the industrial North especially, widespread European immigration—by

Jews, Italians, and Poles, by the white and off-white—encouraged new questions about whiteness and white people. Who could rightfully claim to be white—and thus rightfully claim to be American? Who could and should make no such claims? Such rattling within and around whiteness, so familiar to historians of the urban North and Midwest, of New York and Philadelphia and Chicago, often tightened around questions of nativity. Though perhaps appearing "white," those born elsewhere and immigrating to the United States found their claims to full citizenship and inclusion repeatedly challenged. The American Northeast proved especially volatile around questions of nativity. While the U.S. foreign-born population between 1880 and 1920 remained at between 13 and 14 percent, in the Northeast the percentage hovered between 20 and 25 percent over the same period.[10] European immigrants demanded that the link between whiteness and American-ness, so recently fortified by Jim Crow laws and the disenfranchisement of African Americans, be reconstructed yet again.[11]

That the transformations vexing broader America (modernity, imperialism, immigration, dilemmas of whiteness and citizenship) would prove especially unsettling in New Mexico was due in large measure to New Mexico's exceptional history and demography. Viewed broadly, the history of New Mexico from about 1600 to the present is marked by three periods—Spanish, Mexican, and American.[12] The Spanish period began in earnest in 1593 with the entrance into territory occupied by a range of Indian communities, most of them Pueblo Indians, of a group of Spanish soldiers and settlers. The first of two phases of the Spanish colonization of New Mexico—described by one historian as the "Franciscan century," which focused on conversion of Pueblos to Christianity under the direction of Franciscan missionaries—began late in the sixteenth century. This phase ended with the Pueblo Revolt in 1680, a triumph of Indian resistance that drove the Spanish almost entirely out of New Mexico for thirteen years.[13] The second phase of Spanish colonization was more secular, as civil and military officials administered the colony, and lasted over a century, from 1693 to 1821. The Mexican period in New Mexico commenced in 1821 with the independence of Mexico from Spain. The American period started less than thirty years later in 1848 with the conclusion of the Mexican-American War and has lasted to the present.

Deep-seated differences *between* Indian, Hispano, and American cultures in New Mexico prior to the arrival of the railroad in 1880 were naturally accompanied by divisions *within* each of the cultures. According to historians, settled agricultural communities, stemming from migrations from the north and west, had emerged in the Rio Grande valley, running south to north through the middle of what would become New Mexico,

1. "Colossus of Roads," from an 1882 New Mexico business directory. Notice how the railroad, military power, and imperial expansion converge on the human body. Courtesy of the Museum of New Mexico, neg. no. 67866.

by 1200. In 1600 there were about 50,000 Indians, clustered under the broad term "Pueblo Indians," living in New Mexico. This group was geographically dispersed, politically decentralized, and linguistically diverse. The bulk of the population, about 80 percent of the 50,000 Pueblos, were Eastern Pueblos who lived in more than fifty small agricultural villages, none larger than 2,000 inhabitants, most with less than 400, in the Rio Grande valley. These villages, stretching from around what is now Albuquerque in central New Mexico to the north, were politically autonomous with little in the way of broader centralized government. Six distinct languages, which one historian has described as "mutually unintelligible," further divided the Eastern Pueblos. The remaining Pueblos, the Zuni and Hopi, were located in west-central New Mexico, near present-day Gallup and Grants. These Western Pueblos, with a population of about 3,000 each, spread over several villages and were also distinct, each speaking a separate language. Small-scale agriculture predominated among both Eastern and Western Pueblos, though prowess at hunting conferred considerable social prestige. Indeed, skill at hunting was one of many markers creating internal divisions within Pueblo Indian society. Besides gender divisions—where women were charged with maintaining and reproducing, as well as literally constructing, the home, and men were responsible for external matters like protection from outside enemies—differences of age and ability were critical aspects of social inequality.[14]

Over the next 250 years, many of the Pueblo villages were abandoned during periods of drought and epidemic, but a great many survived into the nineteenth century. Some in fact, like Taos Pueblo and Picuris Pueblo, were chosen to host U.S. Indian schools (the subject of chapter 2). In addition to the settled Pueblo Indians, nomadic Indians also lived in New Mexico. While their exact number and composition are difficult to determine (Spanish census enumerators were far less meticulous with non-settled populations), it is clear that a significant Apache, Navajo, and Ute population emerged in New Mexico during the 1700s.

Like Indians, New Mexico's Hispano population in the era before the arrival of the railroad was hardly monolithic or without its own internal social divisions. Indeed, social inequality also marked life in Spanish villages. While small-scale farming dominated the economy, only a few New Mexicans owned substantial land holdings. These Spanish elites, known variously as nobility, *ricos*, or *patrones*, occupied the highest positions in New Mexico society. Economically, Spanish elites relied for their wealth on agricultural production and their considerable land holdings. Legal protections bolstered elite control, defending their rights and privileges, like the ability to bear arms and to punish harshly those of inferior status who had insulted them. Spanish law, though prohibiting slavery in general, also permitted a form of domestic servitude, where Indians captured in raids or warfare could be forced to work as servants. Still, for all their power, elites were vastly outnumbered in Spanish villages by two other groups: landed peasants and *genízaros*.[15]

Landed peasants, as the term suggests, owned small plots of land and possessed certain rights within Spanish society, but were generally unable to amass the necessary wealth or political power to attain leadership positions in Spanish villages. Compared, however, to the third major group in Spanish society, the *genízaros*, landed peasants could claim a certain standing and respectability. *Genízaros* were Indian men and women who had been captured from nomadic tribes, largely Apache, Navajo, Ute, and Comanche, and pressed into domestic servitude in Spanish households. Torn from their home communities and families, *genízaros* occupied the most subordinate and powerless positions in Spanish society. They had neither the protection of Pueblo villages, which had been relatively free of Spanish intrusion since the Pueblo Revolt of 1680, nor the racial status afforded Spanish peasants. As such, *genízaros* played an important role in the New Mexico social order. Spanish elites acquired the domestic labor (cooking, cleaning, etc.) necessary to demonstrate their privileged social status, and Spanish landed peasants, by defining themselves in opposition to the supposedly inferior and dishonorable *genízaros*, claimed respectability and a middle position within Spanish New Mexico.[16]

Besides the above differences of wealth and social status, racial classifications helped further divide the Hispano population. In 1789 one census of New Mexico recorded 10,664 Indians, 14,533 "Spanish," and 5,736 inhabitants claiming mixed ancestry. Both of the sizable populations claiming Spanish and mixed descent likely also included a large number of New Mexicans of African ancestry. A census taken in Albuquerque several decades earlier found nearly 200 families in the village. Of those, 43 had at least partial African ancestry. Historian Martha Menchaca notes that the census enumerator, Father Joseph Yrigorian, made further racial distinctions. Yrigorian, she says, "found that 36 were *mulatto* (Spanish and Black), 3 *coyote* (Indian and *mulatto*), and 4 *lobo* (Indian and Black)." Despite this racial diversity in New Mexico, Menchaca is careful to point out, "white governors and missionaries [still] ruled the colony."[17]

The arrival of the railroad in 1880 in New Mexico had irreversible consequences for the land and its diverse mix of people. For one, the railroad arrived in New Mexico during a critical transition period in American Indian history.[18] The mid- to late nineteenth century represented an especially difficult period for American Indians. Beset by continued, even accelerated, U.S. military and white settler violence (exemplified by the attacks on California Indians during the Gold Rush era of the 1850s and the 1864 Sand Creek and 1890 Wounded Knee massacres), American Indians also faced an array of new instruments of conquest. A policy of assimilation, the belief that Indians could, under proper American tutelage, be taught to be civilized, emerged as a powerful counterweight to eradication efforts. The Dawes Act, passed in 1887, provided one prong of this effort to assimilate Indians. The act, designed to encourage Indian men to become independent farmers, distributed communal Indian lands to individual Indians (and, not incidentally, offered excess land on Indian reservations to white settlers). Advocates of assimilation argued that Indian farmers and their families, endowed with private property and a sedentary agricultural lifestyle, would be well on their way toward civilization. Indian boarding schools were a second prong of this reform effort. The first Indian boarding school began in 1879 in Carlisle, Pennsylvania, and by 1902 there were twenty-five schools and over twenty thousand students at government day and boarding schools nationwide.[19]

The Dawes Act, so important elsewhere in the nation, had little effect on Pueblo Indian land ownership in New Mexico. In the seventeenth and eighteenth centuries, Spanish administrators had imperiously "given" land in New Mexico to particular Pueblo Indian communities, who of course had already occupied that land for decades, if not centuries. The United States, under the provisions of the Treaty of Guadalupe Hidalgo, which ended the Mexican-American War in 1848, pledged to recognize the land grants issued to the Pueblos. At the same time, the settled agriculture communities of the Pueblos suggested to American officials that the Pueblos were more "civilized" than other Indian communities; one official observed, in a subtle attack on Hispanos, that the Pueblo Indians were "the most law-abiding, sober, and industrious people of New Mexico." As a result, except for the Zuni and Hopi, who had been assigned reservations by the federal government in 1877 and 1882, respectively, Pueblo Indian communities were not designated as federal "reservations" subject to full government oversight and vulnerable to the type of homesteading provisions advocated by the Dawes Act. Thus, although Pueblo land rights throughout the nineteenth and early twentieth centuries were deeply contested, the Dawes Act did not have a major effect on the lives of most Pueblo Indians.[20]

The establishment of U.S. Indian boarding schools, on the other hand, as I will explain in chapter 2, had a profound impact on the Pueblos. According to U.S. Census records, the Pueblo Indian population in New Mexico in 1900 was 8,488, spread over nineteen "reservations" (Taos, Picuris, San Juan, Santa Clara, San Ildefonso, Pojoaque, Nambe, Tesuque, Cochiti, Santo Domingo, San Felipe, Santa Ana, Zia, Jemez, Sandia, Isleta, Laguna, Acoma, and Zuni) and a handful of boarding schools (Santa Fe's Saint Catharine School and Indian Industrial School and the Albuquerque Indian School). Over 90 percent (7,875) of Pueblos lived on tribal lands, the largest of which were Zuni (1,525), Laguna (1,077), Isleta (1,021), and Santo Domingo (771). The remaining 613 attended boarding schools in Albuquerque and Santa Fe. Most Pueblos, with the exception of children enrolled in boarding schools, worked as farmers on their reservations and "interacted very little" with either Hispanos or Anglos. In 1900 there were an additional 4,341 non-Pueblo Indians (defined in the U.S. Census as "Nomad Indians") living in New Mexico: 2,911 were Navajo living on the Navajo reservation (2,441) and in nearby villages (470), 819 were Jicarilla Apache, 480 Mescalero Apache, and the remainder either living in Hispano villages (38) or, like Pueblo Indians, attending boarding schools in Albuquerque and Santa Fe. Navajo, Apache, and Ute living on reservations in New Mexico primarily farmed or raised sheep.[21]

Where the 13,000 Indians in New Mexico accounted for less than 7 percent of the population in 1900, nearly half of the state (93,356 of 195,310) were "Hispanos."[22] Scholars of New Mexico, and many New Mexicans themselves, have used and continue to use "Hispano" to designate all New Mexicans of Spanish Mexican descent in the context of late-nineteenth-

and early-twentieth-century New Mexico. Despite the considerable class differences separating wealthy from poor Hispanos, discussed below, their shared cultural heritage (largely Catholic and Spanish speaking) and their comparable vulnerability to Anglo racializing projects persuade me to identify New Mexicans with Spanish surnames as Hispano unless Indian ancestry is made specific, as in census documents that enumerate an individual as "Indian" or newspaper articles that mention either Indian background or identify an individual as a resident of one of the Indian villages, like Isleta or Sandia.[23]

The class background of Hispanos is difficult to determine with great precision. It is clear that much separated wealthy Hispanos, many of whom identified with and aspired, like many Anglos, to the norms of broader American (white) respectability, from the much larger group of poor Hispanos, who were frequently marked, even by elite Hispanos, as working class, "native," and "mixed-blood." However, because the U.S. Census records, which are the most basic historical sources for determining class, designated both Anglos and Hispanos as "white," differentiating Hispano from Anglo class data is far from straightforward. Nevertheless, historians have made some estimates of the class composition of Hispano New Mexicans.

In turn-of-the-twentieth-century New Mexico, elite Hispanos were characterized by their large land holdings, extensive involvement in mercantile and livestock trade, and political power. A general consensus has emerged among historians that elite Hispanos never accounted for more than 10 percent of New Mexico's Hispano population, totaling less than ten thousand people in 1900. According to historian Charles Montgomery, elite Hispanos represented less than 5 percent of New Mexico's Hispanos. Montgomery cites similar percentages for Hispano elites, 2 percent and between 5 and 8 percent, respectively, from the work of Carey McWilliams and Deena González. According to Sarah Deutsch, twenty families, the large majority of them Hispano, owned 75 percent of New Mexico's sheep in 1880. Of the twelve major donors of land helping to establish the Albuquerque Indian School, for example, four (Santiago Baca, Mariano Armijo, Perfect Armijo, and Juan Armijo) were Hispanos. By another estimate, about twenty-five Hispano families controlled seats in the New Mexico legislature.[24]

Those Hispanos not among the elites, representing the vast majority of Hispanos, on the other hand, owned little land and held sparse political and economic power. After 1880, political and economic transformations, which I will discuss in more detail in subsequent sections, forced most Hispanos away from small-scale agriculture and ranching and toward wage labor. Hispanos adapted quickly to these shifts, and by the beginning of the twentieth century, many had become wage laborers, entering the workforce in occupations as diverse as sugar beet production, live-stock raising, and railroad construction. Still, Hispano wages remained low and most Hispanos struggled mightily to make a decent living. In Albuquerque, to take one example, Hispanos were overrepresented in the number of unskilled and manual laborers. In 1885 almost 80 percent of all employed Hispanos worked as unskilled laborers, in jobs such as day la-borer and horse-cart peddler. Semi-skilled occupations, including cooks and railroad laborers, accounted for 2 percent of Hispanos, while 7 per-cent of Hispanos worked in skilled professions, such as carpenters and machinists. Fifteen years later, in 1900, the situation had only slightly im-proved as two-thirds of Hispanos were unskilled laborers, 6 percent were semi-skilled, and 12 percent were skilled workers. At the other end of the spectrum, the 6 and 10 percent of Hispanos in professional and manage-rial occupations in 1885 and 1900, respectively, nicely approximates the above estimates of the percentage of Hispano elites in New Mexico. In-deed, Albuquerque's First National Bank was founded in 1881 by Mariano Otero and N. T. Armijo, from two of New Mexico's most prominent His-pano families.[25]

To provide some context to these numbers, an average Hispano rail-road worker earned $1 per day, for a twelve-hour workday, which trans-lated into about $25 per month and $300 per year. In Albuquerque, as the above statistics suggest, even a semi-skilled labor position such as rail-road worker was beyond the reach of most Hispanos. The great majority of Hispanos thus in all likelihood earned considerably less than $300 an-nually. By contrast, teachers at the Albuquerque Indian School, who were overwhelmingly Anglo, earned a yearly salary of around $600 in 1902, while the superintendent earned $1,700 yearly and the school physician $1,100 per year. Property value offers another point of comparison. In Al-buquerque in 1900, the median value of property owned by Anglos was $900, while non-Hispanic foreign-born property owners held a median value of $750 in property. The median value of property owned by His-panos in Albuquerque, by contrast, was $320.[26]

Still, despite class differences between Anglos and Hispanos and within Hispano society, the nineteenth century was an era of considerable ex-pansion for Hispanos. Geographically, by one account, Hispano culture spread in influence from covering 5,350 square miles in 1790 to 85,000 square miles by 1900. The Hispano population also grew markedly, from about 16,000 in 1790 to 54,394 in 1850 to nearly 100,000 in 1900. Until the arrival of the railroad, most Hispanos continued to depend on small-scale agricultural production and ranching, and most lived in small vil-lages of less than one hundred inhabitants. The village of El Cerrito, as described by Richard Nostrand, offers a useful example of Hispano expansion in the nineteenth century. Located sixty miles southeast of Santa Fe along the Pecos River, El Cerrito was founded in the 1830s by Hispano stock-raising (primarily sheep) families. In 1900, 136 individuals, representing 30 families, lived in El Cerrito. According to Nostrand, "All were Hispanos, who, for the most part, were related; all owned their homes free of mortgage; and all probably owned several acres of irrigable floodplain on which they grew household foodstuffs and livestock forage." Of the 30 heads of household, 18 raised sheep or cattle, and wool was the most important product of the village. Of the remaining 12 heads of household, there were 4 day laborers, 2 farmers, a blacksmith, a carpenter, and 4 men listed without occupations. One woman appeared in the census as a laundrywoman. None of the villagers were listed in the 1900 census as being able to speak English.[27]

This was the cultural setting that "Anglos" (mostly American-born individuals of northern European ancestry and a handful of recent northern European immigrants, including prominent Jewish merchants and businessmen and immigrants from southern Europe) encountered upon arriving in New Mexico. Many Anglo newcomers came to New Mexico in search of opportunities, scouring the mining industry, sheep and cattle ranching, and farms big and small. In 1900 nearly 100,000 Anglos lived in New Mexico, constituting about half of the population. Fifty years earlier, in 1850, only about 1,500 Anglos had lived in the region. Of those, more than half were either military officers and soldiers or ancillary personnel such as carpenters, blacksmiths, interpreters, and laundrywomen. Anglos clustered in Santa Fe, where their total of 800 accounted for only 15 percent of the population, and other villages like Albuquerque, Cebolleta, Socorro, Las Vegas, and Taos. Over the next half century, especially after 1880, the Anglo population grew rapidly. Of those not native to New Mexico in 1880, Texas, California, Missouri, and Ohio donated the most people. Foreign-born New Mexicans in 1880 largely included those born in Mexico, Ireland, and "the German empire." In 1900 the leading states of origin were Texas, Missouri, Colorado, and Illinois. Of the foreign born, most were German, Irish, Italian, or had been born in Mexico. Twenty years later, in 1920, Texas, Missouri, and Oklahoma were the leading non–New Mexico birthplaces of New Mexicans, while Mexico, Germany, Ireland, and Italy were the most common birthplaces of New Mexico's foreign-born population.[28]

While farmers and ranchers predominated among the newcomers, Anglo merchants, including significant numbers of German-born Jewish immigrants, as well as carpenters, blacksmiths, teachers, miners, doctors, lawyers, and priests and ministers also settled in New Mexico. By 1900 other Anglos worked at jobs associated with the railroad (superintendent, telegraph operator, engineer) or found work in New Mexico's assorted coal, gold, silver, copper, and quartz mines. In Albuquerque, for instance, unlike the high percentages of Hispanos engaged in unskilled labor, such occupations accounted for only 5 percent of the Anglo workers in 1885 and 15 percent in 1900. Over a third of Anglo workers in Albuquerque (36 percent) worked in professional, proprietary, or clerical occupations. Only 10 percent of Hispanos, recall, were employed in such high-paying and high-status jobs. Compared to Hispanos, foreign-born New Mexicans, excluding a very small percentage with Spanish surnames, were similarly prosperous in Albuquerque. Over a third of foreign-born Albuquerqueans in 1900 held professional, proprietary, or clerical jobs, while only 10 percent worked as unskilled laborers.[29]

In general, Anglos enjoyed far greater material wealth and occupational success than Hispanos and Indians in New Mexico. Although it is important when possible to distinguish between those of European ancestry born outside the United States and U.S.-born Anglos, the distinction, I argue, was relatively minor in New Mexico. Such differences were minimized by the presence of large numbers of Hispanos and Indians. New Mexicans, as the following chapters will demonstrate, were far more likely to emphasize the racialized differences between Indians, Hispanos, and Anglos, including both those native to the United States and the foreign born. Another set of newcomers to New Mexico also helped minimize differences of nativity within Anglo society. Although New Mexico's African American population was tiny, even by the endpoint of this study in 1920, African Americans, like Indians and Hispanos, were critical players in both Anglo assertions of superiority and whiteness and the racialization projects pervading New Mexico. In 1880 barely a thousand African Americans lived in New Mexico, .8 percent of the population. In 1900 the number had risen to 1,600, but was still less than 1 percent of the population. Ten years later, in 1910, the population was again about 1,600, but the percentage of the population had dropped to .5 percent. Only in 1920 did the actual number (5,733) and percentage (1.5 percent) rise together. Like Hispanos, African Americans were primarily unskilled workers. In Albuquerque in 1900, 40 percent of African American men worked as unskilled laborers, with another 32 percent in domestic service. Only 8 percent of African American men held either professional, proprietary, or clerical occupations. The median value of property owned by African American men in Albuquerque was $400, slightly higher than the median for Hispanos of $320, but well below the $900 median value of property owned by Anglos. As will become clear over the course of the book, African Americans, though peripheral in terms of actual population and physical presence in New Mexico, were absolutely central in symbolic terms and played prominent roles in New Mexico's multiple and multi-layered racialization projects.[30]

The convergence in New Mexico of small numbers of African Americans and much larger numbers of Anglos sparked unprecedented economic development for the region. New Mexico raw materials, from cattle and sheep to timber and mineral resources, entered national markets aboard newly constructed railroad systems. Likewise, labor practices transformed from more informal, though hardly equal, relationships between workers and their bosses based on reciprocal obligations to a more distant, impersonal labor market where workers sold their labor to national and international corporations. At the same time, as María Montoya has documented, American and European investors injected considerable capital resources into New Mexico, persuaded by boosters that New Mexico represented an untapped bonanza for the canny speculator. In southeastern New Mexico, for instance, a land grant owned by Luz and Lucien Maxwell, an intermarried Hispana-Anglo couple with deep roots in New Mexico, was purchased by a group of European and eastern U.S. investors, led by an Englishman who owned the majority of the shares.[31]

Law was another important arena in the assertion of Anglo power in New Mexico.[32] As David Reichard has observed, legal efforts to transform the sexual practices of Hispanos were an especially critical component of American incorporation. Reichard, tracing adultery charges in New Mexico, finds that the Edmunds-Tucker Act of 1887, which "created new federal crimes such as adultery, incest, and fornication," led to the prosecution and conviction of scores of New Mexicans for sexual offenses. Between 1889 and 1905, he notes, almost 140 men and women were convicted of violating the *federal*, not the territorial, law against adultery.[33] Such prosecutions for adultery disproportionately targeted Hispanos. Those imprisoned for adultery convictions were also overwhelmingly Hispanos. Of 139 documented prisoners, 88 were Hispanos, 39 were Hispanas, accounting for a total of 127 Hispanos in jail, while only 9 were Anglo men, 2 African American men, and 1 African American woman.[34]

In typical imperial fashion, the political incorporation of New Mexico lagged far behind its economic assimilation. After the conclusion of the Mexican-American War in 1848, military rule had lasted in New Mexico until 1851, when a formal territorial government was established according to the provisions governing the entrance of new regions into the United States. This territorial system, established with the Northwest Ordinance in 1787 and lasting through much of the nineteenth century, stipulated that the president would appoint a governor, secretary, and three judges who would effectively administer the territory. While adult white males, including Hispanos, could elect a lower house of representatives, the president selected the members of the upper house.[35] Together, both houses elected a nonvoting delegate to Congress. According to this system of territorial government, a territory could apply for statehood when its total population passed sixty thousand. Once the territory had drawn up and ratified a state constitution, Congress would have to approve the constitution and vote in favor of admitting the new state and the president would have to sign the act admitting a new state to the Union.[36]

Although New Mexico easily fulfilled the population requirement (in 1850 its population was 61,547; in 1860, 93,516), its territorial period nonetheless lasted until the granting of statehood in 1912. During that sixty-year period, sixteen states (California, Minnesota, Oregon, Kansas, West Virginia, Nevada, Nebraska, Colorado, North Dakota, South Dakota, Montana, Washington, Idaho, Wyoming, Utah, and Oklahoma) entered the Union. Over that period, struggles for New Mexico statehood suffered numerous setbacks, from the deaths of key political allies to partisan Republican and Democratic bickering. A constant theme, however, in the repeated denials of statehood was, for broader America, the unsavory mix in New Mexico of Hispano and Indian peoples.[37]

Of great significance in the statehood debate was the fact that "White" and "Native-born" in New Mexico described a much different population than nearly anywhere else in the United States. Ninety percent of New Mexico's population around the turn of the century were listed as "White" in the census. Moreover, in a context where one's place of birth was a critical marker of American-ness, only 7 percent of New Mexicans, well below both the national and northeastern averages, were not native born in 1880. In 1900 the percentage of foreign born was again only 7; in 1920, 8 percent of New Mexicans were foreign born.[38] That is, a sizable number of both "Whites" and "Native-born" American citizens in New Mexico were, unlike most of America, Hispanos. Such demographics raised a furor in the United States. New Mexico, in the eyes of broader America, was teeming with "a mongrel population too ignorant and lazy to assume the privileges of full citizenship" and "unfit for statehood." Others suggested that "the population of the territory is of the mongrel breed known as Mexicans—a mixture of the Apache, Negro, Navajo, white horse-thief, Pueblo Indian, and old-time frontiersman with the original Mexican stock."[39]

Concerns about potential political equality and full citizenship for New Mexicans—fears that, for instance, Hispanos and Indians, most of them "white" and nearly all born in the United States, would have an equal voice and vote in electing senators and presidents—echoed the justifications in other imperial settings, like Puerto Rico or the Philippines, for denying colonized peoples, at least for the foreseeable future, full citizenship. Likewise, the establishment of an elaborate educational system for Indians that was designed to replace Indian culture with American norms mirrored similar efforts to transform "Native" children into proper citizens in Puerto Rico and the Dutch East Indies. Differences of degree, far more than differences of kind, separated the "mongrel breed known as Mexicans" in New Mexico from the "little brown brothers" in the Pacific and the Caribbean. As a result, New Mexico at the turn of the twentieth century resembled not as much its continental partners, California and Texas, as its mates abroad, the newly colonized islands of Cuba, Puerto Rico, and the Philippines. New Mexico thus appears not as the last gasp of westward expansion, but as the first step in American imperialism emerging around the turn of the twentieth century.[40]

Imperial projects, of course, never proceeded without opposition. Indians and Hispanos resisted Anglo incorporation with courage and creativity. As chapter 2 will document, Indians selectively adapted aspects of Anglo culture like the school system for their own uses. Indians also turned to the American courts and brought repeated challenges to Anglo attempts to settle on and acquire Indian land.[41] Among Hispanos, anticolonial resistance proceeded along many fronts, including violent attacks by armed Hispano militants in northern New Mexico, known as *gorras blancas*, or white caps, who protested the seizure of Hispano lands and water rights through the widespread destruction of property such as railroad tracks and bridges, fences, and the burning of homes. Like Puerto Ricans, who turned after 1898 to newly established American courts to make claims (like the right to divorce, previously barred under Spanish rule), Hispanos confidently called upon American courts to adjudicate countless matters, from property disputes to domestic affairs. Hispano-owned and -operated Spanish-language newspapers offered another critical space of resistance, as Hispanos routinely celebrated the endurance of Hispano culture in the face of Anglo incursions. Finally, under American control, Hispano elites continued to assert substantial political power. In 1912, the year New Mexico achieved statehood, 26 of 54 state legislators had Spanish surnames, and Hispanos held the positions of lieutenant governor and secretary of state. In 1921, 27 of the 54 legislators had Spanish surnames, Manuel Martinez was secretary of state, and Bonifacio Montoya and J. M. Luna served on the three-person corporation commission.[42]

In this unsettled context of Anglo incorporation and Hispano and Indian resistance, New Mexicans, native and newcomer, struggled mightily to stabilize their newly seized and seizing world. How, in a land both deeply foreign and strangely familiar, did turn-of-the-twentieth-century

New Mexicans create, or re-create, social order? I will argue that in this context, bodily comportment took on special meaning. New Mexicans a century ago turned to the supposed "truths" of human bodies in order to bring sense and order to their world. Physical bodies and "body practices"—arms and legs, heads and shoulders, tongues and cheeks, spit and excrement; the varied chosen and involuntary activities concerning the human body such as type of clothing, bathing habits, elimination of waste, patterns of speech; as well as the more subtle tendencies in presenting one's body to others like flipping the hair; posture during sitting, standing, or walking; movement of eyes during conversation; or the negotiation of shared space on a streetcar—can offer a deep symbolic reservoir for a range of social groups. Social bodies, whether nations, communities, or families, often draw upon images of human bodies, "natural symbols," in order both to establish legitimacy and to discredit and belittle opposition. The argument that a regime should "naturally" have a "head of state," for example, directly compares the social body with the physical body, suggesting in this case that a thriving political entity needs a head every bit as dearly as a thriving human does. Attacks on immigrants as contagions to an otherwise healthy national body similarly extract meaning and authority from physical human experiences of disease and infection.[43]

Many societies, including New Mexico of a century ago, focus special attention on the body's entrances and exits, on those points where social and physical danger are most threatening. Images of the ineffective control or maintenance of human bodies—as in improper excretion, salivation, lactation, consumption, and so on—frequently represent perceived threats to the maintenance of social order. Bodies that lack control over a variety of bodily functions receive great criticism and abuse both literal and figurative. Acceptable, proper, legitimate bodies, on the other hand, characteristically manage more adequate control over the various functions of their bodies. As an example, take this account from a New Mexico newspaper. In 1895 one article observed that "the man of real force is the man who has complete control of himself." Defining a "real man" by denying negative attributes rather than asserting positive ones, the article claims a real man is "neither a bully nor a braggart, seldom arbitrary, passionate or unjust."[44] Respectable men, that is, were dispassionate and just, in full control of themselves and their actions. The legitimate body appears as a coherent, uniform body, while the dangerous body is a hybrid, made up of mixed and disparate parts.

Anthropologist Mary Douglas explains that seemingly "natural" and straightforward symbols and images of the human body, the ways different parts of the body are represented in relation to other parts, reveal complex systems of social distinction and hierarchy. Take, for instance, representations of the relationship of "head to feet, of brain and sexual organs, of mouth and anus." All are used repeatedly to "express the relevant patterns of [social] hierarchy." Peter Stallybrass and Allon White expand on Douglas's groundbreaking work. They argue that bourgeois identity emerged in opposition to a heterogeneous mass of excluded "grotesque" bodies. Unlike the "closed, homogeneous, monumental, central, and symmetrical" bourgeois body (the body of classical beauty), the grotesque, vulgar, hybrid body is characterized by "impurity (both in the sense of dirt and mixed categories), heterogeneity, masking, protuberant distension, disproportion, exorbitancy, clamor, decentered or eccentric arrangements, a focus on gaps, orifices, and symbolic filth."[45]

The search for order in turn-of-the-twentieth-century New Mexico, literally the incorporation of New Mexico, began, as do all searches for order, with human bodies. New Mexicans—principally Anglo civic leaders like government officials, lawyers, judges, physicians, business owners, and newspaper editors—placed great significance on an individual's ability to govern their own body, to manage and properly regulate their body's entrances and exits. Bodily comportment, especially for Indians and Hispanos, figured prominently in determining respectability and propriety, as well as fitness for citizenship.

This "re-approximating the edges" of the ragged New Mexican social order, determining through bodily comportment which individuals and groups merited membership and which deserved to remain on the margins of legitimate civic participation, speaks directly to the intertwining of race and sexuality in the structuring of social inequality. New Mexico, in recent years, has for good reason received heightened scholarly interest as a particularly rich location for the study of race and citizenship. Such studies, however, have tended not to focus in any substantial sense on gender and sexuality.[46] As a result, historians of New Mexico have paid little attention to the role of sexuality and embodiment in, as Nancy Stepan puts it, "the story of citizenship and its limits."[47] Like Stepan, I am moved by the need to understand the complicity of sex, race, and embodiment in determining opportunity in American history. Understanding such complicity has never been easy; race and sex are notoriously, even perversely, flexible and unpredictable mechanisms, at times contradictory, at times complementary, at times mutually exclusive. By focusing on the racialization and sexualization of bodily comportment, my approach offers a far more sensitive register of the racial and sexual structuring of opportunity both in New Mexico and in the broader United States.

I use the term "racialized" here to imply an externally imposed set of categories that differentiate and hierarchically organize social groups according to scientific and quasi-scientific physical embodied features. Racialization entails a claim by a privileged few to superior social position and abstract leadership skills by virtue of their embodied physical characteristics. At the heart of the dynamic, repetitive process of racialization projects is the unequal distribution of power based on physical differences of race. This definition, of course, is historically quite specific, representing the emergence of racial science in the eighteenth and nineteenth centuries and the modern significance placed on visual cues to identity.[48]

Like racialization, the process of "sexualization" can vary considerably based on historical context. Likewise, a sexual identity (prostitute, man, woman, pervert, mother, masturbator) links body practices with group identities, associating certain groups with certain forms of genital activity.[49] To extrapolate a sexual identity from a particular body practice, to *sexualize* a body practice, is at times to associate a body practice that is entirely unrelated to sexuality or genital activity with an identity based on genital activity and/or difference. Licking whipped cream off a human body, for example, in a certain sense is entirely unrelated to sexual intercourse, yet in turn-of-the-twenty-first-century America at least, such a body practice almost invariably suggests a particular sexual identity (for some, a sexually adventurous person; for others, perhaps a sexually *un*adventurous person). Likewise, standing with one's hands on hips hardly appears linked to genital or sexual difference. But notice the difference between standing with one's thumbs facing forward and fingers to back and vice versa (try it!).

Each of the following chapters fleshes out different aspects of the imposition of an embodied social order in New Mexico. Chapter 2 discusses New Mexican Indian schools, where Anglo educators sought to train students in the bodily requirements of citizenship. This racialization of Indian boys and girls (linking physical characteristics like length of hair with abstract qualities such as capacity for citizenship) helped Anglos articulate a social order where those conforming to Anglo standards of bodily comportment received the greatest rewards and those who deviated, the greatest punishment. Courtrooms and sexual offense trials, the subject of chapter 3, present a similar scenario for Hispanos. As in Indian schools, bodily comportment (sexual history, alcohol consumption, mobility in public space) was a critical indicator of racial difference. While Hispana rape victims were especially vulnerable to Anglo racialization efforts, which targeted the women's sexual reputations, Anglo women also faced often-painful physical examinations and potentially humiliating courtroom appearances. Chapter 3 concludes with a discussion of the critical role of elite Hispanos in forcing Anglo attorneys to adopt new arguments regarding Hispano defendants, accusers, and witnesses. The racialization of Hispanos, and to an extent Hispanas, was impeded by wealthy Hispanos whose presence and social prominence in New Mexico prevented, unlike elsewhere in the country, the widespread condemnation of the supposed sexual voracity of Mexican-origin peoples.

Chapter 4 picks up this discussion through an examination of bodily comportment in ceremonies and public events in New Mexico. In newspaper accounts of parades, festivals, and religious ceremonies, Anglo editors routinely denounced most Indian and Hispano ceremonies and celebrated Anglo festivities, yet were notably restrained in their descriptions of events potentially significant to wealthy Hispanos. Chapter 5, focusing on domesticity and marriage, will explore further the accommodations forced upon Anglo newcomers by the economic and political strength of Hispano elites. The chapter will also track an important shift in Anglo racializing projects, one spurred by Anglos' inability to denounce and demonize Hispano peoples with impunity. Instead, I will argue, Anglos turned to two groups as exemplars of irregular and dangerous domesticity: African Americans and prostitutes. Like Indians and Hispanos in other settings such as Indian schools, rape trials, and public ceremonies, negative depictions of the embodied actions of African Americans and prostitutes provided the backdrop against which Anglos could portray their own supposed superiority and fitness for citizenship.

Chapters 6 and 7 will address directly what previous chapters spoke of only peripherally, the considerable time and energy that Anglos spent racializing themselves. Anglo newcomers to New Mexico, recall, hailed from a broader America of imperialism and immigration where dilemmas of whiteness and citizenship were prominent. In New Mexico, the link between whiteness and social status was even more tenuous. As wealthy Hispanos constantly pointed out, Anglo newcomers were not the only white people to claim whiteness. Thus, one of the critical racial projects in New Mexico was the "naturalization" of whiteness. By the naturalization of whiteness, I mean the process through which whiteness comes to be seen as the basic condition of humans, where the natural, normal, average, healthy, accepted state of humankind is that of being white. In this context, racialized descriptions (Indian, Hispano, Mexican, black, etc.) would only be necessary to describe those individuals and communities who *diverged* from the norm, who were different or abnormal. When whiteness is naturalized, it becomes so accepted, so normal that commenting on or observing an individual's whiteness becomes unnecessary. In regimes of naturalized whiteness, for instance, there would be no need to describe a white man walking down the street. Noting that a man walked down the street would be enough to suggest that the man in question was white. Put another way, to draw from a much different context, one of the greatest tricks of whiteness is to convince us that whiteness never existed.[50]

In New Mexico, where racial identity was so distorted, the link between Anglos and the privileges of whiteness was not automatically accepted and assumed; whiteness was not naturalized. Wealthy Hispanos had long claimed that their physical attributes (the sexual restraint of Hispanas, the sexual virility of Hispanos, the unmixed purity of their European blood lines, their light skin) reserved for them the privileges of social status, deference, and civic leadership. Anglo settlers thus needed to claim for themselves the privileges of whiteness.

As in previous chapters, chapters 6 and 7 will focus on bodily comportment and racialization. Rather than focus on the supposed inadequacies of the body practices of Indian and Hispano racial others, however, these two chapters will describe Anglo embodiment. Anglos, after all, in order to demonstrate their superiority, needed to point out both the failings of Indian and Hispano bodies *and* the successes of Anglo bodies. In chapter 6, on medicine, Anglo physicians take center stage. In the pages of the *New Mexico Medical Journal*, articles written by and for doctors emphasize the superior bodily comportment of physicians. Doctors' supposed exalted relationship with the body, their self-control, sexual restraint, capacity for abstract scientific thinking, masterful knowledge of the human body, and intolerance for gender ambiguity in turn offered "proof" of Anglos' heightened fitness for full participation in broader American political and economic life. The following chapter extends this analysis of naturalized whiteness into spaces of mass consumer goods and advertisements for the new array of goods carried into New Mexico aboard the railroad. Here again, celebrations of Anglo bodily comportment (their unblemished skin, moderate appetites for food and the ingestion of alcohol, appropriate fashion, disciplined bowels) helped sustain claims for social superiority. At the same time, the chapter highlights Hispano claims to whiteness and charts the development in New Mexico of a shared, Hispano and Anglo, white body.

The concluding chapter will point to the implications of this study for broader understandings of modernity, imperialism, Chicana/o history, and the intersections of race and sexuality in American history. The conclusion will also address some of the inherent unsettling aspects of colonial rule, the pervasive anxiety of imperialism and the spots where the hasty patchwork of empire was at its most obvious. Covered beneath a new colonial order, New Mexicans like those described in the subsequent chapters tossed and turned against each other in the disorder and turmoil following the arrival of the railroad in 1880. Though in places carefully tucked, this newly spread quilt also proved at times remarkably frayed. On occasion, though certainly not always, the boundary between social order and out-of-control racial and sexual bodies proved insufficient. While anxiety, contradiction, and smoldering desire are hardly the stuff of toppled regimes, postcolonial theorists remind us that conquest and social order demand far more sophisticated maneuvers than the swiveling of a Gatling gun or the drawing of a saber. Once military violence ends, conquest does not cease but enters a new stage. José Limón, following the lead of Antonio Gramsci, makes a critical distinction between wars of maneuver and wars of position in the nineteenth-century American Southwest. Wars of maneuver, according to Limón, pitted armed social groups against one another within a context "in which clear victory [was] still an open question." In wars of position, on the other hand, "one side has achieved nearly complete dominance." In the war of position, public intellectuals, newspaper editorialists, and civic leaders replaced the war of maneuver's generals and soldiers as the leading men, and sometimes women, of conquest. In other words, the war of position—a war waged with increasing frequency with the end of direct military battles in the nineteenth-century West—emerged in settings like New Mexico and was waged by and upon the bodies of New Mexicans.[51]

To illustrate, let me end with a specific example. In 1903 Mary Dissette, a supervising teacher for the United States Indian Service, sent a detailed and wide-ranging report on the day school at Taos Pueblo to the superintendent of the U.S. Indian school in Santa Fe. During the course of the letter, Dissette expanded at length on issue after issue, expressing alternating regret, surprise, dismay, sympathy, and disgust at the "present arrangement" in Taos. Amid the more mundane observations—improvement of buildings, requisition orders, and enrollment figures—were a flurry of blunt and biting assessments of the day school, the tone of which proved typical not only of Dissette, but of newcomers in general to turn-of-the-century New Mexico.[52]

Shocked at the physical appearance of the male students, Dissette reported that she directed Antonio, a Pueblo assistant at the school, "to shingle every head . . . make them pantaloons in American style, and insist on their being worn." Taos was the only school, she snapped, "where those disgraceful leggings were worn in school and it had to be stopped." Besides the governor of the pueblo, whom she mildly upbraided for being "very indifferent about school matters," Dissette reserved for Antonio her greatest criticism. She described him as "too much taken up with courting a girl very much his inferior," and found it all too discouraging to "see a young man who has had his opportunities making the clothes of his intended on the sewing machine." Lack of manly disposition and industry aside, Antonio also struck Dissette as "almost completely subjugated" by the Taos Indians. Indeed, Antonio, Dissette assured the superintendent, was "fast going in the same direction" as Lorenzo, "one of the biggest *Indians* in the village" (emphasis in original), who visited Dissette "clad in buckskin leggings, moccasins, his long hair trimmed with fur and his face covered with red paint."[53] Like so many New Mexicans, Antonio and his improper body practices appeared to an Anglo newcomer as grievously unfit for citizenship.

In the above example, and throughout the following chapters, human bodies (heads and toes; arms and legs; ingestions and secretions; bodily fluids like tears, saliva, and semen; genitals, skin, and hair) proved fundamental to racialization. In a tumultuous land, where familiar racial binaries proved ineffective, bodily comportment was indispensable. The evaluation and characterization of human bodies and body practices in New Mexico helped define citizenship, structure opportunity, and provide the scaffolding around which new sets of social hierarchies were to be constructed.

Now, a century later, New Mexico remains an eccentric space within the American nation. Like the legendary coyote trickster figure of southwestern folklore, the state still occupies the margins of the American polity and continues to be resistant to conventional binary forms of racialized order. In exploring further such links between bodily comportment and modern American racial and sexual order in New Mexico, I ask readers to cast their eyes beyond the traditional focus on race relations in major East Coast metropolitan areas and contrasting sexual norms between whites and African Americans. Like the settled and unsettled of New Mexico who met for the first time at the railroad depot but did not linger, I will explore other arenas in New Mexico. It is my hope that this survey of New Mexico offers readers a sense of the dreads and delights lurking in the wind, howling beneath the stars, and clouding the sunsets of the Land of Enchantment.[54]

COMPROMISING POSITIONS

RACIALIZING BODIES
AT PUEBLO INDIAN SCHOOLS

In 1920 a day-school inspector for the United States Indian schools addressed a circular to all teachers. The circular directed each teacher at the beginning of every school day to "inspect all pupils for cleanliness and personal appearance." Teachers, according to Inspector Beahm, "should demand that each child have clean hands, clean faces, clean nails, and clean teeth." Furthermore, in terms of personal appearance, the inspector recommended that "hair should be combed and neat and shoes cleaned." Beahm suggested that the "wide-awake teacher" should be "constantly on the watch for evidence of defects, disorders, and diseases."[1]

To aid educators in their constant vigilance in "discovering these evidences" of sickness, the inspector then helpfully outlined an array of disease and defect classifications. He listed eight broad categories, each of which included between five and fifteen specific warning signs or symptoms. The categories ranged from "Eye Disorders and Defects" to "Neverous [sic] Disorders" to "Incorrect Posture." Conditions like "enlarged glands in the neck" or "granulated lids" appeared to carry similar diagnostic weight as "irritability," "offensive breath," and "excessive perspiration of feet." Huddled together under "Neverous [sic] Disorders" were the following: "Fits, Fainting, Spasmodic Movements, Twitching of eye, face, or other part of the body, Moroseness, Sex Disturbances, Irritability, Timidity and Undue Embarrassment, Undue Emotion of any sort, and Solitary Habits." Other notable features included "Blank expression, Peculiar reading posture, Eruptions, Pallor, Lassitude, Exaggerated knee-action in walking, Flat Chest, Protruding Abdomen, and Stooping Posture." The circular ended on a hopeful note. "Many of the above conditions," the inspector allowed, "can be corrected by you and in other cases, the field matrons and physicians will be glad to advise and assist if you will call upon them." [2]

Polingaysi Qoyawayma, a Hopi boarding school student and eventually a teacher herself, similarly emphasized bodily regulation in a list of suggestions for Indian children that she and her students developed. The list reads:

> We must have clean hands.
> We must have clean faces.
> We must not have sores on our bodies.
> We must not have bugs on us.
> We must wear clean clothes.
> We must polish our shoes.
> We must have our hair cut.
> We must not be ashamed to speak English.
> We must not be afraid of white people. [3]

Clearly there is much of interest in Beahm's memo and Qoyawayma's list, not the least of which is the clustering of clear, at least to contemporary eyes, medical conditions like sore throat, chronic cough, vomiting, and sores on the bodies, which could signal life-threatening diseases like tuberculosis, diphtheria, and measles, with somewhat more vague ailments like blank expression, bad breath, sweaty feet, and emotions like fear and shame. [4] Both sources illuminate the central relationship in New Mexico between bodily comportment and racialization. A shuffling gait or a stooped and hunched posture, for instance, represents more than an innocent observation. "Shuffling," "stooped," and "hunched" evoke particular images (notably, those of monkeys, gorillas, chimpanzees) associated with beings far lower along a racial hierarchy and allude to the widespread belief, as we shall see, among Anglo educators that Indian peoples were in general "dirty" or "filthy." Teachers in the memo are cautioned to be alert to signs that their students were literally walking closer not only to the earth, but toward primitivism and savagery and away from Anglo civilization. Moreover, Qoyawayma's list establishes a clear connection between unclean hands and faces, long hair, and Indian culture. "White people," on the other hand, are associated with cleanliness, health (the absence of sores and pests on the body), and proper shoes and clothing. [5]

As the above examples make clear, the education of Indian children at United States Indian schools was a critical space of embodiment and racialization. This racialization project, directed at Indian children and their broader Indian communities, centered on Anglo assertions of the supposed inferiority of Indian culture, and the corresponding superiority of Anglo culture, and depended on bodily comportment. Anglo teachers and administrators emphasized both sexual contagions (miscegenation, adultery, fornication) and more general bodily pollutions and incoherences (language and speech, hair length, clothing, alcohol consumption, dancing, use of medicine, students' comportment in and out of the classroom) as typical of Indian culture.

In the late nineteenth and early twentieth centuries, Anglo policy makers, united by a shared belief in the sanctity of the monogamous nuclear family and the key role of private property in advancing stages of "civilization," used boarding schools as a primary instrument in attempting to acculturate and transform Indian youth.[6] The first off-reservation boarding school for Indians in the United States opened in 1879 in Carlisle, Pennsylvania, and by 1902 that number had reached twenty-five, with schools throughout America. David Wallace Adams notes that in 1900, of 21,000 Indian students attending both day and boarding schools in the United States, 17,700 of them were enrolled in either off-reservation or reservation boarding schools. Despite the great distance between New Mexico and Pennsylvania, Pueblo Indian students attended the Carlisle school in substantial numbers; nearly one hundred were in attendance in 1889.[7]

In New Mexico, modern schools for Indians began with the founding of a Presbyterian mission school in 1873. In 1884 a government boarding school opened in Albuquerque, and a second school was created in Santa Fe in 1890. Day schools were also established in the Pueblo villages, one in Laguna Pueblo in 1871, two more in Jemez and Santa Ana in 1885. By 1922 thirteen government day schools had been established, including schools at Laguna, Acoma, Isleta, San Felipe, Santo Domingo, Cochiti, and Jemez. Nearly 750 Pueblo children attended day schools that year. Boarding schools in Albuquerque, Santa Fe, and outside New Mexico accounted for another 500 students in 1922, and over 400 additional children attended Catholic mission schools outside of Pueblo villages. Thus, according to one historian, by 1922, of the total Pueblo Indian school-age population, "only 283 out of a total of 1,941 school age children were not in school."[8]

While day schools naturally were filled with children from nearby villages, students at boarding schools represented Indian communities from throughout New Mexico. In 1887, for example, San Felipe (39), Isleta (36), Laguna (18), Santa Ana (10), Zia (8), Acoma (8), Cochiti (5), and Sandia (5) sent children to the Albuquerque Indian School for a total of 129 Pueblo students attending the school. That year, another 39 students attended from other Indian communities: Pima (23), Navajo (8), Papago (7), and Mescalero Apache (1).[9]

Indian students may have been newcomers to boarding schools and American-style education; however, their teachers were strangers to both the land and the culture of New Mexico. Anglos predominated among the employees of the government schools in New Mexico. The staff of the Albuquerque Indian School in 1885 were the following: "RWD Bryan, superintendent; the Misses Tibbles, Wood, Patten, and Butler, teachers; Mrs. Bryan and Miss Wilkins, matrons; Mr. McKenzie, instructor in carpentering; Mr. Loveland in painting; Mrs. Loveland and Mrs. Sadler in sewing; and Mr. and Mrs. Henderson in cooking and care of the tables." Note both the exclusively English surnames and the fact that all of the employees designated as "teachers" were women and single (they were identified as "Misses" and not "Mrs."). Like the broader Anglo community, most educators were recent arrivals to New Mexico. At the Santa Fe Indian School, one survey found that of 65 teachers employed between 1891 and 1911, 31 hailed from the Midwest, 10 were from New England and the South, and 11 had moved from the Plains states. Only 13 had origins in the Far West, many presumably, if not all, from outside New Mexico. The survey of the Santa Fe Indian School also revealed clear gender divisions among Indian school employees: 57 of the 69 teachers were women, 45 of them single, while only 12 were men, 3 single and 9 married. School administrators, on the other hand, were disproportionately male. In 1900, of the 100 Indian school superintendents and assistant superintendents throughout the United States, only 9 were women.[10]

The imprint of American modernity is everywhere evident in such efforts to educate Indian children and reform Indian communities. Margaret Jacobs has adeptly explored interactions between Pueblos and Anglos in New Mexico, with a special emphasis on education. She highlights the relationship between modern changes in the broader American gender ideology of the turn of the century and the encounters in New Mexico between Anglo female reformers and Pueblo women and men. She correctly observes that Anglo women stood at the forefront of efforts both to reform and assimilate Native Americans and (later) to preserve and protect their customs and cultural artifacts. Jacobs argues that a major aspect of reformers' efforts to "civilize" the Pueblos, and Native Americans in general, was to enforce transformed, and supposedly more equitable, modern gender roles.[11]

Within this modern context, Jacobs understands Indian education and reform efforts as primarily concerned with shaping, through various forms of coercion, Native Americans into American citizens. In this respect, although she does not explicitly engage literatures of colonialism and imperialism, she is (or should properly be understood to be) in conversation with scholars of American and European imperialism. Pedro Cabán, for instance, highlights the central place of education in American colonial policies in Puerto Rico. For American officials, the Americanization of Puerto Rican children was fundamental to the success of the island's political and economic transformation. Cabán observes: "Because these territories were so densely populated the United States did not have the option of relocating the indigenous people and replacing them with its own citizens. Instead colonial policy was designed to Americanize these people into loyal colonial subjects." Between 1898 and 1911, the American colonial administration in Puerto Rico built over three hundred school buildings, a total that would rise to over a thousand by 1930. Teaching staff similarly expanded, from 1,100 in 1902 to 4,500 in 1931. So linked were education and colonial rule for Americans that Puerto Rico's commissioner for education supervised the largest government agency (by both size of budget and employees) on the island. Even as late as 1929, education still accounted for roughly a third of total U.S. government expenditures in Puerto Rico.[12]

Resistance to colonial educational policies likewise characterized both Indians in New Mexico and Puerto Ricans. Through ingenuity, courage, and some small measure of good luck, Pueblo Indians had managed to retain their land and limited resources, and to exercise some degree of autonomy and control over their own communities during the nineteenth century. Moreover, unlike flagship schools in Indian education like the Carlisle Indian School, which was located in central Pennsylvania, far away from substantial Indian communities, Indian schools in New Mexico were relatively close (most within fifty miles) to the villages and townspeople that the educators so roundly criticized. Educators knew full well the implications of such proximity. In addition to anxieties surrounding the sexual misconduct of the students, educators feared that scandals would convince parents to withdraw their children from the schools. As a result, educators were forced to contend, and negotiate with, Pueblo leaders.

Indeed, while Anglo educators' dedication to assimilation and training in American citizenship led to sustained attacks on Pueblo culture, Pueblo students and their families in New Mexico hardly acquiesced to such treatment. Students adopted, and adapted, skills acquired in the schools for their own purposes, strictly adhering to certain regulations and ignoring others outright. Many parents protested poor conditions by petitioning government officials or initiating extensive letter-writing campaigns. Others either withdrew their children from the schools or delayed returning their children to school after vacation periods.

New Mexico Indian schools thus have much to offer those interested in the processes by which Pueblo Indians, and other communities, experienced American incorporation and colonial administration. By placing efforts to control and discipline Indian bodies, the multiple ways that racialization overlapped with instruction in bodily comportment, within a context of imperialism, we can begin to make important linkages to other emerging American colonial spaces around the world like Puerto Rico and the Philippines. In addition to describing the fundamental role of embodiment and bodily comportment in distinguishing Anglos from Pueblos, this chapter will also speak to the colonial aspirations, and insecurities, like the fear that Pueblo Indian parents would refuse to send their children to boarding schools, at the heart of this campaign to impress Pueblos with and into civilization.[13]

In New Mexico, the racializations of citizenship were at their most vital in the classroom. Educators expended considerable energy discussing the curriculum and the bodily comportment of students in the classroom, and tended to stress themes of patriotism and national inclusion as well as academic and industrial tutelage. Students participated in daily (American) flag-raising ceremonies and celebrated holidays such as Washington's birthday, Memorial Day, and the Fourth of July. In 1914, for example, Luella Gallup passed along to a supervisor in Santa Fe a handwritten outline of the daily activities at Cochiti Day School. The outline begins with an overview of the typical school day, starting at 8:45 with "Flag Raising" and a 9:00 school bell. The fifteen-minute morning recess occurred at 10:45, followed by a lunch break from 11:30 to 1:00. The fifteen-minute afternoon recess began at 2:45 and students were dismissed from classes at 4:00. The next section of Gallup's outline notes the dates throughout the school year when the students participated in a special program. In addition to commemorating Thanksgiving, Christmas, Washington's and Lincoln's birthdays, and Memorial Day, November 3 was designated as a day devoted to "Humane Treatment of Animals" and December 7, "Tuberculosis Day."[14]

Another annual calendar of instruction, the 1920–21 calendar for the Santa Fe Industrial School, begins with a list of the nearly forty employees of the school, beginning with the superintendent, and including clerks, a physician, disciplinarians, principals, teachers, a night watchman, and a florist. Students at the industrial school followed a meticulously ordered daily schedule that began with reveille at 5:45 A.M. and a ten-minute roll call and flag-raising ceremony at 6:20. After a half-hour breakfast, all students joined in an unspecified morning drill. Students then alternated between "industrial" and "academic" instruction for the remainder of the morning. Another three hours of either industrial or academic work followed lunch, then a session of "group games, academic department," then supper. Evening sessions changed from day to day. Monday between 7:00 and 8:00 was reserved for religious instruction. Students on Tuesday,

2. Schoolboys brushing teeth, Santo Domingo Pueblo, New Mexico. Seemingly mundane bodily acts like brushing one's teeth were a focal point of efforts by Anglo educators to "civilize" Native American children. Photo by Witter Bynner. Courtesy of the Museum of New Mexico, neg. no. 95252.

Wednesday, and Thursday attended band practice. "Sociables, literary societies, etc." occurred on Friday; "confessional for Catholics" on Saturday; and a "General Assembly on Sunday." Finally a bugle sounded the daily call to "retire" and taps were played at 8:45 P.M. The only other notable feature of the daily program was a "hospital call" scheduled every day for girls at 7:30 A.M. and for boys at 12:25 P.M.[15]

Other correspondence sheds further light on the daily classroom experience in New Mexico. A year before her draft of the daily program at Cochiti, Luella Gallup forwarded a detailed requisition order to Santa Fe. Clustered on the list alongside requests for boxes of colored crayons and six dozen unruled tablets are more intriguing provisions. Gallup asked at one point for four "Perry Pictures," carefully placing the series number of each picture beside the title. The four pictures were labeled "Can't You Talk?," "Cattle of Brittany," "Madonna," and "Race of the Roman Chariots." Such illustrations likely shared space on the classroom walls with the maps of New Mexico and the United States ordered by the instructor. Among the books requested for the school library were *Stories of the Red Children*, the only book listed for second-grade students and the only book explicitly addressing Native Americans. The third-grade library, by contrast, was to receive, among other titles, *Great Americans*, *Seat Work and Industrial Occupation*, and *Gymnastic Stories and Plays*. Besides a variety of types of paper and writing instruments, the most notable other feature of the list is an order for twelve sets of "toy money." Notice here the direct attempts to link academic training—the dull stuff of memorization, grammar, and basic mathematics—along with broader concepts of nationalism and love of country with whiteness.[16]

Some other writers were especially blunt in their attempts to transform Indian children. A letter by Benjamin Rothwell emphasized the energy Anglo teachers devoted to ensuring that Pueblo students would be present at the school at the appointed time. In 1913, noting that it was "very important that we have one," he asked for "a large bell" for the school in Peñasco. A bell was necessary, he reasoned, because "these people have no clocks" and "it seems wrong to fault the children because they cannot know when it is time for school."[17] Another teacher forwarded a list of students and their instances of tardiness and being absent, including their accumulated "minutes lost by tardiness" in the first three weeks of the 1914 school year. Testament to the continued struggle between Anglo educators and Pueblo families and students over the exact details of students' physical presence in the classroom is the fact that Cora Lopez headed the list of punctuality with only eighty minutes lost to tardiness. Of the fifteen students listed, only one other fell below two hundred minutes late. More than half had collected, in the first three weeks of school, over four hundred tardy minutes.[18]

Training citizens, however, required more than raising flags and playing money. Students required bodily discipline as well as patriotism, posture as well as posters, if they were to abandon the supposedly primitive ways of their parents and communities, and approach whiteness. Administrators reminded teachers to take advantage of the pedagogical opportunities presented by previously overlooked and underutilized periods during the school day, such as recess. Day-school inspector Beahm, for instance, asked teachers in 1920 to devote a specific fifteen minutes every morning and afternoon, and a full hour on Thursday afternoons, to "Supervised Play." While recess was a hardly a novel idea in 1920— Luella Gallup's 1914 daily calendar included both morning and afternoon play breaks—Beahm proposed specific objectives and settings for the period of "supervised play." According to Beahm, the exercises "should be conducted on the outside when the weather is at all suitable and should consist of setting up exercises, various group games, and other play." Under the watchful eye of teachers and housekeepers, recess was to accomplish two main goals. The first goal focused on mostly physical attributes: improving "posture, carriage, and grace of movement" and developing "strength, skill, and endurance." The second goal aimed at "such mental and moral qualities as alertness, initiative, courage, courtesy, sense of fairness, honesty, good sportsmanship, perseverance, and leadership." Importantly, Beahm included under the first goal focusing on physical characteristics, the aim of developing "a good wholesome vocabulary of playground English." The inspector regrettably left no further specifications regarding "playground English," however he concluded his circular by noting sternly that "during these periods only the English language should be tolerated."[19]

As the Beahm memo demonstrates, characteristics that educators associated with whiteness (posture, courtesy, punctuality, abstract thinking, "wholesome vocabulary" of English, American citizenship, Christianity) were celebrated while Indian-ness was denounced and demeaned. One of the main goals of the classroom therefore was to clearly differentiate whiteness from Indian-ness. This racialization centered on carefully monitoring and reforming the bodies of Indian children. In the above documents, certain required activities, like the flag raising and the celebration of national holidays, link particular body practices with whiteness and American identities. The circular on appropriate recess activities and comportment links speaking English, one of the primary indices of assimilation to Anglo culture, with physical "exercises." As for punctuality, Anglo teachers attempted to demonstrate the idea that being physically present at a certain place at a certain expected time was critical to educational—if not moral, financial, and social—success. By so linking punctuality with white norms, educators depicted tardiness, alongside poor hygiene, unstructured learning, and non-English languages, as racially "other" and incompatible with American citizenship.

Imagine the effects of these calculated regimentations, hourly and half-hourly lesson blocks, patriotic celebrations, and attention to health and hygiene, on a Pueblo student on her first day of school. As she would soon discover, much depended on a student's ability to demonstrate effectively her claim to citizenship. Careful cultivation of the body would have been impressed upon her at the outset, clothed as she would have been in government-issued uniforms and inspected as she had been for medical infirmities and physical deficiencies. Almost immediately, she would have noticed the strict time schedule, the shuttling at precise intervals between activities and exercises. Something else would have been inescapable for the student on her first day of school: this scrutiny and control of the body was linked to America. America was everywhere in the classroom, from the raising of the flag that signaled the new day rising to the celebrations of presidents' birthdays, Memorial Day, and the Fourth of July. Maps of New Mexico and the United States reminded students that the land they inhabited, New Mexico, was part of a broader land, the United States. The point for a student would have been clear: education was linked to bodily coherence was linked to American citizenship.

As we have seen from the classroom experience, students and educators in New Mexico could hardly escape the relationship between bodily coherence and fitness for citizenship. Bodily incoherence struck educators as absolutely incompatible with the broader goal of Indian education: developing American citizens. Concern over porous boundaries crystallized around the following body practices: speech, bathing, clean clothes, elimination of waste, hair length, clothing style, dancing, and consumption of alcohol.

One of the main objectives of Anglo educators throughout the government school system—and perhaps the best documented example of Anglo attempts to transform the behavior, and help reform the identity, of Indian students—was teaching Indian children to read, write, and speak English. As their counterparts in Puerto Rico would enforce simultaneously in the Caribbean (of the five objectives in the Puerto Rican educational program, Pedro Cabán notes, the first was "imparting English language skills"),[20] American educators prohibited, under dire penalty, the speaking of Indian languages. An 1890 directive informed schools throughout the country that students should be forced under threat of punishment to speak only English with one another. One school was especially vigilant, organizing students into an elaborate military-style rank system based on their ability to speak English and even promoting and demoting students accordingly. In a similar effort to force Indian students to adopt the English language and supposedly become more like proper American citizens—and, not incidentally, to facilitate their acquisition, transfer, and inheritance of property—schools also forced students to adopt Anglo names. As one historian correctly notes, the renaming projects "constituted a grave assault on Indian identity."[21] In their memories of their education at New Mexico schools, former students often highlighted language and naming. Mrs. Walter K. Marmon, for instance, recalled having her name changed from Bau-mac-a to Suzy at the Santa Fe Indian School. "They changed the names of many of the other little girls and boys," she added. She also remembered, while at the Carlisle school in Pennsylvania, being required to report every week whether they spoke their own language rather than English. As punishment, the students "were given some menial tasks, we scrubbed floors in the big assembly hall." Clemente Vigil told an interviewer that his father's name had been changed to Allen Withers, while his uncle became James D. Porter.[22]

In this racializing project, Anglo educators also sought to impress upon their charges the benefits, and supposed link to higher "civilization," of proper bathing habits and cleanliness. Over the course of 1914, Mary Dissette in Santo Domingo directed several letters to Santa Fe. She reported, among other bits of business, that she and her assistant "bathed all the girls today and dressed them from the skin out." "Boys," she added, "will be put through tomorrow." By October, however, Dissette had evidently become frustrated in her bathing efforts. She noted that the "wind does not blow and we have no more water than we did last year." As a result, she continued, "I am frantic to bathe these filthy children and can't do it." She concluded the letter by noting that "we have a change of clothing ready for them," presumably meaning that clean clothes were waiting to be placed on clean children. A month later Dissette again addressed bathing, pointing out to the superintendent that "the girls toilet and bath room has an outside door which makes it impossible to keep it warm enough for bathing." Illustrating the importance educators like Dissette placed on cleanliness, she added that twice a week "the classroom work is disorganized" for the sole purpose of providing "a place warm enough for pupils to dry off and dress in."[23]

As comments like "dressed them from the skin out" and Mary Dissette's evident desire not to place clean clothes on unbathed "filthy" bodies suggest, educators emphasized the pedagogical value of clean clothes, its link to civilization and whiteness. In another letter, Dissette explained to the superintendent some of the tension and misunderstanding at the school over laundry. Two Pueblo assistants, Monica and Santiago, apparently were in "a wrath over having any laundry work done on the place," and, according to Dissette, "want[ed] to reduce the school to the unsanitary level of their own home and village life." The year before, Dissette, faced with a lack of water at the school, had given each child half a bar of soap each week and instructed them to wash their clothes at home. The plan failed, however, because the laundry was "always badly done and often not done at all," a fact that Dissette believed "did not disturb Monica and husband [Santiago] at all." "And when the teachers found themselves infected with vermin," Dissette added bitterly, "it was rather a good joke."[24] Even letters addressing wholly different subjects reiterated the link between Pueblo life and lack of cleanliness. A teacher from Sandoval asked for help in convincing the mother of Santiago Shije to send her son to boarding school in Santa Fe. Santiago, "quite a bright lad," the writer asserted, would be far better served attending school than "playing in the filth and dirt at home."[25]

Anglo fear of contagious disease, both for themselves and on behalf of students, inspired a slew of further descriptions and denunciations of Pueblo health and hygiene. Mary Dissette recommended in 1915 that all students from Santo Domingo be detained in Santa Fe until "every dog and cat in this village has been shot and burned, every house where there has been sickness and death fumigated and whitewashed, all old rags burned, and a general sanitary campaign carried out." Dissette directed blame for the epidemic at Pueblo homes, "such culture beds of disease germs as these hovels."[26] From the Zuni agency, one inspector reported that the "native medicine men and medicine women still have a considerable influence over the tribe," adding that their influence was "frequently very detrimental to proper care of the sick." Moreover, despite noticing some improvement, the inspector noted, "the majority of Indians are prejudiced against treatment in the hospital," and "many are not even willing to submit to treatment by the physician in their own homes."[27]

Bantering freely about Pueblo "filth" and "immorality" and "barbarous practices," Anglo educators also denounced Pueblo customs surrounding defecation, elimination, and waste. In one remarkable letter, Mary Dissette suggested the creation of "commodes for the use of the sick." Secure in the belief that "there is no surer way of preserving disease germs and propagating that fever" than the Pueblo practices of elimination while sick, Dissette advocated "teach[ing] the Indians to use these [commodes] rather than the floor of their dwellings as they do now for . . . they will probably plaster the floor over again with mud and consider it thoroughly clean." Dissette then provided detailed specifications for the construction of the commodes. Preferring the use of wooden boxes to "chambers or their own pottery jar" because the boxes could be "burned up if they become foul," she recommended boxes of eighteen square inches by eighteen inches high, adding helpfully that "a low seat is bad for bowel troubles." The boxes were to have a hole in the top and no bottom, as well as a cover. Another smaller box, about a foot square, was to be made, filled with clean earth, "ready to be slipped into place" beneath the larger box.[28]

Indian students recognized the intensity of educators' interest in personal hygiene. In her memoirs, Polingaysi Qoyawayma describes how Anglo teachers and missionaries subjected Hopi Indians to humiliating baths and showers in the name of cleanliness and health. Curious about the Anglo mission schoolhouse that had just opened near her home, and lonely because it seemed that "all the children except herself had gone to school" (her parents joined several other families in resisting the decision by a village leader to commit all children to the mission school), Qoyawayma visited the school one day. As soon as she entered the door, however, the schoolmaster ordered that an older girl should first "take [her] and clean [her] up." Only after they "scrubbed her from head to toe" was she given a "ticking dress" and sent to the classroom. Several years later, at another government school, despite her unfamiliarity with showers and her terror that the "Water Serpent," described by her mother as a dangerous spirit who could impregnate a woman with his breath, would attack her through the gushing water, Qoyawayma was compelled "to bare her body and stand beneath that stream of water, to be seen and perhaps breathed upon by the Water Serpent." "Worst of all," she recounts, "she had seen women stripped and marched through a dipping vat like so many cattle because, so the white man claimed, an epidemic threatened the reservation residents."[29]

In the opinion of Polingaysi Qoyawayma, only slightly less painful than the memory of naked Hopi women forced by Anglos to march through disinfecting showers was the image of "grown Hopi men crying because white men had cut their hair." According to Qoyawayma, "In ancient days, her mother had told her, it had been considered a sin to cut the hair, except as ritual decreed. When the white men came, they insisted that the Hopi men have their long hair cut. When they refused, the white men cut their hair by force, disgracing them in the eyes of their people." Others echoed Qoyawayma's observation that length of hair represented a particularly vivid point of contention between Anglos and Indians. In an oral history interview, Andrew Becenti, a Navajo, observed that "Navajo used to let their hair grow and they used to braid their hair up, they don't want to cut their hairs off." Late-nineteenth-century anthropologist Frank Hamilton Cushing agreed that convincing Zunis to cut their hair was critical to their learning the "right ways of living [and] the right ways of working."[30]

Length of hair also drew sustained criticism from school correspondents. Writing from the Taos Pueblo in 1902, Alice Devine articulated the central role that length of hair played in distinguishing, in her words, "white man's ways" from "the old customs." Devine reported some limited success in enforcing the superintendent's recent order to "induce Indians to wear short hair, cease painting the face, and do away with customs detrimental to progress." Despite an initial setback when a Pueblo assistant was dismissed for refusing to cut his hair on the grounds that it would bring upon him "persecutions" from the Taos Pueblos, Devine noted that the subsequent assistant, Antonio Romero, "honors his position." In a splendid example of the ease with which educators associated appropriate body practices with civic respectability, Devine praised Romero because he "wears short hair, dresses in most becoming citizens' dress, is true and faithful, and fearless, both in the schoolroom and among his people."[31] In other cases, teachers considered the cutting of children's hair a worthy first step in their efforts to transform Pueblo traditions. Roy Stabler wrote from Santa Fe that his meeting with tribal officials led to "no big result" other than being allowed to cut the schoolchildren's hair. The painting of faces continued, though Stabler seemed to get some satisfaction from the fact that "they do not paint themselves profusely any more." Worse, the returned students appeared "far more obstinate to deal with than the older people."[32]

Besides language, hygiene, and length of hair, the choice of clothing appeared as a similarly racialized action in New Mexico schools as teachers targeted their students' adoption of "citizen clothes" (or lack thereof) as critical markers of whiteness. Teachers subtly and not so subtly emphasized the connection between wearing Anglo-style clothes and success both in the classroom and in the broader culture. As with questions of hygiene, boarding and day-school students were well aware of this emphasis on the part of educators on proper clothing. An anonymous informant recalled owning two sets of clothes at the Santa Fe Indian School: "We have everyday clothes and what do you call it a dress parade uniform, which is when we wear drilling in military drills, we wear those uniforms." Polingaysi Qoyawayma describes the "worn ticking dresses, cheap shoes, Hopi shoulder blankets, and trading post shawls" of Hopi girls and "the boys [being] just as unkempt in their homemade floursack shirts and denim pants." As K. Tsianina Lomawaima notes of the Chiloco boarding school in Oklahoma, "Clothing was a clearly marked terrain of power in the boarding school, especially in the girls' dormitories." Lomawaima adds that the surveillance of female students extended beyond their clothing to include a tracking of girls' menstrual cycles. "One alumna," she writes, "recalls the 'blue bag' full of rags issued to girls during their menstrual periods" that helped matrons monitor "each girl's cycle."[33]

Indian school administrators and teachers, however, hardly limited themselves to discussions of well-managed bodies inside the classrooms. Educators clearly had a sense that the success of the Indian school required reforms both in and out of the classroom; lapses on the part of students, and their teachers, could all too easily ruin years of training. Sexual misconduct in particular jeopardized both individual and institutional success. Sexual bodies out of control, whether student, teacher, or administrator, posed a special threat to the goals of Indian schooling and thus drew considerable attention. Indian school correspondents commented upon a wide range of sexual topics, including the need for clear gender distinctions, appropriate and inappropriate forms of sexual behavior in the schools and the surrounding villages, and acceptable and unacceptable bodily habits and practices.

In the first place, bodily comportment that suggested an unclear and porous boundary between men and women seemed to Anglo teachers and school administrators emblematic of less advanced civilizations and peoples. In opposing such "primitive" practices, educators installed a system of strict gender segregation, demanding clear differentiation between the sexes (certain behavior from Pueblo boys and other, quite different, behavior from Pueblo girls), and imposing physical boundaries between boys and girls. One educator's recommendation to his male students that they cut their hair and not "wear it like girls" linked body practices like hair length with masculinity and male identity. In describing a certain student as being willing to allow their hair to be trimmed, Anglo educators often portrayed that student not simply as compliant and well behaved, but as male. Petra Chavez Romero of Jemez Pueblo, who attended the Santa Fe Indian School between 1910 and 1916, remembered the physical division of boys from girls in the schools, each with their own buildings, and both "a line across the dining room" and a fence separating the two playing fields. "Girls never played with boys, or anything like that."[34]

Efforts at sexual differentiation and the enforcement of clear gender boundaries as integral to whiteness were even more obvious in the curriculum. Teachers repeatedly planned different activities, outings, and instruction for boys and girls. As the daily calendars, as well as the letters on clothing and cleanliness suggest, boys and girls could expect to be physically separated during everything from medical checkups to daily bathing and dressing. While Pueblo societies, as Margaret Jacobs observes, "practiced a well-defined sexual division of labor," Anglo educators hardly sought to replicate Pueblo gender roles. Rather, the goal was always to enforce Anglo notions of proper masculinity and femininity. It is difficult, for instance, not to see the Pueblo students' sense of themselves as male or female not being directly affected by sitting, day after day, hour after hour under pictures of "Madonna" and "Race of the Roman Chariots."[35]

Besides advocating clear gender differentiation, school officials routinely reported harsh punishments imposed on students who violated rules designed to maintain sexual order. In one case, the superintendent of the Haskell Institute in Kansas received a letter from the Santa Fe school concerning the applications to Haskell of Nerio and Crecencio Tafoya. Although the letter praised the "boys' records," calling their behavior "very good" and "perhaps deserving of further education," they had not been allowed to return to school in Santa Fe. The "cause of their discharge" was the discovery "during the spring that these two boys had gained entrance into the girls' dormitory one night." Due to their "indescretion [sic]," Nerio and Crecencio Tafoya had been expelled from school.[36] The two Tafoya boys were not the only students expelled for sneaking into girls' dormitories. The assistant superintendent of the Santa Fe boarding school sent a letter in 1913 to the head of the Carlisle Indian School in Pennsylvania regarding Felipe Cata, who, according to the letter, had "felt it necessary to misrepresent facts" in a letter written to the Carlisle school requesting a transfer there. He had apparently not mentioned the "real reason for his desire to transfer," which in the opinion of the assistant superintendent was that "he got into the girls' dormitory one day last spring and I expelled him." Like the Tafoyas, Cata was "a very intelligent and promising young man." The Santa Fe official concluded by noting, "I feel Felipe is a bright young man, and until I saw his letter to you I had no reason to suppose he was not truthful. I hope he will overcome this serious fault."[37]

3. Apache parents visiting their children at the Ramona Indian School, Santa Fe, New Mexico, ca. 1890. The proximity and enduring strength of Native American communities posed important challenges to Anglo educators. Photo by Dana B. Chase. Courtesy of the Museum of New Mexico, neg. no. 14213.

In 1914 Superintendent C. R. Jeffries posted a letter from the Mescalero Indian agency to the U.S. Indian school in Santa Fe. Jeffries described a romance between Encarnacion Rodriguez, "a girl who was recently transferred to your school [in Santa Fe] from Mescalero," and Sam Kenoi of the Mescalero agency. Rodriguez apparently "became entangled" with Kenoi and "caused considerable embarrassment to every one concerned." Jeffries noted that Kenoi was likely to attempt to write to Rodriguez and suggested that the superintendent "give her mail matter a little special attention for awhile, with the view of heading off any elopement, or other such scheme." He concluded by noting that "the young man [was] perfectly capable of planning" a scheme of that sort.[38]

Sexual transgressions outside the schools, in the surrounding Pueblo villages, similarly drew the concern of Anglo educators. In 1914 Superintendent H. F. Coggeshall reported the resignation of Deputy Special Officer Valentine Naranjo at San Juan Pueblo. According to Coggeshall, who apparently reviewed the testimony of witnesses in the case, Naranjo, while on duty, "went to the house of Jose Antonio Montoya, a San Juan Indian deputy, at the time he knew Montoya was under arrest and in custody of a constable at El Llano, a Mexican settlement some three or four miles distant from San Juan." Coggeshall stated that Naranjo "followed

Montoya's [unnamed] wife into the house and that on Montoya's unexpected return to the pueblo and to his home, Valentine was found alone in Montoya's house with Montoya's wife." Coggeshall concluded that "improper relations existed between Valentine and Montoya's wife, or at least that improper advances were made, or attempted, to Montoya's wife by Valentine." The superintendent also noted that Montoya's wife was "not altogether as blameless as she maintains." Although Valentine Naranjo "had rendered efficient service as an Indian deputy" and "been faithful and industrious," in the opinion of Coggeshall, he had acted with "conduct unbecoming an officer." The superintendent thus suggested "severance of his connection with the service."[39]

In 1916 John Rhodes, a farmer at the Santa Clara Pueblo, reported that Victor Naranjo, "a Santa Fe student now working in Colorado with the school boys there," was "the father of Eliza Cajete's child." According to Rhodes, Naranjo had acknowledged being the father of the child and even baptized the infant in his name. Promising to marry Cajete, but lacking the money to do so, he had traveled to Colorado to earn enough cash to pay for the wedding. In anticipation of the nuptials, the marriage banns had already been read once and "will be again next Sunday." Unfortunately, Rhodes noted, a letter from Naranjo had just arrived canceling the wedding plans. As a result, Naranjo's guardian, Severo Naranjo, apparently asked Rhodes to write to the superintendent requesting that the wayward young man be ordered home. Rhodes added that Naranjo "ought to bring all his money with him as the ceremony will cost fourteen dollars and both Eliza and the child need some clothes." Three weeks later another letter, the last record of the tale of Naranjo and Cajete in the school archives, was sent from the superintendent to Rhodes. In it, the superintendent reported that he had expected Naranjo to marry Cajete and did not understand why he had changed his mind. Moreover, according to the letter, Naranjo had been allowed to leave school for the purposes of marrying and establishing a family. Consequently it was "a matter for the Superintendent of the Pueblos [not the superintendent of Indian schools] to adjust it if he is unwilling to marry the girl whom he got into trouble last year."[40]

In denouncing sexual misconduct, educators did more than simply report misbehavior. As Ann Stoler reminds us, the effects of colonial discourses on sexuality were not limited to colonial subjects and students. Colonial discourses had constitutive effects, inciting and creating the identities of colonizers and colonial subjects as much as simply reciting them. Placed alongside Pedro Cabán's observations about Puerto Rico and Margaret Jacobs's description of the deeply gendered efforts to reform and regulate Pueblos in New Mexico, Stoler further helps us locate Indian schools more squarely within a colonial context. Viewing colonialism from a more expansive vista than the careful studies of Cabán and Jacobs, Stoler describes a colonial arena in which the discourses and constitutive effects of sexual desire represent one of several major avenues in determining citizenship and belonging.

Like European colonizers whose sexual discourses "secured the distinctions of individual white bodies and the privileges of a white body politic," New Mexico Indian school educators sketched their own identities in their denunciations of sexual misconduct and bodily incoherence among the Pueblos. Anglo educators, after all, were no more secure in their whiteness and fitness for citizenship than other Anglo newcomers to New Mexico. Such educators were products of turn-of-the-century America, where vexations of whiteness, proper masculinity and femininity, and modernity proliferated. As inhabitants of New Mexico, Anglo educators had few more political rights and privileges than their Pueblo students. They could not vote for president or national representatives and were, at the turn of the twentieth century, inescapably associated with the same "mongrel breed" known as New Mexicans that were routinely denounced by broader America. Like physicians, as I will describe in more detail in chapter 6, who pleaded for acceptance as full Americans from the far outskirts of America, the Anglo denunciations of Pueblo failures of bodily integrity helped educators constitute themselves, by contrast, as both fit for citizenship and white.[41]

For instance, Anglo educators, in their discussions of "mixed" and "pure"-blooded students and the supposedly troublesome racial boundaries among Indians in New Mexico, defined themselves, in contrast, as racially pure and white. Schools distinguished between "full blood," "mixed blood," and non–Native American ancestry in New Mexico, with the most common differentiation, unsurprisingly given the demographics of New Mexico, between "Indians" and "Mexicans." Only students demonstrating some degree of "Indian blood" were permitted to attend the government schools. Comments on the precise amount of "Indian blood" ranged from the detailed to the off-handed and casual. One teacher reported that "Luciano Gallegos and the Hurtado family have Indian blood, the former not Pueblo, the latter Santa Ana."[42] In another case, Felipe Valdes wrote from San Jose that "the father of three half-breed girls wanting to attend" the Santa Fe boarding school had contacted him. The mother, according to Valdes, is "a pure Navajo, brought from the Navajo country when a child." A year later Valdes passed along a note of introduction in Santa Fe for Rafael Aragon, a "full blooded Navajo." Aragon, in Valdes's words, was accompanying "two half-breed girls" to the boarding school.[43]

This concern with racial identity, the "blood" of students and their families, appears throughout the Indian school records. In 1908 U.S. Indian Service superintendent Charles Burton wrote to Santa Fe, asking school superintendent Crandall to look into the case of Mrs. Isobel [*sic*] Trujillo, "a full-blood Navajo woman," who had requested that her two grandchildren be allowed to attend the Santa Fe boarding school. Burton asked Crandall to accompany him to visit the family and "investigate this woman's story," apparently with the sole aim of determining through personal, face-to-face contact with her whether Trujillo was in fact a "full-blood Navajo woman." Several weeks later Burton wrote to Crandall again, reporting that he (Burton) had visited the Trujillo family and was "perfectly sure that she [was] a full-blood Navajo women [*sic*]."[44] Discussions of racial identity extended beyond the rights to education at the government schools. In 1905 Dr. M. S. Martin wondered from Española about his obligations to care for non-Pueblos who became sick. Martin reported that he had "been attending the wife of Thomas Dozier, the 'squawman,' " and wanted advice as to whether she was "entitled to [his] services, gratuities, the same as though she lived in the pueblo."[45]

Just as denouncing the racial ambiguity of Indians could serve to accentuate the supposed racial purity, and whiteness, of Anglo educators during a period of unclear racial boundaries throughout America, so, too, could the racialization of Indian villages—descriptions of their purportedly deviant and destructive bodily comportment—help emphasize both the inferiority of Pueblos in general and the superiority of Anglos and white culture. Anglo teachers and administrators saw a clear link between the success of their "uplifting mission" and occurrences, attitudes, and behavior outside the schools, especially in the villages. The consumption of alcohol and participation in Indian public events like feast-day celebrations and dances represented other sets of contested (and, in the eyes of educators, incoherent, uncivilized, and racially inferior) forms of bodily comportment. The consumption of alcohol by Indians appeared especially troubling, invoking repeated denunciations in the correspondence. In December 1913 Reverend G. Haelterman of Santa Cruz received a long letter from the superintendent of the Santa Fe boarding school. The letter assured the reverend that the Indian office had the "authority and law to meet the situation of trespass on Indian lands, the introduction of liquor on Indian lands, and the sale and furnishing of liquor to Indians." After several weeks of "get[ting] things in shape for [their] campaign against the liquor traffic among the Indians," the superintendent confidently informed Haelterman, "I now have a white man" ready to gather evidence "against those furnishing liquor to the Indians." Several months earlier,

Reverend Haelterman had asked the superintendent to "come after that Morris of Santa Cruz, who has been handing it [alcohol] out so freeley [sic] to all Indians who came along no matter from where." According to Haelterman, Santa Clara, San Ildefonso, and San Juan Pueblos benefited most conspicuously from Morris's charity. "If any man deserves the stripes and a big number on his back," exclaimed the clearly exasperated minister, "it is that fellow." [46]

That same month, Superintendent Coggeshall detailed the arrest of Jose Maria Tafoya of Santa Clara Pueblo. "The boys" (likely special deputies employed by the Indian service) apparently found Tafoya "very drunk," but not in possession of any alcohol. As Tafoya "acted very nasty about being pinched," the deputies decided to detain him. There being no jail in Santa Clara, they took him to the house of one of the deputies. Coggeshall had rushed to the house to pass judgment on the wayward Tafoya, but without any hard evidence against him, "after a good raking, the only thing to do was to turn him loose." The letter then describes the arrest of Eulogio Gonzales, a "Mexican" charged with attempting to furnish alcohol to a "San Ildefonso Indian." [47]

Descriptions of excessive alcohol use stitched together discourses on body practices and racial otherness. Dominant Anglo discourse rarely associated alcoholic excess with either whiteness or proper masculinity; drunkenness appeared more often as characteristic of nonwhite or quasi-white groups. Moreover, in New Mexico and elsewhere, legal prohibitions restricted the sale and transport of alcohol to the Pueblo Indians, effectively adding potential criminality to the charge of drunken debauch. Accounts of alcohol consumption (which always appeared as excessive and out of control, rather than socially acceptable, appropriate, or ritually based) tended to differentiate rather strictly between those Indians acting sober and those behaving exactly the opposite. The latter group, the drunk and intemperate, thus were associated with "primitivism" and "savagery" and unfitness for citizenship. Anglo educators, in contrast, depicted themselves, as well as those Pueblo men and women who followed their lead, as exemplars of American respectability. [48]

Correspondents similarly worried about Pueblo feast days, especially the dancing that occurred during such celebrations. In 1914 Mary Dissette reported from Santo Domingo that twenty-eight of her students "did not go to the San Felipe feast and our Indian assistants did not go either." Instead, teachers and students "made a *clean* day of it" (emphasis mine). They "mopped and oiled every floor, cleaned yards, and served all a picnic lunch." And, Dissette reported, "they thought it lots nicer than the fiesta." [49] From Picuris, Mrs. Starr Hayes wrote to Superintendent Crandall requesting a letter from him to the effect that he did not wish to have

"Ramita," presumably an assistant at the Picuris school, participate in any feast dances. Hayes apparently refused to release Ramita when her father Julian Duran asked "if he might have Ramita for the dance last Friday when the Governor was installed." Hayes claimed that Duran "was quite ugly about it," but that ultimately he relented. Ramita, she proudly announced, "did not dance, of course, as I told her not to, and she would not have done so because . . . I had explained to her that you wished her to set a good example by not taking part in any of the dances."[50]

Deeply concerned with the potentially harmful effects of Indian festivities on the goals of Indian schooling, Anglo educators also celebrated the involvement of their students in more acceptable, "American"-style events. One letter from a school official to Jesus Joaquin, a former student living in Tucson, noted that "the boys are very busy with their football games."[51] In reply to a request from the manager of the University of New Mexico baseball team that the UNM squad and the Indian school team face off for a game, an assistant superintendent noted that while "we will be glad to play the game," the team could not pay any of the game expenses. Furthermore, according to the official, "Mr. Gurule, our disciplinarian who accompanied our team to Albuquerque last year, feels that our boys did not have a square deal in the game." "Unless we can be assured that you will be ready to be fair," he continued, "we would hardly want to play again."[52] Financial and fair-play problems aside, school administrators clearly had few problems with Pueblo students participating in the organized exertions of Anglo sporting events.

Educators also encouraged Pueblo students to participate in Christian religious events at the schools. One former student remembered Christmas gifts arriving in "precious boxes," and during one Christmas "each one of us little girls received one of those [boxes] containing a doll and sewing kit." In a letter to Juanito Naranjo of Española, the father of three girls at the Santa Fe boarding school, one official acknowledged receiving a five-dollar bill in the mail from Naranjo, presumably to pay for the girls' transportation back to Española during the Christmas holiday. The administrator also noted that one daughter, Leucaria, was "in the Christmas canata" and would likely not depart for home until December 24.[53]

Besides applauding Indian participation in Anglo events, educators vigorously defended those Indian men and women who chose not to participate in feast-day celebrations and other Indian public events. Juan Pedro Melchor and his wife, for instance, managed to convince Luella Gallup to write a letter to Superintendent Coggeshall describing the family's involvement in a land dispute. The letter from Gallup to Coggeshall begins by observing that "the Indians are making trouble for Juan Pedro Melchor." Apparently to persuade Coggeshall to take up their case, Gallup described Melchor and his wife as the couple who have "refused for some time to take any part in the pueblo ceremonies." The Melchor family's credentials thus established, Gallup recounted the land dispute in essence as an example of unfair Pueblo encroachment on the rights of an aggrieved landowner.[54]

Letters like Gallup's accentuate the complex nature of Indian education and colonial rule in New Mexico. In New Mexico, recall, Pueblo Indians held a certain amount of power, and negotiations between Indian parents and community leaders and Anglo educators were inevitable. On the one hand, many Pueblo parents sent their children to government schools, while others cut their hair, adopted "citizens dress," and refused to attend annual fiesta days and feasts. Pueblos and Anglos similarly seemed at least in partial agreement on the care of the "insane," especially those threatening or engaging in violence. One doctor's requisition for medicine from Picuris noted, "I have a case of change of life, menopause, at Taos Pueblo and the woman is losing her mind." Adding that a Picuris boy was "suffering from convultions [sic]," the physician requested "for these two cases about two pints of Elixir of Chloral and Potassium Bromide."[55] In several cases, Pueblos seemed willing, even eager, to commit such people to asylums. According to one letter, the governor and the father of "a violent insane man at Picurice [sic] named Cruz Lopez" apparently "want[ed] him sent to [the] asylum." The man had to be "watched all the time" and had only recently "injured a child." Though unable to transport him all the way to Santa Fe—the letter quotes the Picuris leaders as saying they were "too poor" to afford to do so—they offered to take him as far as Embudo.[56] A year later a letter announced that the Taos Pueblos decided to send an "insane woman" with the reputation of being "quite violent at times" to the asylum at Las Vegas. One of the Taos leaders, "Old Ventura," apparently justified their decision because "they are citizens and have the right to put her there."[57]

At other times, events within the schools themselves strained relations between Anglo educators and Pueblo communities. When the Albuquerque Indian School opened in 1884, leaders at Santo Domingo and Jemez Pueblos were at first suspicious of sending their children to boarding schools. Only when new officials were appointed did the leaders agree to support boarding schools for their children. Nonetheless, Pueblo leaders and parents continued to approach government schools with caution. "There has been a persistent, systemic effort to prevent the people from patronizing these schools," one official complained in 1894, "and recently some of the patrons have been induced to have their children removed from Albuquerque by a writ of habeas corpus."[58]

Moreover, as we have seen, while educators promised to instill in their students the habits and customs of "civilized" peoples, which included sexual propriety and clear and unambiguous gender roles, the educational setting itself undercut such ambitions, bringing boys and girls from throughout New Mexico into intimate and potentially romantic and sexual settings. Sexual misconduct on the part of Anglo educators could similarly threaten the educational goals of the educators. In an 1891 report, Robert Gardner, the U.S. Indian inspector, addressed charges brought by three female employees of the Albuquerque day school against school superintendent W. B. Creager. According to Sallie Gause, a teacher, Creager repeatedly propositioned her, offering her money and a better position in the school if she would have sex with him. At one point, Creager came to her room and asked her to leave the door unlocked so that he could enter her room late at night. Creager also told Gause, in her words, "that his wife was an invalid, and that she did not object to his going to some nice woman." Minnie Walter, assistant matron and nurse, was similarly forced to fend off Creager during a trip she, the superintendent, and Juan Leite, a Pueblo driver, made to Isleta Pueblo. During the trip Creager promised to raise Walter's salary if she would, in her words, "permit him to have sexual intercourse and be his mistress at the school." Walter replied that she would rather "lose [her] life and all [she] had, than lose [her] virtue." Undeterred, Creager promptly asked her if she knew of "a young lady or [would] find him one to use for that purpose." He once again invoked his "invalid wife," who he asserted, "would not care if he got a clean, nice woman to cohabit with." When Walter suggested that "there were public houses of that kind in town and that he had better go there," he answered that Walter was "pure," and that "he did not want any second hand woman." Finally, Lillian Carr, an assistant matron, described how Creager "made indecent and immoral proposals to her in the cottage at the school used by Superintendent Creager as his residence." According to Carr, he "threw his arms around her and attempted to force her to his bed," but she managed to "disengage herself from his embrace" and escape the cottage. Creager was also charged by one of the teachers, Mary Benbow, with "being a profane man and using profane language in her classroom."[59]

Inspector Gardner subsequently interviewed the three women, Superintendent Creager, and a number of other school employees about the allegations. Given Creager's absolute denial of the accusations and in the absence of any eyewitnesses to the attacks (Pueblo driver Juan Leite apparently did not qualify as a reliable witness), Gardner concluded that there was "no one to support the charges [the women] made." "The subject," he noted, seeming to throw up his hands in frustration, "now resolves itself into one of veracity." Fortunately, Gardner observed, the matter seemed resolvable without any firm decision on his part. Creager apparently had applied for the position of president of the University of New Mexico, and believed, according to Gardner, "from statements made him by members of the board . . . that his application will be favorably acted upon." Mary Benbow, who Gardner believed spoke truthfully about Creager's frequent use of profane language, similarly transferred to the Navajo agency school. As for Sallie Gause, "who has not been appointed," Gardner noted tersely, "I don't think she should be." Minnie Walter, though reputed to be "an excellent matron and nurse," appeared to the inspector "to talk too much for her own good and the good of the school, thereby being a disturbing element." He recommended that she also not be reappointed. Finally, he reported that Lillian Carr did not wish to continue at the day school and had secured a job with the Albuquerque public schools.[60]

News that the allegations had apparently spread beyond the narrow confines of the school was an added, and especially intriguing, complication of the case. As "the Subject of Conversation and Criticism," the affair struck the inspector as not entirely to "the benefit or success of the school." Most troubling was the likelihood, in Gardner's view, "that the parents of the children attending this school, or those to attend in the near future, would object to sending their children to this school, alleging as a cause that the superintendent was not a moral man." Anglo educators, for all their faith in the superiority of whiteness, were well aware that their civilizing mission in education (and their jobs) could not continue without the support of Pueblo parents and community leaders. If displeased or offended, Pueblo parents had a certain ability to withdraw their children from the schools. With such a worrisome possibility in mind, Gardner thus suggested that "under the present existing circumstance a change might be for the better."[61]

Other Anglo educators similarly bemoaned the persistent nature of Pueblo resistance to Anglo incursions. In 1920 an administrator described the ongoing efforts to "secure the attendance" of Pueblo children at the government school at Taos Pueblo. While himself "a little bit loath to use force in placing these children in school," the writer nonetheless advised "regulations" that would more effectively persuade attendance. The administrator then turned to an attack on the political leadership at Taos Pueblo. "Conditions at the Taos Pueblo," he said, "while in some respects good, are in others a disgrace. The fact that a long haired, dirty, ignorant Indian, because he happens to have been selected by a bunch of Indians of his own class for Governor, can set at naught all efforts of our Government to bring education and civilization to his people is little more than a caricature on our Department." Among the charges leveled against the governor were levying fines against those who work with whites, arranging certain marriages, controlling work orders and schedules, and, appearing no less serious in the eyes of the writer, "prevent[ing] the returned, educated young Indians from wearing citizens clothes in the Pueblo."[62]

Finally, take the example of Matthew Derig, who along with his wife was a teacher at Santo Domingo. In response to a 1902 directive prohibiting long hair and the painting of faces, Derig submitted a handful of suggestions to the superintendent. Addressing the comportment of students who had returned to their villages, Derig noted, "I regret to say that all of them wear long hair and all of them, as I verily believe, on various occasions, paint their faces and join in the dances; they also wear blankets together with their garments." Dances struck the teacher as particularly dangerous, not only interfering with the regular schedule of school work, but "dissipat[ing] the energies very much of the young and old." The "long siege and practice" of the dances, which Derig claimed could last several days, occurred throughout the week, even "occasionally on Saturday and Sunday." Furthermore, the dances were evidently "secret." Some eight secret dances had been performed in the last nine months, with the children kept absent from school each of those days.[63]

Most troubling, for Derig, was the issue of young men's hair. According to Derig, students typically attended school with long hair. The only exceptions were a boy whose hair Derig "had trimed [sic] close because he did not keep his hair clean," and two boys whom the teacher managed to convince to "cut their hair like boys and not wear it like girls." After the arrival of the directive, Mr. and Mrs. Derig apparently went on a bit of a haircutting spree, immediately trimming "the hair of nine boys modern style," and eventually "making, in all, fourteen boys, who had their hair trimmed white boys' style."[64]

Unfortunately for the Derigs, a mere two hours after school let out on the day of the trimming, "the governor and interpreter with several other Indians" paid the couple a visit. The governor told the Derigs that while the Santo Domingos consented to the cutting of the children's hair short when they went away to boarding school in Santa Fe, they made no such concessions when the children stayed at the Santo Domingo school. Derig reported that he spent an hour trying "to reason it out with him," but finally agreed not to cut the boys' hair in the future, but merely to advise parents and children as to the manifold benefits of short hair.[65]

The imprints of American colonial aspirations in New Mexico are unmistakable in the stuttering attempts like those of Matthew Derig to impress upon Pueblo students and their families the imperatives of proper bodily comportment. Indeed, the enduring presence and political influence of Indian leaders forced Anglo educators into a colonial educational model that bears striking similarity to educational institutions emerging elsewhere in America's turn-of-the-twentieth-century imperial domain. Pedro Cabán, for instance, has highlighted several objectives of the American educational program in turn of-the-twentieth-century Puerto Rico. He points in particular to American plans that included "imparting English language skills," conducting Americanization projects such as "instilling civic values, and patriotism for the United States," and impressing upon students the importance of proper, at least according to American models, gender roles and the "preservation of a male-centered family unit." As the preceding chapter has demonstrated, such objectives were almost identical to the goals of Anglo educators in New Mexico Indian schools. So, too, did the multiple forms of Indian resistance in New Mexico echo Puerto Ricans' refusal to comply completely with American imperial demands on the island.[66]

This chapter has suggested that central to the racialization projects of Anglo educators in New Mexico was teaching and enforcing the proper regulation and maintenance of bodily and social boundaries. Like the rest of New Mexico, the struggles between Pueblo students, many of them earnest and energetic learners, and Anglo educators, similarly enthused and excited about their professions, over bodies and body practices reveal much about race, citizenship, and colonialism along one of America's most ragged of edges. As the following chapter will make clear, Anglo educators were among the many newcomers to New Mexico who found themselves compelled by their exceptional circumstances to compromise. In racialization projects directed at Hispanos in New Mexico, a group, recall, comprising nearly half the population and controlling significant wealth and political power, the stutter steps of empire evident in New Mexico Indian schools emerged once again in another realm of imperial aspiration: the courtroom.

CARNAL KNOWLEDGE

RACIALIZING HISPANO BODIES
IN THE COURTS

In 1848 the United States and Mexico signed the Treaty of Guadalupe Hidalgo to end the Mexican-American War. Among the provisions of the treaty were guarantees that Mexicans in the newly annexed sections of the United States would have their property rights honored and protected. The treaty also stipulated that those Mexicans who chose to remain in the United States would be granted full American citizenship. Article IX of the treaty reads in part, "Mexicans who, in the territories aforesaid, shall not preserve the character of citizens of the Mexican Republic . . . shall be incorporated into the Union of the United States, and be admitted at the proper time . . . to the enjoyment of all the rights of citizens of the United States."[1]

Despite these legal assurances, Mexicans throughout the Southwest found themselves vulnerable under the newly imposed American legal system. Military strength may have initiated American occupation, and to an extent sustained it, but it was in the courts where many of the most profound battles occurred. Indeed, American lawyers, judges, and court officials were critical to American conquest and incorporation. In New Mexico, legal battles between Hispanos and Anglos over property rights were especially fierce, prompting several scholars to note recently the similarities between the role of legal institutions in conquest in New Mexico and the rule of law in other colonial settings like the Caribbean and Africa.[2]

This chapter will extend such analysis into the realm of trials for sexual assault and the embodied racialization of Hispanos. The chapter will also introduce a broader discussion of elite Hispanos, who were a critical segment of New Mexico's racial order. Due to the presence and political and economic power of elite Hispanos, Anglos were hesitant to label all Hispanos as dangerous and sexually violent, lest they offend powerful individuals and families. As I will demonstrate, the alterations that the presence of elite Hispanos demanded were critical factors in the exceptional nature of racialization and colonial order in New Mexico.

Denouncing the sexual behavior of nonwhite men and women has been a common strategy in efforts, in both America and elsewhere, to deny political rights to particular communities and individuals. In the American South after the Civil War, vicious white terrorists murdered and sexually mutilated hundreds of African American men for alleged sexual attacks on white women. Such allegations, as historians and contemporary observers noted, were frequently fabrications fueled by stereotypical notions among white Americans about the supposed sexual voracity of African American men. Moreover, the targets of such lynchings were often economically and politically successful African Americans like shop owners and businesspeople. Attacks on the sexuality of African American men (besides stereotypes about the sexual deviance of African Americans, lynching victims were often castrated) thus accompanied attempts to deny African Americans economic and political success. In a like manner, in Puerto Rico in the 1890s, middle-class white men and working-class Afro–Puerto Rican men found common cause, and political unity, in a shared denunciation of the purported sexual aberrance of working-class Afro–Puerto Rican women.[3]

Sexual and racial politics were no less intertwined in sexual offense cases in New Mexico. In New Mexico, most sexual assault cases involved Spanish-surnamed men and women; a great many of them, given the large percentage of Hispanos in New Mexico, were likely Hispanos rather than Indians with Spanish surnames. This chapter will draw evidence from approximately 150 rape charges in New Mexico between 1880 and 1920. With the exception of a handful of cases from the New Mexico Supreme Court, most of the rape charges summarized here originated in four counties: Bernalillo, Doña Ana, San Miguel, and Santa Fe. Those counties were four of the most populated counties in turn-of-the-century New Mexico, covering, respectively, the territory's largest cities: Albuquerque, Las Cruces, Las Vegas, and Santa Fe. In 1880 these four counties accounted for almost half (47%) of New Mexico's total population; in 1900 they made up two-fifths (42%) of the territory.[4]

TABLE 3.1. SURNAME OF WOMEN BRINGING RAPE CHARGES*

	Spanish	Non-Spanish	Mixed	Unknown	Total
Bernalillo County	20	13	0	0	33
San Miguel County	41	9	1	3	54
Santa Fe County	12	4	2	0	18
Total	73	26	3	3	105

Source: New Mexico State Records Center and Archives, Santa Fe.
*Only the name of the assailant, not the accuser, was available in most Doña Ana County records.

As table 3.1 indicates, Spanish-surnamed women brought the clear majority (70%) of rape charges in the three counties. Like their accusers, the men accused of rape also overwhelmingly had Spanish surnames, once again in the range of 75 percent (table 3.2). In San Miguel County, for instance, almost 90 percent of the rape indictments charged Hispanos. Only in Bernalillo County did the percentage of Spanish-surnamed defendants drop below 60 percent, and it did not dip by much (57%).

In the cases where the names of both the accuser and the assailant are available, 64 percent of the rape charges were filed against Spanish-surnamed men for sexually assaulting Spanish-surnamed women (table 3.3).

Likewise, the majority (58%) of the rape indictments brought against Anglo men, only thirty in all, resulted from attacks on Anglo women. In Santa Fe County, not a single rape charge was entered against an Anglo man for raping an Hispana and only one occurred in San Miguel County. The twenty indictments involving assailants and accusers with different surnames included eleven Spanish-surnamed men raping non-Spanish-surnamed or mixed-heritage women, and five Anglo men raping mixed-heritage women or Hispanas. In the four remaining indictments, two mixed-heritage men (Jose Maria Clark and Florencio Pfeiffer twice) were charged with raping Spanish-surnamed women and one (Jose Cutler) for raping a woman with a non-Spanish surname.

To a certain extent, such findings should come as little surprise considering the near-majority Hispano population in New Mexico during this period. Still, it is striking that between roughly 1880 and 1910 in Santa Fe and Las Vegas combined, two of New Mexico's biggest cities with the largest percentage of Anglo newcomers, only one Anglo man was accused of sexually assaulting an Hispana. New Mexico in this respect closely resembled broader America. White men throughout America exercised

TABLE 3.2. RAPE ASSAILANTS BY COUNTY AND SURNAME

	Spanish	Non-Spanish	Mixed	Total
Bernalillo	19	11	3	33
Doña Ana	32	9	0	41
San Miguel	47	6	1	54
Santa Fe	12	4	2	18
Total	110	30	6	146

Source: New Mexico State Records Center and Archives, Santa Fe.

TABLE 3.3. RAPE ASSAULTS BY COUNTY AND SURNAME

	Both Spanish	Both Non-Spanish	Mixed	Surnames Unclear	Total
Bernalillo	16	7	10	0	33
San Miguel	39	4	8	3	54
Santa Fe	12	4	2	0	18
Total	67	15	20	3	105

Source: New Mexico State Records Center and Archives, Santa Fe.

great sexual latitude, especially in terms of their privileged access to a wide range of sexual partners, including nonwhite women (and men).[5] That Anglo men would disproportionately be unlikely to be accused of sexual assault in New Mexico follows a familiar American pattern.

In certain respects, the following trials for sexual assault in New Mexico also followed familiar American models. In New Mexico, sexual assault cases consistently served as spaces for the racialization of poor, non-elite Hispanos, the linking of the bodily comportment of Hispano victims, defendants, and witnesses with supposed threats to public safety and the well-being of the society at large. The portrayal of non-elite Hispanos and Hispanas as sexually deviant helped Anglos solidify the distinction between the proper bodily comportment of Anglos and the illicit bodies of Hispanos. This racialization process was an insidious aspect of more general sexual discourses in rape trials that especially targeted women. Like rape trials throughout the country, rape trials in New Mexico differentiated between the sexually temperate and normal, and thus credible to judges and juries, and the supposedly untrustworthy sexually deviant. The perils and humiliations facing women brave enough to bring rape charges, the expanding modern medical discourse of perversion and desire, anxious and uncertain masculinity, all appear to have weathered rather well the journey to New Mexico. In other respects, in a tension I will highlight throughout the book, sexual assault trials, especially when involving elite Hispanos, followed new and unprecedented trails.

Imagine as the chapter progresses the effect of these trials on, say, an Hispano juror, or indeed upon other members of the court or even the audience seated in the gallery, including women (though as the following trial makes clear, women's attendance at rape trials could be a source of some contention). The juror would likely notice that both sets of attorneys, as well as judges and the occasional juror, tend primarily to discuss, describe, and evaluate the embodied actions of the female rape victims. Where she walked, what she wore, how she pushed the attacker away, the words of protest she uttered, all came under the often suspicious eyes of the courtroom. The body practices of the accused—the men's inclination for insobriety and public misbehavior, their tendency toward violence, their ability or inability to control their passions, their reputations for fidelity—also materialize before the court, the jury, and the assembled audience.

The juror, furthermore, might take note of how the descriptions of particular body practices often turned around whether they represented "normal" or "abnormal" behavior. As will become apparent, abnormal bodily comportment, in addition to sexual assault, included the following: literal and threatened physical violence; "shingling," or cutting the hair of another; hysterical, sobbing, complaining, or pleading ("calling for the Holy Virgin") speech; carnal intercourse or cohabitation with nonrelated persons; engaging in prostitution; drinking alcohol to excess; walking along city streets at night without clear purpose; expressing sexual desire for older women; failing to call attention immediately to a sexual assault; failure to resist a sexual assault with the appropriate vigor; and women speaking of "private" matters (i.e., matters relating to female sexual organs) in public. Normal body practices, on the other hand, covered the following: calmly reading a newspaper; going to sleep early; drinking little, if any, alcohol; marital, preferably reproductive, sexual intercourse; male "clean" habits with respect to women, such as not "running after" women; male sexual desire for women of an appropriate age (above the age of consent); and gynecological examinations of women by "regular" male physicians. These actions of the human body in rape trials were racialized and sexualized, coming to be associated, as in Indian schools, with racial superiority or inferiority, sexual propriety or deviance, and fitness for citizenship.

The following case of *New Mexico v. Prudencio Martinez* offers a useful example of the sexual politics at the heart of New Mexico's emerging racial order.[6] According to the transcript of the trial, at a quarter to ten on a cold, wet night in Las Vegas, New Mexico, in early February 1908, Mary Ragan heard a noise outside her back door. Glancing at the clock, she pulled open the door and found one of her boarders, Margaret Carling, stumbling up the stairs sobbing uncontrollably. Mud caked Margaret's face, hands, and clothes, and her hat dangled from the back of her head. She staggered around the kitchen, according to Ragan, "not hardly know[ing] what she was doing," with "the front of her waist . . . all torn open." Margaret Carling, Ragan testified, "looked very bad." After fifteen minutes, recovering slightly from "her hysterical condition," Margaret Carling managed to report to Mary Ragan and her husband that she had been raped.[7]

Margaret Carling had come to Las Vegas two years earlier, in 1906, from Ontario, Canada, at the age of eighteen without family or friends in New Mexico. She worked as a telegraph operator at the Colorado Telephone Company from five in the evening until nine o'clock at night and usually walked home alone. On the night of February 10, Carling left work at a little after nine and noticed two unfamiliar men coming across Main Street from Old Town toward her.[8] She sped up her pace and even started to run, but the men followed, catching her and dragging her into an alley behind the *La Voz del Pueblo* newspaper building. Testifying that the men spoke Spanish throughout the attack, except for threatening her in English to shoot her if she screamed, Carling described how Prudencio Martinez and Felipe Garcia covered her mouth, threw her down into the mud of the alley, and raped her.

The first witness in the trial, Dr. McClanahan, claimed to have "attend[ed] [Margaret Carling] in a professional capacity" the day after the attack. The doctor examined Carling "with instruments," noting that "her external female organ" was "bruised" and that "the mucus membrane in the virgina [*sic*] had been bleeding." The doctor testified that he found Margaret Carling in "a very nervous condition." According to McClanahan, Carling was "unable to answer for herself," forcing Mr. Ragan, her landlord, to describe "what the trouble was." Though unable to speak, Carling nevertheless apparently "complained a great deal of a great deal of pain" during the examination. The doctor concluded from his examination that "she had been roughly handled." He stated, "The external lips [of the vagina] were bruised and reddened, that is, as if the hand had been pressed against them forcibly." When asked by prosecuting attorney C. W. G. Ward if "the person of Margaret Carling had been violated," McClanahan answered, "I should say, yes." Ward ended by prompting

McClanahan to describe the position of his patient during the examination as partially dressed and lying on a couch.

It should be noted that Dr. McClanahan's examination of Carling's genitals drew no pause in the trial transcript. Nobody, not even the defense attorney, accused him of impropriety or an irregular use of his eyes, hands, or fingers. In fact, the uncanny resemblance between the details of the rape itself and the explanation of the medical examination—both causing outcry and pain, both forcing Carling to be prone and partially dressed—probably served to highlight the difference between a normal relationship between a physician and a patient and an abnormal event such as rape.

McClanahan's special status as a physician was further emphasized when the next witness, Mary Ragan, took the stand. Another member of the prosecution team, S. G. Davis, announced to the judge that he and defense attorney George Hunker had agreed, if satisfactory to the judge, that "the remainder of the hearing of the present case, at least so far as the ladies who are to testify is concerned, shall be private." In other words, in the opinion of the lawyers, the court gallery should not hear the testimony of a woman—presumably including both Mrs. Ragan and Margaret Carling. Of course, no such objection arose during Dr. McClanahan's testimony, despite, as I have noted, the apparently far more "private" nature of his account. Regardless, the judge agreed to the motion and cleared the gallery. While police testimony and medical findings drew no criticism, both Ragan and Carling's testimony in court assumed an inescapable air of impropriety and the forbidden.[9]

Rather than challenge Carling's reputation for chastity and honesty, or her willingness to engage in consensual sexual intercourse, Prudencio Martinez's defense team argued, quite simply, that Prudencio Martinez could not have raped Margaret Carling, that he was nowhere near that alley on the night of February 10. According to Martinez himself, and his parents and siblings, the young man had been home reading *La Revista Católica*, a local newspaper, the entire evening. Several members of his family testified that Martinez rarely visited saloons and spent most of his evenings either reading or going skating with his sisters. The defense also argued that Margaret Carling had mistakenly identified Martinez as one of her attackers, never, they claimed, actually picking him out of a lineup. Finally, defense witnesses stated that Felipe Garcia, who pled guilty and testified that he was Martinez's accomplice in the attack, had a poor reputation for sobriety and was untrustworthy.

Faced with expert testimony, Carling's positive identification, and the confession of Felipe Garcia, Prudencio Martinez's defense team faced a difficult task. George Hunker's opening statement began by challenging the claim that Garcia and Martinez had spent the evening drinking before attacking Carling. Hunker argued that Garcia had lied about Martinez's involvement and that Martinez passed the entire evening of February 10, from five o'clock onward, at home with his family. After questioning a handful of witnesses about Felipe Garcia's reputation for "truth and veracity" (all answered "bad"), Hunker called to the stand successive members of the Martinez family: sisters Felipa, Guadalupe, and Rosaria, father Nicanor, and mother Celsa Garcia de Martinez. All five recounted essentially the same story. According to their account, Prudencio Martinez arrived home around five in the evening, ate dinner with the family, and, while his mother and sister Rosaria prepared tripe in the kitchen, read *La Revista Católica* alongside his father, who read first silently and then aloud to the two daughters a book about "the mines in Siberia," until going to bed at ten o'clock. Martinez emerges in his family's testimony as stationary and stable, sitting and reading the newspaper, enveloped safely in the family home in Old Town, while his mother and sisters labor over the tripe well into the evening. Despite this attempt to depict the Martinez family as *gente decente*, in historian Leticia Garza-Falcón's apt phrase, Prudencio Martinez was ultimately convicted in the rape of Margaret Carling.[10]

Anglo prosecutors in *NM v. Martinez* went to great lengths to racialize Prudencio Martinez, to associate alcohol consumption, movement along city streets, and speaking Spanish with Hispano, non-Anglo behavior and identity. Prosecutors were quick to link Prudencio Martinez and Felipe Garcia, who, it was noted, both spoke primarily in Spanish during the attack, in Old—that is, Hispano—Las Vegas. Prosecutors described two drunk Hispanos stumbling up from Old Town to wreak havoc on an innocent young woman. Mobile, predator-like characters in the prosecution's account, Garcia and Martinez were said to have not only crossed the bridge from Old to New Town, but were reported to have spent the evening bouncing from saloon to saloon, at times even drinking on city streets, and came upon Carling while walking.

At the same time, Martinez's defense team notably refrained from attacking the sexual reputation of Margaret Carling. While the bodily comportment of Martinez was racially marked, Carling's embodied actions received no such scrutiny. That her sexual past and the details of the attack were not scrutinized and evaluated with excruciating precision should not, of course, obscure the wrenching aspects of Carling's experience. She was still forced to endure a painful medical examination and a potentially humiliating court appearance. Many women, especially Hispanas, as will be made clear, faced far worse in terms of hostile questioning and attacks on their sexual reputations. Sadly, few rape victims, Anglo or

Hispana, could expect better treatment in the courts than Margaret Carling received.

Andrea Cordova, for example, was one of many Hispanas who was forced to endure a legal system all too willing to assail her reputation for sexual propriety and respectability. On the morning of August 30, 1893, Geronimo Pino knocked at the door of the home Andrea Cordova shared with her two brothers in the small village of Socorro, forty miles south of Albuquerque. Pino asked for Cordova's brother Juan, then for her brother Lorenzo, and after Cordova replied that both were gone for the day, he attacked her. He forced her to the floor, raped her, and then "took out a pair of scissors out of his pocket" and "shingled" Cordova's hair, wrapping the hair in his hand and putting it in his pocket. He told her that he would "have no other pleasure than to kill [her] and hang [her] to a tree," and stomped on her arms, "lacerating them" and resulting in her "flesh all being torn up." During the attack, Cordova "was calling out for the Holy Virgin, because [she] was in great tribulation and very much scared." After Pino ran from the house and down the hill, Cordova stumbled to the doorway and screamed for help. She yelled to her aunt and close neighbor Luisa Morena, begging her, in Cordova's words, "to come see how Geronimo Pino has left me." Significantly, Cordova both actively resisted the violent attack and reported the crime immediately after Pino left her house. Further evidence of Cordova's resistance emerged in the testimony of two witnesses. Both Julian Torres, a neighbor, and Luisa Morena, Cordova's aunt, testified that they noticed tufts of hair spread out over the floor of Cordova's house. Torres described the house as having the "appearance of a scrap or fight."[11]

The trial began with Andrea Cordova describing the attack for the prosecution. During the cross-examination, Geronimo Pino's attorney grilled Cordova about the chronology and specific details of the attack. The defense lawyer asked her if she knew what rape was (she answered affirmatively, "To use a person without their consent") and if Pino had cut her hair and "stamped on [her] arms with his feet" before or after the rape (after the rape, she said). The defense team also asked Cordova for the whereabouts of her husband and whether she knew, had lived with, or had engaged in "carnal intercourse" with a man named Dionicio Padilla. She answered that she and her husband had separated years earlier and that she did not know his whereabouts. She also claimed never to have met, let alone to have had "carnal intercourse" with, Dionicio Padilla. When defense attorney Freeman asked if she had "had carnal intercourse with any man since [her] husband went off," prosecutor H. M. Dougherty objected to the question. Judge H. B. Hamilton sustained the objection, but wittingly or not revealed the deeper intentions behind that particular line of questioning by announcing that while the defense could not attempt to prove certain acts, it could try to "show her character; whether she is a prostitute or not."[12]

Cordova's aunt Luisa Morena also testified for the prosecution, stating that she witnessed her niece running out the house "arms bleeding and her hair cut off" and Geronimo Pino "leaving her [Cordova's] yard." The prosecution's only other witness was Julian Torres, a neighbor who testified that he had seen Geronimo Pino enter the house of Andrea Cordova that morning. After a short time, Torres stated, he heard a woman screaming and came out of his house to find Andrea Cordova crying, her clothes in tatters, and blood "streaming down her arms." Cordova then led Torres into the house, where he saw "the blood and the hair of this woman" strewn on the floor. On his way to Cordova's house, Torres testified that he noticed Geronimo Pino making his way from Cordova's house down to the railroad tracks.[13]

In addition to attempting to prove Cordova's reputation as sexually deviant—by claiming that she committed adultery and cohabitated with men who were neither her husband nor her family members—Geronimo Pino's lawyers argued that Cordova had complained only of a fight with Pino, *not* a rape. Her statement to her aunt after the attack, "see how Geronimo Pino has left me, torn to pieces," the defense claimed, represented a report of a "mistreatment," not a sexual assault. Both witnesses Torres and Morena testified under cross-examination that Cordova never actually mentioned the word "rape." Finally, although the trial record makes no mention of her age, defense lawyers repeatedly referred to Cordova as an "old woman." Freeman asked Pino, himself hardly a child at thirty-eight, "Did you ever rape that old woman?" Accentuating Cordova's age and presumed unattractiveness, the lawyer then asked Pino if he ever tried to rape Cordova and "did [he] ever want to?" Pino answered no to all three questions.[14]

Still, faced with three witnesses all testifying to his guilt, the defenders of Geronimo Pino needed to do more than simply sully the character of his accuser, Andrea Cordova. They would also have to fortify the reputation of their client. Pino's lawyers attempted to characterize Pino's actions both on the day of the assault and throughout his life as unremarkable, expected, and normal. That he claimed not to have had any desire to rape an "old woman" such as Cordova did more than simply depict Cordova as sexually undesirable—making her, according to the logic of the argument, unlikely to be the victim of a sexual assault. As an added result, Pino could emerge as normal because he claimed not to find her desirable. Another step in the effort to normalize Pino's behavior occurred earlier in his testimony, when he stated that he had an occupation as a "farmer and stockraiser" of cattle and sheep and had been married for eight years. Though Pino testified that he and his wife did not have any children, he made a point to state, "I have none now." Asked how many of his children had died, Pino answered two. [15]

Finally, Pino's defense attorneys called to the stand several acquaintances of Pino, each of whom testified to his good character and conduct. Estevan Baca, for instance, who stated that he had known Pino for over twenty years, was asked about Pino's "reputation for chastity." Pino's lawyer asked Baca if Pino had a reputation for "being a man of clean habits, so far as his intercourse with women is concerned," and whether Pino had "the reputation of running after women, or raping, anything of that sort." Baca answered that, as far as he knew, Pino's reputation was "good." Abran Abeyta likewise testified that the "propriety of [Pino's] relations with women" was good. In all, Geronimo Pino's lawyers argued that their client had been gainfully employed, was married, had fathered two children, had no odd or deviant sexual desires (such as wanting to rape an "old woman"), and held a good reputation for chastity and propriety toward women. In contrast, the defense linked Andrea Cordova with alleged adultery and carnal intercourse, advanced age, supposed physical unattractiveness, and evidence that Cordova had not immediately mentioned that she had been raped. Over the objections of the prosecutor, Antonio Armijo testified that Cordova and Dionicio Padilla had lived together for several years. Another witness, Claudio Tafoya, claimed that Abran Gutierrez had said that "he had carnal intercourse with her." A handful of subsequent witnesses went on to contend that Cordova's reputation for chastity was "bad" and that Geronimo Pino's reputation was "good." Apparently, however, the jury was unconvinced by Pino's defense team. On December 14, 1897, Geronimo Pino was found guilty of raping Andrea Cordova. [16]

The dogged attacks on the sexual reputation of Andrea Cordova, an Hispana, stand in marked contrast to the generally respectful treatment afforded an Anglo woman like Margaret Carling. In addition to the defense attorneys who denounced Cordova during the trial, the trial judge encouraged the vilification of Cordova by giving attorneys permission to "show her character; whether she is a prostitute or not." No such official encouragement for defense attorneys to question the sexual reputation of Margaret Carling occurred in *NM v. Martinez*. In both cases, women were violently attacked and forced to endure painful and potentially humiliating physical examinations and courtroom questioning. Yet, only in the case of an Anglo woman attacked by an Hispano was the female victim protected from direct questioning of her sexual reputation. The sexual politics supporting racialization projects in New Mexico could hardly be more clear. Hispanas in general could expect extensive and humiliating testimony regarding their sexual reputations. Anglo women attacked by Hispanos, on the other hand, faced less scrutiny of their sexual lives. Regardless of whether the victim was an Anglo woman or an Hispana, as will become apparent, Anglo men and elite Hispanos accused of rape could, through their attorneys, attack with relative impunity the sexual reputation of their accusers.

The following trial illustrates the considerable latitude permitted Anglo defendants in impugning the sexual reputations of their accusers. The trial also demonstrates that racialization projects directed at Hispanos and Hispanas in New Mexico were not limited to trials involving Hispanos. Indeed, denunciations of the bodily comportment of Hispanos in general emerged even in cases not directly involving Hispanos. According to fifteen-year-old Bertha Strossner, sometime in the middle of the afternoon on November 26, 1890, the day before Thanksgiving, V. P. Edie, an older man that she and her mother had known for several months, came to her house in New Albuquerque and asked if she wanted to go for a buggy ride to Old Albuquerque. Strossner accepted the invitation, but rather than driving directly to Old Town, Edie stopped first at the home of a "Mexican lady" for a glass of wine. Over the course of the afternoon and early evening, Edie and Strossner stopped at several places for wine, though Strossner contended that she only "tasted a little bit of it and threw the rest out."[17]

Returning to his home in New Albuquerque, Strossner claimed Edie then dragged her into the building, locked the doors, and raped her. Leaving the young woman locked in the room, Edie then went out for food, returning with oysters and wine. He attempted to rape Strossner again. When she resisted, he pulled out a pistol and shot her in the hand. Edie then went to sleep. Strossner, bleeding from the gunshot wound and still locked in the room with Edie, "sat up in a chair" all night, crying. The next morning Edie gave her money and instructed her to ride the streetcar to Old Town and buy breakfast there. He threatened to kill her if she did not claim, if asked, that "a Mexican had done the shooting." Returning from Old Town that morning of Thanksgiving, Strossner ran into her mother and, as instructed by Edie, told her a "Mexican" had shot her. Strossner did not mention either the rape or the involvement of V. P. Edie. Strossner did not tell her mother the truth until six o'clock that night.[18]

The trial of V. P. Edie began with the testimony of Bertha Strossner. After extended examination and cross-examination of Strossner, the prosecution called only two additional witnesses. Strickler Aubright, an Albuquerque physician, described the gunshot wound on Strossner's hand, and George Moore, a neighbor of Edie, testified that the layout of Edie's room was such that Strossner would not have been able to escape or summon help during the attack. Edie's defense team focused on proving Strossner's consent, arguing that she willingly had sexual intercourse with Edie and had in fact been seen drinking and flirting with him in public days before. The lawyers claimed that Strossner inflicted the wound on her own hand and that she herself, not Edie, had concocted the story of the "Mexican."[19]

During cross-examination, defense attorney Neill Field asked Strossner if she knew W. L. Trimble, who owned a livery business in Albuquerque. Despite Strossner's answer of no, Field asked her several more questions about Trimble, including if she had been in "Mrs. Fisher's saloon" a few days earlier with Edie, her mother, and Trimble. "Were you at that time and while this man Trimble was there," Field queried, "were you sitting on Mr. Edie's lap?" Strossner answered no and prosecuting attorney W. H. Whiteman promptly objected to the testimony, arguing that the past relationship between Strossner and Edie was "utterly irrelevant" to the case. Field responded to the judge that "if the woman had been in a compromising situation with the man, prior to the time of the alleged rape," that it was relevant to determining "if there was any rape committed, or whether she consented to the intercourse." Field continued, "If I could show voluntary sexual intercourse between these parties at any time and place anterior . . . I would have the right to give that fact in evidence." Judge Lee agreed with Field, noting that "what relation had existed between them and what they had been doing" had "some weight" in determining consent. The "weight" of the nature of the relations between Strossner and Edie, of course, was whether the young woman had behaved improperly with Edie, *not* what constituted improper behavior. Both sets of lawyers described a woman sitting on the lap of a relative stranger as well outside the realm of acceptable things a young woman did with her body.[20]

The extent of Strossner's sexual experience proved to be one of the more important elements during the trial. In *NM v. Pino*, defense attorneys had asked the victim, Andrea Cordova, if she knew what constituted rape. Cordova replied succinctly that it was the use of a woman's body without her consent and the matter was quickly dropped; however, Cordova's sexual reputation was repeatedly challenged. She was accused of promiscuous sexual behavior and even compared to a prostitute. In the Edie trial, defense lawyers similarly attacked Strossner's sexual reputation, grilling her about her understanding of rape, sexual intercourse, penetration, and even the difference between penetration by a penis and penetration by a finger or other "foreign" objects. Defense attorney Field asked Strossner, "How do you know that the instrument that entered your body were his privates? Did you ever see a man's private parts?" Strossner answered no, and Field continued, asking her how she knew "it was not his finger." Strossner replied, "Because he had both arms around [my] shoulders." Field promptly turned to another line of questioning, quizzing Strossner about whether she could say "how far, whatever it was that he put into [her], went into [her]." Despite an objection, the judge ruled the question valid, leading the witness to reply that she could not tell how far Edie had penetrated her. Field continued, asking Strossner if she "[saw] his organ at all" during any part of the attack or, indeed, if she even knew "what part of the man it is attached to." Strossner answered that she knew very little about sexual intercourse, that she only knew what Edie had done to her because her mother had vaguely mentioned, at some unspecified point, that "that is what men do to women." The cross-examination of Strossner ended on an absurd note. When Field asked her if she knew what part of the man the "organ . . . is attached to," she answered, no, prompting him to ask if she knew "whether it is under the arms or in his back." Strossner answered, "No, sir," and thus ended her testimony.[21]

At issue in the Edie case was a familiar double-edged sword. If Strossner, at sixteen years old, knew what constituted penetration and sexual intercourse, then she possessed a knowledge and sexual experience unusual, even improper, for a young woman of her age. If, on the other hand, she understood little about sexual intercourse, and managed to present herself as innocent and virginal, her accusation of sexual assault would also come under scrutiny as defense lawyers could ask Strossner how, if she was so ignorant of matters of sexual intimacy, could she know that Edie had raped her. Lawyers in effect could attempt to challenge her accusation of Edie by challenging her claims to sexual innocence. The main point for defense lawyers, of course, was establishing Strossner's reputation as a sexually promiscuous young woman, one who fully consented to sex with V. P. Edie.

Despite their adversarial postures, however, both sides seemed to agree on certain issues. The impression that emerges from such defense tactics—and the failure of the prosecution to object in any serious way to such tactics—is that a certain consensus existed surrounding how a young woman learned about "male organs" and "what men do to women." No proper and respectable young woman, the transcript implies, would learn of sexual matters by actually engaging in sexual relations. The only normal way for women to acquire knowledge about sexuality was from speaking to another woman, preferably a mother or close relative.[22]

In a decision rendered in Spanish, the significance of which I will soon discuss, V. P. Edie was convicted of rape and sentenced to five years in the penitentiary. As in each of the above trials, and indeed in every trial discussed here in detail, the defendant was found guilty. Regardless of the strategy that the defendant or his lawyer adopted, that strategy proved, at least until appeal, a failure, and unless an appeal was forthcoming, the defendant would be sent to prison. The victim in each case, despite the traumas associated with rape, could find at least partial solace from her successful charges. Family, friends, and acquaintances would similarly experience the effects and consequences of the trial. The reverberations of the trial, however, did not end there. A public event like a trial could have broader effects as well. In addition to the consequences for those most intimately involved, such trials could have productive effects on observers and audience members. Observers would likely have noticed that certain body practices were represented as acceptable and normal, and linked to Anglos, while other body practices appeared disreputable and suspect, and were associated with Hispanos, especially poor Hispanos. The trials thus helped racialize citizenship, helping differentiate those with legitimate claims to citizenship from those deemed unfit for civic membership.

In the case of *New Mexico v. V.P. Edie*, notice the racialized significance placed on the consumption of alcohol, as well as the explicit mention of "Mexicans" and, as in *NM v. Martinez*, questions of appropriate transit. In New Mexico, the attention paid to the drinking habits of rape trial participants associated those who did not drink alcohol, who maintained bodily coherence, with whiteness (and, especially for women, sexual respectability), and those who did imbibe with racialized groups. Felipe Garcia, recall, described his visits to several Las Vegas saloons with Prudencio Martinez before the attack on Margaret Carling. Bertha Strossner claimed that "at some kind of a store" in Hispano Old Town, Edie ordered her a glass of wine and "she just tasted a little bit of it and threw the rest out." Under cross-examination, Strossner stated that until that day, she had never "tasted anything to drink." Throughout the trial, she consistently said that, except for her small sip of wine before pouring out the glass, she drank only soda. Describing the encounter a few days earlier with Edie, her mother, and W. L. Trimble, Strossner continually denied that either she or her mother, or Edie for that matter, were drunk. Though Strossner and the prosecution were adversaries with Edie's defense attorneys, both sides apparently agreed that the consumption of alcohol—like the tardy reporting of rape and the lack of vigorous resistance to attack—was hardly characteristic of respectable young women. During the testimony of W. L. Trimble, ethnicity surfaced directly. Trimble was asked if he knew that Strossner and her mother were both German and whether he was familiar with "the habits of German people." Next, Trimble was asked if it was "a common custom among German people for the women to go to beer saloons." Although the witness stated that he was not familiar with German drinking customs, the questions provoked no objections. The implication of course was that consumption of alcohol was a habit associated with a particular group, not a characteristic of all Americans or all New Mexicans or even all those of European descent. Rather, drinking alcohol was associated explicitly with racial and ethnic difference.[23]

In such associations, New Mexicans drew upon distinctions common to broader America. Throughout turn-of-the-twentieth-century America, sobriety and the temperance movement provided critical markers of whiteness. Eric Lott has noted during the mid-nineteenth century "an attempt to shore up 'white' class identities by targeting new enemies such as immigrants, blacks, and tipplers," while David Roediger observes that "black antebellum Northern urbanites were probably more temperate than whites, but neither popular language nor the mobs wanted to recognize that fact." Elliott West similarly argues that for white middle-class Protestants, the temperance movement "represented a 'symbolic crusade' to protect older values threatened by the social forces of urbanization, industrialization, geographical mobility, and the 'new' immigration of non-Protestants from southern and eastern Europe." John Kasson quotes a mid-nineteenth-century observer of New York City as describing "scenes of drunkenness and beastly debauch" as part of the city's racialized life as "a dark continent, populated by 'primitive' natives."[24]

Another association made in several of the trials linked the consumption of alcohol and a racialized type of transit. In both *NM v. Edie* and *NM v. Martinez*, the drinking parties passed between old and new sections of town, between the older, predominantly Hispano Old Albuquerque and Old Las Vegas and the more recent Anglo developments. Prudencio Martinez and Felipe Garcia were accused of spending the evening before they attacked Margaret Carling carousing from saloon to saloon, and Felipe Garcia testified that he and Martinez crossed the bridge over to New Las Vegas near the end of their evening. Both prosecution and defense teams in the Edie case described several hours spent by Edie and Strossner traveling from bar to bar between New and Old Albuquerque. Both parties agreed that early in the afternoon on November 26, Edie invited Strossner to go for a ride in his buggy. Neither disputed the fact that the two stopped at several local saloons during the course of the day. Strossner mentioned that their stops included the home of "a Mexican lady" where they had a glass of wine and another establishment in predominantly Hispano Old Town. Edie was a bit more specific about their itinerary, noting that they visited Badaraceo's saloon in the nearby village of Duranes, Ysidro Apodaca's bar in "Los Griego," another bar in "Los Candelaria," where the two "got out of the buggy there awhile and was in the Mexican's house," and Homer's in Old Albuquerque. The association of drinking alcohol with movement between racially marked sections of town reinforced the distinction between temperate and sober whites in New Mexico, an identity that included select Hispanos, and groups and individuals marked as mobile, intemperate, and racially different. [25]

Like Hispanas in general, and certain Anglo women, Mexican immigrants, male and female, were similarly portrayed as sexually aberrant. On June 19, 1912, twenty-five-year-old Ricardo Alva and twelve-year-old Refugia Zuniga Torres were walking along railroad tracks in northern New Mexico. An automobile approached, pulling to a halt near the tracks, and three men, Lincoln County deputy sheriff W. E. Dudley, deputy sheriff L. O. Mace, and E. O. Mares, an interpreter, climbed out. The men stopped Alva and Torres and asked the couple where they were going. They discovered that Alva, a boarder in the rooming house of Torres's mother, and Torres were on their way to distant Raton, where they planned to marry. The officers promptly arrested Ricardo Alva on the charge of rape and escorted Refugia Torres back to her mother in Dawson. Torres was under fourteen, the legal age of consent in New Mexico.

During the subsequent trial, Deputy Sheriff Dudley recalled in great detail his encounter with Alva and Torres. The sheriff described his conversation with the two, managed as it was with the help of interpreter Mares. Alva, Dudley claimed, told him that he and Torres had sexual intercourse "twice that morning and one time before on No. 5 hill, making three times in all." Dudley also claimed that during the automobile trip back to her home, Refugia pointed to a bridge and "told [him] that they had intercourse there." Finally, Dudley reported searching under the bridge. "I could see by the tracks under there," he said, "that it seemed as if they had been lying down or sitting down." [26]

Late in 1912, Ricardo Alva was found guilty of rape and sentenced to the state penitentiary. Claiming both that no direct evidence corroborated Refugia's assertion that the two engaged in sexual intercourse and that the presiding judge failed to instruct the jury on pertinent matters of law, Alva's defense team quickly appealed the verdict to the state supreme court. The appeal was denied. Judge J. Hanna, writing for the New Mexico Supreme Court, noted: "We are of the opinion that the evidence in this case leaves nothing to be inferred." [27]

In certain respects, events in *NM v. Alva* differed little from sexual assault trials elsewhere in turn-of-the-twentieth-century America. [28] The case indeed highlights transformations in age-of-consent laws in New Mexico and throughout the country. Ricardo Alva was convicted under a statute that had undergone several revisions over the preceding two decades. Between 1865 and 1897, the age of consent for "a female child" in New Mexico was ten years old. In 1897 the age was lifted to fourteen, and in 1915 (three years after Alva's trial), the age was lifted again, this time to sixteen. At the time of the trial, the state considered "a female under the age of fourteen incapable of giving her consent to an act of sexual intercourse with a man."[29] The case also hints at the complex relationship between parents and the court. Under defense examination, Virginia Zuniga, Refugia Torres's mother, revealed that by contacting the authorities upon her daughter's disappearance, she had simply hoped to have her daughter returned to her. She had not, she said, in fact made any written complaint to the police or "ask[ed] any person, officer or otherwise to punish the defendant, charging that he either ran away with [her] daughter, or caused her to run away, or that he had committed rape, or had sexual intercourse with [her] daughter." The prosecution challenged Zuniga's claim, charging that she, and not her daughter, wanted to marry Alva and claiming that Alva "was staying at [Zuniga's] house sleeping with [Zuniga] and having connection with [Zuniga]." District attorney George Ramley even asked Zuniga, "Was [Alva] not living with you on the left hand side, I mean by that, was he not your bed-fellow a part of time?" To which Zuniga answered curtly, "No sir." Possible romantic involvement aside, the case suggests the zeal with which attorneys attacked the sexual reputation of particular witnesses, in this case Mexican immigrants (Ricardo Alva as Virginia Zuniga's man "on the left hand side"), and the willingness, even eagerness, of New Mexico courts to prosecute age-of-consent violations even beyond the wishes of the parents.[30]

As in previous trials, attorneys on both sides of the aisle, with few objections by the judge, forced Refugia Torres to describe the most minute details of the sexual encounter. Among the questions asked of the, by then, thirteen-year-old Torres, were "Did he put his privates in your privates?" "Did he take up your dresses?" "Were you standing up or lying down?" "Whereabouts on the road did he have intercourse with you?" and "Do you know whether any of his clothes were unbuttoned or not?" The following are transcripts of Torres's testimony during the trial, the first from the prosecution, the second from the defense.[31]

Q (district attorney George Ramley): Now, just what did he do to you?
A (Refugia Torres): He done things with me.
Q: Did it hurt you?
A: I don't know.
Q: Did it feel good?

A: No sir.

Q: Now, what did he do to you, Refugia, tell us just exactly what he did and how he did it.

A: I can't say it very well.

Q: Say it as well as you can.

A: I have already said he done bad things with me.

Q: When he got on top of you what did he do?

A: Things.

Q: What things did he do, just explain?

A: Bad things.

Q: Did he put something into you?

A: Yes sir.

Q: What part of him did he put into you?

A: On me.

Q: Where did he put it into you—point out to this jury where he put it into you—just point to the place—there is nothing to be ashamed of.

A: Right in the center of me.

Q: What part of his did he put there?

A: The same part.

Q: (defense attorney J. Leahy): How do you know whether he put any part of his body into your body?

A (Refugia Torres): Because.

Q: Because of anything that was said between you, or because you could feel?

A: I don't know.

Q: Do you understand what it means by intercourse between a boy and a girl?

Ramley: Object to that because it has been asked and answered.

[Objection sustained]

Q: How long were you and the defendant on the ground?

A: I don't know.

Q: Were you on the ground as much as five minutes?

A: I don't know.

Q: When you were on the ground did he say anything to you, or you to him?

A: I don't know.

Q: Did you know what he was doing?

Ramley: Object to that as not proper re-cross-examination; and further for the reason that it is immaterial whether she knew what he was doing or not.

By the court: I will let her answer.
A: I don't know.

In both examples, lawyers struggled to induce Torres to describe, in open court, the details of her encounter with Alva. For its part, since the question of consent was irrelevant due to Torres's age, the prosecution sought to establish simply that Torres and Alva had engaged in sexual intercourse. Hence, when the prosecutor asked Torres, "What part of him did he put into you?" and "Where did he put it into you?" he was attempting to prove that Alva and Torres committed what the court defined as "carnal knowledge"—the penetration of the penis, however slightly, into the vagina.[32] The defense, on the other hand, unable to address questions of consent and coercion, challenged Torres's account of the events. Asking Torres, "How do you know whether he put any part of his body into your body?" and "Do you understand what it means by intercourse between a boy and a girl?" the defense attorney clearly hoped to convince jurors that Torres and Alva had not in fact engaged in sexual intercourse.

Torres's hesitancy to provide specific details in public, to speak in open court of her sexual intimacies, clearly frustrated the lawyers. Her determined effort to resist speaking publicly of sexual activities was typical of trials for sexual assault in New Mexico and throughout America.[33] Besides focusing on proof of vaginal penetration by a penis (and thereby excluding other potential forms of assault), trials throughout the country often centered on women speaking in public of sex. A woman's "inappropriate" silence, not screaming for help during the attack, not reporting the attack promptly, or untoward articulation in the witness stand could easily damage her credibility regardless of the outcome of the case.

Citizenship, in a strictly legal sense, was also a regular topic during *NM v. Alva*. Ricardo Alva was born in Guanajuato, Mexico, and had lived in the United States for five years. Virginia Zuniga had emigrated from San Luis Potosí, Mexico, in 1905 with her daughter Refugia and son Sostenes. After Alva's conviction, his lawyers tried unsuccessfully to argue that Refugia Torres's Mexican birth certificate, and her age, were unreliable (taking the odd strategy of challenging not the age printed on the certificate, but the spelling of her name). To such legalistic understandings of citizenship, Deputy Sheriff Dudley added a sexual component. Speaking of age-of-consent laws in New Mexico, he testified that he spoke to Alva about "the customs of Mexico and the customs over here, and showed him the difference, and spoke to him about the difference, that down in Mexico they did all those things but here in the United States they handled those things differently."[34] National (legalistic) citizenship and sexual habits and customs here are conflated, expanding the notion of citizenship to include both one's legal membership in a nation and one's sexual customs. In this respect, New Mexico has much in common with turn-of-the-century America. Gail Bederman has demonstrated that in the United States, a racial hierarchy developed based on notions of "civilization" and "savagery." One of the hallmarks of "civilization," according to Bederman, was supposedly "normal" forms of sexual conduct like marital sexual intercourse. Less civilized, nonwhite people especially African Americans, by contrast, purportedly practiced deviant sexual customs. Ricardo Alva's sexual "customs of Mexico" indicated his supposed inferiority and distance from civilization. Like African American men throughout the country, Alva appears here as sexually aberrant.[35]

At the same time, in New Mexico, where racialization followed such a different path than elsewhere in the country, rape trials bristled with a new and unprecedented energy. *NM v. Alva*, though typically American in many respects, also highlights the links between sexual practices, national differences, and the contortions of American territorial annexation. New Mexico extends the above arguments about sexuality, "civilization," and "savagery" into far more complicated racial and colonial terrains. In *NM v. Alva*, an apparently solid distinction between Mexico and the United States (pitting sexual customs "here in the United States" against those "down in Mexico") quickly dissolves. Though New Mexico was putatively "here in the United States," simple distinctions between domestic and foreign, "American" and "other," did not and could not suffice, not with the demographic, political, and economic strength of Hispanos. As Deputy Sheriff Dudley surely knew, it was one thing to claim that "down in" Mexico "they did all those things." It was quite another to claim that "Mexicans" in general, including Hispanos in New Mexico, practiced such sexual customs. Dudley therefore was forced to make a clear distinction between Hispanos from New Mexico and natives of Mexico. "Ricardo is an *Old Mexico* Mexican," he carefully noted, "and being in that country, there is a whole lot of provincialism" (emphasis mine).[36] Dudley's cautiousness is typical of American newcomers, who sought, within trials for sexual assault and in general in New Mexico, to assert the superiority of American "customs over here" without at the same time insulting or enraging "*New Mexico* Mexicans."

This far more complicated interlacing of national identity, race, and sexual customs draws the work of historians of American black/white race relations into conversation with historians of the American Southwest such as Tomás Almaguer and Martha Menchaca, who have ably described the racialization of Indian and Chicano communities in the aftermath of the Treaty of Guadalupe Hidalgo. Both Almaguer and Menchaca recognize the relative ability of Chicano communities to position themselves—

through legal appeals, strategic intermarriages, certain shared European and Christian religious traditions, and linguistic affinities—along a middle rung of the developing racial hierarchy in the Southwest, below Anglo-Americans, yet in many respects with clear advantages to Asian Americans, African Americans, and Native Americans. As Sheriff Dudley's measured words suggest, nowhere was this middle position more evident than in New Mexico. In emphasizing territorial annexation and resistance, Almaguer and Menchaca nonetheless pay less attention to emerging gender and sexual hierarchies structuring, and structured by, the imposition of colonial order in the American Southwest.[37]

Focusing on bodily comportment in rape trials like *NM v. Alva* and in other arenas in New Mexico helps fill in this critical gap between the linkage of race and gender/sexuality in a biracial setting and the processes of racialization and incorporation in a place of profound cultural heterogeneity. Bodily comportment in New Mexico, in other words, illuminates the process by which racial and sexual differences, conjoined, serve to structure societies marked by heterogeneity and colonialism. To illustrate further, take the following two examples from *NM v. Alva*, one focusing on what was absent from the trial proceedings, the other addressing that which, however subtly, appeared.

In the first place, nowhere in *NM v. Alva*, or for that matter in any of the trial transcripts that I have investigated, is there talk of "Hispano rapists" or Hispano predispositions to aberrant sexual behavior, as most certainly occurred with African American men in other regions of the country. The juries in all three trials were composed of large numbers of Hispanos. In the Martinez case, eleven of the twelve jurors had Spanish surnames; in the Edie trial, all twelve had Spanish last names and announced the verdict in Spanish. Although records for the Pino trial list only the foreman, named Joseph Patterson, the site of the trial, Socorro County, was predominantly Hispano, making it probable that the jury in *NM v. Pino* was also largely Hispano.[38] Given the preponderance of Hispano jurors, prosecutors were understandably reluctant to associate Hispano defendants with aberrant and violent sexual acts. Such tactics, like associating Hispanos in general with sexual promiscuity or violence, as occurred elsewhere in the nation, primarily with African American men, could have disastrous results in New Mexico. It is not, after all, inconceivable that V. P. Edie's attempt to convince Bertha Strossner to report that a "Mexican" shot her in the hand played a role in his conviction by a largely Hispano jury (his verdict, recall, was read in Spanish by the foreman of the jury). The easy link between rapist and racial otherness thus severed, officers of the court were compelled to turn elsewhere for evidence of aberrance and sexual deviance and turned to human bodies and questions of bodily integrity. New Mexico's peculiar demography and heterogeneity thus magnified the importance of certain bodily acts like alcohol consumption and public movement.

One need only glance at an American newspaper from the era to notice how exceptional New Mexico truly was in turn-of-the-twentieth-century America, an era marked by Jim Crow and lynchings and widespread denigration of the supposed sexual voracity of African American men.[39] Thus, while certain aspects of rape trials in New Mexico were indistinguishable from trials elsewhere in America, New Mexico's peculiar social dynamics forced certain adaptations. In light of the large numbers of Hispanos in New Mexico with political and economic power, many of whom sat on juries during rape trials, charges of sexual violence that included references to racial predispositions to aberrant sexual behavior on the part of Hispanos were not promising avenues of discussion for prosecutors. Instead, prosecutors, and defense lawyers, turned, as did New Mexicans throughout the period, to human bodies and determinations of bodily integrity and incoherence in order to argue for the guilt or innocence of the accused. Sexual habits and body practices proved invaluable in this context, coming to the aid of faltering racial binaries (sexually proper white Americans and sexually voracious racial "others") and distinguishing respectable practices and individuals from suspect, and illegal, customs and criminals.

The contortions required of American annexation are similarly visible in the testimony of thirteen-year-old Refugia Torres. Torres, a Mexican immigrant girl with few claims to wealth or status, was reluctant to speak publicly of her sexual life. Her reluctance reflects an attempt to protect her own sexual respectability in the face of intrusive and prying questions. Chicanos throughout the American Southwest around the turn of the century made similar claims to respectability. Leticia Garza-Falcón has argued that for the Tejano community the assertion of their own fundamental honor and *decencia* was critical to their resistance to Anglo-American dominance in Texas. Still, in Texas and in California, such claims were easily dismissed and denigrated as Anglo power proved virtually unassailable. New Mexico offered a much different scenario. Hispanos' claims to be, in Garza-Falcón's words, *gente decente* in New Mexico proved especially effective, due in large measure to the enduring prominence of Hispanos in political and economic affairs. Similarly, A. Gabriel Meléndez points to the great symbolic value of the Spanish language in nineteenth- and early-twentieth-century *Neo-Mexicano* print culture. Publishing Spanish-language newspapers and encouraging the retention of Spanish, especially among children, was central, according to Meléndez, to *Neo-Mexicano* efforts to resist Anglo incorporation. Refugia

Torres's testimony resonates with both analyses as the bilingual Torres (recall that an interpreter was involved in the capture of Alva and Torres) fought mightily, against considerable opposition from both prosecution and defense lawyers, to portray herself as a proper and respectable young woman. Moreover, her testimony is notable in that her protestations elicited not denunciations but relative restraint on the part of lawyers. To a degree unprecedented elsewhere in the United States, Hispanos exerted power in New Mexico, and trials and legal matters were places for negotiating, as well as exerting, power. As a place of relative power for Hispanos, New Mexico offered a place where Hispanos' claims to *decencia* were not, compared to elsewhere in the Southwest, denigrated or immediately dismissed.[40]

As *NM v. Alva* illustrates, the "mongrel" land of New Mexico shuttled between clear and refracted reflections of trends from broader America. The cases of *New Mexico v. Bonifacio Mares* and *New Mexico v. Claudio Armijo* similarly point to the enduring strength of Hispanos in New Mexico as well as the oscillation in New Mexico between familiar American concoctions and strange new brews. In both cases, as occurred throughout broader America, a victim's credibility depended on the prompt reporting of a sexual attack. In each trial, the victim did not report the attack until months later, a delay that would prove critical in each case. At the same time, the two trials notably avoided a common feature of American rape trials: the vilification of nonwhite men as sexually voracious and innately prone to sexual violence. Likewise, in both cases, the Hispano defendants were relatively wealthy. Bonifacio Mares was a store clerk, and Claudio Armijo's family employed domestic servants. Recall from the introduction that the considerable majority of Hispanos worked as manual or semi-skilled laborers, not as clerks in stores, and that only a very small percentage of Hispanos could afford to employ domestic labor.

As recounted in *New Mexico v. Bonifacio Mares*, early in the morning, just after dawn, one December day in 1898, Virginia Montoya, twenty-two and a domestic servant in the household of the Graff family, walked through the door of Bloom's butcher shop in downtown Las Vegas, New Mexico. Bonifacio Mares, a clerk at the shop, and the only employee present that early in the morning at 7:00 A.M., took Montoya's order, wrapped up the package, and then, in Montoya's words, "he turned around the corner right quick and he went to the door and locked the door and took hold of me at once and took me into another room." There, Mares raped Montoya, threatening to kill her if she reported the attack. Montoya did not report the rape until four months later when, after suffering a miscarriage, she told her mother that Bonifacio Mares had raped her.

The trial opened in June 1899, six months after the attack. The prosecution called four witnesses, including Virginia Montoya and her mother, Deluvina Valdez de Montoya, as well as Miguela Chavez and Dr. Felipe Romero, who were both called to treat Montoya during her miscarriage. After Montoya described to the court the violent attack, her mother testified that in April her daughter had become sick. "Where was she sick," she was asked. "What was the matter with her?" "She had a miscarriage," her mother answered, "and at the same time she was sick for a good while after that." The defense called to the stand Bonifacio Mares, the defendant; Charles Bloom, Mares's employer and the owner of the butcher shop; and Charles Hernandez, a character witness. Mares's defense attorney made much of the fact that Montoya did not report the rape until four months later, when she told her mother of the attack. The defense attorney also attempted to prove that Mares and Montoya could not have possibly been alone in the store at that early hour, calling witnesses to testify to the busy nature of the butcher shop, even at seven in the morning. Bonifacio Mares also testified in his own defense. When asked if customers often frequented the store at that time of day, he answered, "All the time. They are most generally waiting for me at the door." Asked to describe some of his regular customers, Mares replied, "Every one comes there, Americans, Mexicans, Chinamen." Thus besides attempting to discredit Montoya's account of the attack (arguing instead that their sexual acts had been consensual), Mares's defense team tried to prove that the store was far too busy for Mares to have been able to lock the door and attack Montoya without drawing attention.[41]

Mares was convicted of the rape and appealed the case to the New Mexico Territorial Supreme Court. The appeal argued that, based on the supposed scarcity of evidence presented during the trial, Mares should not have been convicted of the crime. Mares's lawyers cited the following section of the New Mexico rape statute: "On the trial of an indictment for rape, where the accused testifies in his own behalf, and denies the accusation, there must be some corroborating evidence or circumstance, however slight, or a reasonable probability of the truth of the assault, to justify a conviction." Judge J. MacMillan, writing for the court majority, heartily agreed. Reversing the conviction, he wrote, "There is not in the whole case, any corroborating evidence, nor a single corroborating circumstance, and the probability of the commission of the alleged offense is so far outside of the domain of reason that there was absolutely nothing for the consideration of the jury except the bare improbable statement of the prosecutrix." MacMillan went on to cite, in his view, several "improbabilities" in Virginia Montoya's criminal complaint. It was, he said, improbable that a clerk in a busy store on a busy street at a busy time of day would "assault and ravish a customer." It was also highly unlikely, in his opinion, that "a female 22 years of age, in such a place," would not "make an outcry, and resist, if she desired to protect her virtue." Furthermore, MacMillan doubted that Montoya ("a woman of the mature age of the prosecutrix, who was with her mistress [Mrs. Graff] in the daytime and her mother at night") would "allow such an assault to go uncomplained of to one or the other until she was ill from miscarriage, four months after the alleged occurrence." In all, Montoya's accusation, according to MacMillan, "four months after the alleged assault and wrung from her at a time when she was ill from miscarriage, has no value whatsoever."[42]

A considerable delay between the attack and the filing of criminal charges was also significant in *New Mexico v. Claudio Armijo*. The trial, which occurred in Las Vegas, New Mexico, in 1919, involved a violation of New Mexico's law making sexual intercourse with a female under the age of sixteen a felony. According to the transcript of the trial, in November 1917, Maria Francisca Vigil, who at the time was fourteen and five months old, was working as a domestic in the home of William and Altagracia Booth, the brother-in-law and sister of the defendant Claudio Armijo. Armijo lived in the same house in Las Vegas with his sister and brother-in-law where Vigil worked. Vigil testified on the day of the attack that she had been scrubbing the floor when Altagracia Booth announced that she and her children were going out and, in Vigil's words, "told [her] to lock the front door." Vigil, however, continued washing the floor and then "heard some noise." "I went," she said, "and threw the water outside and someone slammed the front door, and I went to see who it was, and it was Claudio Armijo, and he locked the front door, and I went to try to open it, and I could not open it, and then I went to the back door and it was locked too. . . . So I could not get out." "Then," she continued, "he caught me and done such thing with me." As an indication of how traumatizing the attack was for her, when asked if she went home afterward, Vigil replied, "No sir, I could not walk."[43]

In May 1918 Vigil's mother and two friends of the family, apparently suspecting that she was pregnant, confronted Vigil, and she told them of the attack. On June 28, 1918, Vigil gave birth to a child. During the subsequent trial, the prosecution called several witnesses, including Maria Vigil herself, her mother and father, and several acquaintances, who testified both to Vigil's age at the time of the assault and to her report that Claudio Armijo was the father of the baby. Her mother testified that her daughter "told [her] that the boy forced her and that he had promised to marry her." "She had said 'She didn't want to,'" her mother continued, "and that he had promised her to marry her."[44]

During Vigil's testimony (which is introduced in the trial transcript with the comment "this witness testified in English language"), the prosecuting attorney asked Vigil, "Did he actually have sexual intercourse with you?" Vigil answered, "Sexual intercourse? . . . Like what?" The judge then interrupted the testimony and asked the court interpreter to "give some translation that is commonly used for sexual intercourse . . . if you know of any." It is unclear how, or even whether, the interpreter responded to the judge's request because the prosecutor immediately stepped in and directed Vigil to "just tell what happened." Vigil did so, describing the sexual attack and her resistance, which included "ripping him" with her hands and "holler[ing]." Armijo's defense team, on the other hand, tried to argue that Maria Vigil had not even been an employee of the Booth family in November 1917, at the time of the attack. The defense also attacked Vigil's reputation for sexual propriety, calling to the stand Cristobal Montoya, who testified that he had "gone around with Maria Vigil" and "taken her places." When asked where he and Vigil has gone together, Montoya answered that they "went to the picture show [the Mutual Theater] and near her house."[45]

Claudio Armijo was convicted of the statutory rape, sentenced to five years in prison, and ordered to help pay for the support of the child. He appealed the verdict. During the appeal, as in the previous trial, the absence of what the New Mexico Supreme Court considered corroborating evidence became a major issue. In the court's decision to overturn the verdict and order a new trial, Justice C. J. Parker stated flatly, "The charge made against the defendant is an absolute and palpable fraud, designed to victimize an innocent young man." Judge Parker pointed out that several reputable, in his eyes, witnesses had testified that Vigil had not been working in Booth's house in November 1917. Furthermore, Vigil had only reported the attack six months later, when her pregnancy became noticeable. Parker, citing a previous decision regarding corroborating evidence and rape accusations, conceded that if "there were a single unequivocal fact, established by a single witness, shown . . . to be fair and willing and able to tell the truth," the verdict should be allowed to stand. Absent such evidence, however, Parker determined, and his fellow judges agreed, that a new trial should commence.[46]

In both trials, judges upheld the defendants' appeals, reversing the conviction in the case of Bonifacio Mares and ordering a new trial for Claudio Armijo. The fact that both victims delayed by several months bringing their accusations clearly was significant to the court, as were questions of the women's consent to sexual intercourse. Like other Hispanas described in this chapter, Virginia Montoya and Maria Vigil faced determined attacks on the credibility of their testimony and their sexual reputations. So, too, did Anglo women like Bertha Strossner endure scathing assessments of their intimate lives. Even Margaret Carling, who had been treated with relative respect and care by the court, still faced a painful physical examination and was forced to testify publicly about her rape. The bodily comportment of non-elite Hispanos like Prudencio Martinez, Geronimo Pino, and Ricardo Alva was also extensively critiqued. In contrast, lawyers and judges in the cases of elite Hispanos like Bonifacio Mares and Claudio Armijo were notably mild, treating the men much as they did Anglo men under similar circumstances. One judge even described Armijo as a victim and "an innocent young man." Thus, the racialization of Hispanos in New Mexico exacted the greatest toll from poor Hispanas, while allowing male Anglo and elite Hispano defendants the greatest latitude in challenging the sexual reputations of their accusers.

Though focused on the determination of guilt and innocence, punishment and exoneration, trials were much more than that. Those in attendance (whether juror, officer of the court, or seated in the gallery) would have likely gained valuable lessons about how respectable and disreputable men and women were expected to comport themselves physically in New Mexico. Such demonstrations of normal and abnormal bodies during rape trials in New Mexico spoke to a range of issues, addressing critical questions: what was appropriate behavior in public spaces, who deserved civic membership and legitimacy, who was a citizen. Like Indian schools, rape trials reveal that the racialization of Hispanos depended on the scrutiny and evaluation of individual bodies. As the previous two chapters have suggested, Anglo newcomers turned with disturbing frequency to bodily comportment for evidence of the supposed inability of Hispanos and Indians to claim full citizenship.

The ability of bodily comportment to provide answers to such basic questions about Indian and Hispano citizenship and respectability was especially valuable because imported racial distinctions (sexually violent dark men, promiscuous dark women, tumultuous intermarried families, debased and powerless "foreign" tongues like Spanish) were of little help in the contorted, at least by broader American standards, racial and imperial politics of New Mexico. It is noteworthy that during a period in America of widespread attacks on the sexual voracity of nonwhite men, neither Bonifacio Mares nor Claudio Armijo was depicted as a sexual "beast" or an out-of-control "monster." Imposing judgment and racial order required more subtle distinctions in New Mexico, ones less likely to insult jurors or enrage observers. As the above trials make clear, a focus on human bodies and the supposed racialized truths emanating from bodily comportment like public mobility and consuming alcohol offered a most compelling alternative to Anglos wary of challenging directly the power and social status of elite Hispanos. The following two chapters will examine in more detail the ability of elite Hispanos to force concessions from Anglo newcomers in New Mexico. In both public ceremonies and depictions of marriage and domesticity, racialization in New Mexico entailed considerable accommodation and negotiation between Anglo and Hispano elites.

TRANSITS OF VENUS

CEREMONIES AND
CONTESTED PUBLIC SPACE

In 1909 a newspaper article described the corn dance ceremony at Santo Domingo Pueblo, located twenty-five miles south of Santa Fe. Included in the account of the "strange celebration" are descriptions of "Indians in full regalia, ascending the estufa [stove] and standing on its top" and "a buck in full dance costume." Although onlookers seemed welcome, photographers were, in the article's view, treated with great suspicion "as the Pueblo, and especially the Santo Dominican, regards the camera at his fiesta in much the same manner as a bull does a red flag." The event, the article continues, was highlighted by "old men singing their weird chant and beating their drums." The article ends with a bit of an editorial comment, "Had the harvest dance of Santo Domingo been as widely exploited as the famous snake dance of the Moqui hundreds would come to see it where there are now dozens."[1]

Bodily excess permeates this account. Witness the "weird chants" emanating from the "old men" banging upon their drums and the "buck" dressed in exotic regalia, climbing astride "estufas." Moreover, that the "Santo Dominicans" should react to photographers' camera like enraged beasts ("in much the same manner as a bull does a red flag") appears in the writer's estimation not to be a reasonable desire among the Pueblos for privacy. Instead, the author hints, Pueblos resembled animals and evinced a certain incompatibility with tools of modern life like cameras and photography.

New Mexico newspaper accounts of Indian ceremonies like the above frequently highlighted the supposedly aberrant bodily comportment of Indian participants. Hispano ceremonies like the Penitente rituals, which I will describe in more detail later in the chapter, were similarly criticized as filled with corporeal excess and strange and exotic bodily acts. Anglo public ceremonies by contrast were described as orderly and well managed, with precise organization and restrained, measured involvement by onlookers and participants alike.

The difference between newspaper accounts of Indian and Hispano Penitente ceremonies and the descriptions of Anglo ceremonies is striking. This contrast highlights the emphasis placed on bodily comportment in the creation of a racialized order. Once again, embodied truths exposed a clear divide between those deserving of civic membership and those unfit for full citizenship. Embodied truths thus stabilized an unsettled social order, offering the authority of the human body to Anglo newcomers in desperate need of legitimacy for their rule.

Typical of New Mexico's exceptional racial politics, however, was the relatively mild and respectful treatment that Anglo newspapers afforded most Hispano public events. Anglo newcomers had neither the political and economic power nor the demographic supremacy necessary to control public space completely. Like the Hispano writers and historians, that A. Gabriel Meléndez describes, who challenged triumphal American narratives by documenting a history of their own, native New Mexicans at times made competing claims to public legitimacy and fitness for citizenship.[2] Hispano elites forced Anglos to temper considerably their widespread condemnation of Hispano bodily comportment and adopt a vision of New Mexico that included rather than excluded its Hispano population. As a result, despite the general attack on native New Mexican rituals and ceremonies, certain Hispano public events compelled respectful, even celebratory, press coverage. This chapter will focus on this forced inclusiveness at the heart of Anglo colonial aspirations in New Mexico.

Anglo racializing projects, efforts to claim that Indians and Hispanos were socially inferior, depended on a variety of institutions. Few were more critical than newspapers. The development of New Mexico's territorial press nicely reflects the accelerated pace of Anglo incorporation after the arrival of the railroad, and, like the railroad, the imprints of an emerging modernity are clear in the growth of the press. Before 1880, relatively few newspapers, just over sixty in all, were published and most did not last beyond an initial handful of issues. In California, by comparison, over six hundred different newspapers were published in only twelve years between 1846 and 1858. The first Spanish-language newspapers in New Mexico (*El Crepúsculo de la Libertad, La Verdad,* and *El Payo de Nuevo Méjico*) were printed in the 1830s and 1840s, and the first English-language newspaper (Santa Fe's *Republican*) appeared in 1847. By 1879 only seven fairly viable newspapers existed in New Mexico, none of them dailies. Twenty-one years later, in 1900, the number of daily newspapers had risen to five, and a total of 283 newspapers had been started between 1879 and 1900. In contrast to the pre-railroad era, where news articles were often obtained by clipping and inserting stories from other newspapers, increasingly professionalized journalists in Albuquerque and Santa Fe subscribed to the Associated Press wire service for their stories.[3]

Among the prominent Anglo editors during the turn of the twentieth century were William McGuinness (Albuquerque's *Republican Review*), Thomas Hughes and W. S. Burke (*Albuquerque Morning Journal*), William McCreight (Albuquerque's *Daily Citizen*), J. G. Albright (*Albuquerque Daily Democrat*), and Max Frost (*Santa Fe New Mexican*). Generally, editors of New Mexico's Anglo newspapers had moved to New Mexico from the Midwest. Historian Porter Stratton notes that of 34 American editors, 7 hailed from Ohio, 5 from Illinois, 6 from Kansas, 4 from Missouri, and 2 from Iowa. An additional 2 editors were from Pennsylvania, 2 from Texas, 3 from Kentucky, 1 from Colorado, 1 from Nebraska, and 1 from New York. In terms of foreign origins, Stratton found one each from Mexico, Austria, England, and Canada.[4]

Annual newspaper circulation in New Mexico varied considerably, but rarely rose above 2,000 yearly for a single paper before 1920. Albuquerque's *Daily Citizen* improved its circulation from 1,100 in 1895 to 1,900 in 1899. In 1895 the *Morning Democrat* in Albuquerque cited a circulation of 2,500, while Las Vegas's *Daily Optic* reached a high of 1,930 in 1892. An accurate count of readers is difficult to determine since information on nonsubscription newspaper sales and the frequency of sharing newspapers is unavailable in the historical record. Still, it is likely that annual subscriptions represent a low estimate of the extent of the newspaper audience in New Mexico.[5]

Prior to 1880, the few Anglo newspapers depended heavily on Hispano readership for their survival. Although Hispanos accounted for only one in eight journalists in New Mexico, most newspapers were bilingual, with equal space devoted to English and Spanish versions of the news, editorials, and classified advertisements. After 1880, bilingual newspapers were rare and English-language newspapers predominated. Nonetheless, Anglo newspapers treaded carefully when addressing Hispanos, especially Hispano elites. New Mexico was, after all, a relative anomaly in the continental United States, a land where powerful entrenched forces demanded conciliation and concession rather than naked contempt. As a point of comparison as the chapter progresses, contemplate the differences between Anglo depictions of many Hispano ceremonies and depictions in the wider United States of the public events and bodily acts of African Americans.

In New Mexico, Anglo newspapers routinely described Indian ceremonies like the corn dance that began this chapter. In 1907 one Albuquerque newspaper described an "acequia dance" to be held at Isleta just south of Albuquerque. Noting that the celebration was "one of the most important dances in the Pueblos' calendar," the piece outlines several aspects of the ceremony. The dance, according to the writer, "marks the completion of the work of repairing and overhauling and cleaning out the irrigation ditches in the Indian farming lands adjoining the village." Apparently, Isleta townspeople living away from the village returned for the weekend festivities, including those "called in from their work on the railroad and from wherever they may be." The "big dance" appeared as "a sort of preliminary to the beginning of the agricultural season and the planting of crops." Other dances, the writer remarks, of comparable significance include "ceremonials marking the various seasons of the year such as the harvest dance, corn dances, and others." The article ends by noting that "as usual a large number of Albuquerque people will go down to Isleta and see the dance Sunday and several visitors from the east are expected to swell the crowd." Unfortunately, the piece provides no details on organizers of the *acequia* dance or its participants. [6]

In March 1918 the *Albuquerque Morning Journal* announced the performance of another *acequia* dance at Isleta. According to the article, the Isletas celebrated the "turning of water into the ditches that irrigate their fields." The article describes women and children of the pueblo greeting the men returning from cleaning out the debris from the ditches by "bearing branches." The piece also notes that the *acequia* dance "was common among the pueblos" in New Mexico, that each held some ceremony marking the beginning of the irrigation and growing season. Finally, the article adds that the *acequia* dance would be the final dance until the first of May, when "the San Felipe Indians on that date [would] observe the feast of San Felipe." [7]

Other newspaper articles provided further glimpses of Native American ceremonies. One article announcing a celebration at Tesuque Pueblo, located about ten miles north of Santa Fe, describes "the feast of San Diego, the patron of the Tesuque Indian pueblo." Noting that many Santa Fe residents traveled to the village to witness "this function," the article highlights the exotic nature of the event. In the afternoon, the announcement stated, "the Indians will give their weird dances." Furthermore, the spectacle was "an occasion of unusual rejoicing." Other articles similarly accentuate the differences between Pueblo Indian ceremonies and Anglo public events. Announcing an *acequia* ceremony at Isleta Pueblo in 1907, a headline reads: "Big crowd goes to Isleta to see dance." "Four hundred Albuquerqueans," the headline continues, "witness acequia ceremonial of the Pueblo Indians at ancient village." The Albuquerque newspaper did not simply emphasize the physical space between Albuquerque and Isleta Pueblo, which was located only a handful of miles south of Albuquerque. The spatial divide between Albuquerque and Isleta was imagined as a cultural (between "Albuquerqueans" and "Pueblo Indians") and a temporal divide (Isletas as inhabitants of "an ancient village" in contrast to the presumably modern city of Albuquerque).[8]

Indians in public space more generally, regardless of whether they were participating in formal events or simply traveling along city streets, could be the targets of newspaper disapproval and even ridicule. In early December 1882, a woman fell off a streetcar in Albuquerque. According to the brief newspaper account, she had "exhibited the bad sense" of exiting the streetcar while it was still in motion. Several pedestrians apparently witnessed her fall; however, their reaction remains unclear, just as no record exists of the woman's name, or even if she managed to escape injury. The newspaper reported only a handful of facts about the incident. The unfortunate woman was "a Navajo Indian squaw," and her fall off the streetcar apparently made "some of the pedestrians in the neighborhood think that the transit of Venus had come ahead of time."[9] Throughout the fall of 1882, Albuquerque newspapers had devoted much attention to the astronomical event of the "transit of Venus," during which, at various intervals, the planet Venus passes in front of the sun. One transit occurred in 1874, and another would in December 1882, the same month as the newspaper article. The spectacle of a woman falling off a streetcar thus triggered in the mind of the anonymous reporter, and likely in the minds of the readers, the passage of a planet in front of the sun. In other words, the article is an elaborate joke about anatomy and astronomy, specifically about a woman's excessive weight, "bad sense," and the resulting supposedly humorous accident.

This story of the Navajo woman falling off the streetcar overflows with prescribed and prohibited physical bodily behavior.[10] The conflation of a planetary movement—especially a planet like Venus so intimately associated with female sexuality—with a Native American woman's fall from a streetcar also speaks loudly to questions of social ordering in New Mexico. Bodies out of control, especially those of Indian women, posed troubling questions in New Mexico, even when those women tumbled off a streetcar or suffered the ridicule of pedestrians and newspaper readers. Individuals with poorly controlled bodies could carry disease into respectable households or threaten insurrection or challenge Anglo power. In contrast, New Mexicans behaving well, with correct body habits—unlike the spectacular behavior of the unbalanced, astronomically overweight "Navajo Indian squaw" falling off a streetcar—exhibited good "sense," maintained their balance, and did not stumble even in the face of modern technology; they were, in other words, good and able citizens.

Even less demeaning accounts of Indian ceremonies also portrayed the Indians as inferior to Anglos and requiring tutelage in the basic matters of civilization. One review of an Indian school commencement exercise in 1898 notes blandly that the program had been "rendered in a highly creditable manner." Anglo teachers and school administrators received special praise as did the instructor of the Indian band, which apparently "made good progress" over the year. The article comments that most students had returned home for the summer and were advised that "it will be to their interest to return again at the beginning of the next school year." "There is a bright future," the writer adds, "for those who take advantage of the opportunities at present offered."[11]

New Mexico newspapers targeted other groups besides Indians for purportedly improper public activities. Within Hispano culture, the most dramatic event, according to newspaper accounts, was the Penitente ceremony. The Penitentes, a mutual aid society developed in the absence of regular Catholic clergy in New Mexico, celebrated Lent through a set of rituals that could include self-flagellation and the symbolic re-creation of the Crucifixion.[12] New Mexico newspapers frequently reacted to such rituals with a, by now familiar, mixture of fascination and disapproval. A 1907 article, for instance, describes the "Rites of Penitentes" from Sabinal, a village near Belen in central New Mexico. The basis of the article is the report of Walker Healy, apparently "one of the few Americans who has been able to witness the rites of the Penitentes." According to the article, a "few fanatics" performed the ceremony, making "no concealment of self-flagellation." In some cases, in the testimony of Healy, "the natives' backs were a mass of raw and bleeding flesh from the neck down." Another description of the Penitentes in the same article quotes "Don Margarito Romero, of Las Vegas," who claimed that the group was "a villainous lot of people." Romero asserted that he had spent considerable time talking to members of the group who "agreed solemnly with [him] that it is an inhuman organization and ought to be stamped out." Furthermore, he argued that after the Penitentes had "expiated their sins by beating themselves," they felt "licensed to commit all the devilment imaginable."[13]

Excessive bodily comportment was highlighted in other articles on Penitentes. An editorial from 1892 applauds the "high dignitaries of the Catholic church in the territory" for their efforts aimed at the "suppression of the order known as the Penitentes." In denouncing Penitentes and calling for the "eradication of this monstrous evil," the article points specifically to the supposed bodily outrages committed by the group and the threat that the Penitentes posed to civil society ("they are subversives of all good government"). According to the writer, Penitentes "have been known to cut their flesh with sharp knives and to inflict often fatal wounds; they have flogged themselves with thorny cactus or rawhide whips till they had to stop from sheer exhaustion and loss of blood; they drag heavy crosses barefooted over stony roads for miles; they have crucified some members and it is reported that, in more instances than one, death has resulted in such cases."[14]

Although the precise class background of all participants in Penitente ceremonies is difficult to determine, due in large measure to incomplete historical records, evidence suggests that Anglo newspapers made clear distinctions between Penitentes and elite Hispanos. Recall from the above story that Margarito Romero was addressed in the article with the honorific term "Don." "Don" Margarito Romero was linked in the article with Anglo Walker Healy, both of whom were outside observers who shared condemnations of the Penitente ceremony. An article from Santa Fe in 1898 accentuates the differences between Penitentes and elite Hispanos. According to the article, a Penitente procession in Taos, in northern New Mexico, had erupted into violence due purportedly to "drunken penitentes," including the "drunken sheriff and his intoxicated deputies," who attacked and shot at Anglo bystanders. Narrowly averting a "race war," "Hon. Malquiades Martinez" and "friends" apparently stepped into the fray and "prevented a clash." Martinez here is accorded "much praise" for his actions and is positioned squarely in the middle between the riotous and inebriated Penitentes and the Anglo bystanders in Taos. Described as "rag-tag and bob-tail," the Penitente parade is further differentiated in the story from more acceptable, presumably Catholic, Hispano events. "The procession," the article notes, "was not one held by the church, but one by the penitentes."[15]

Such denunciations of Indian and Hispano public events could at times overlap, as in the following account from Indian school records. T. P. Martin reported from Picuris that a "drunken free fight took place between the Mexicans and Indians" during a "Fiesta" at nearby Santa Barbara. Of the "several Indians [who] were badly beaten up," Lorenzo Vargas was the most seriously injured. According to Martin, Vargas "had his trachea, windpipe, broken and skull mashed in between the eyes and a long cut on [the] side of [his] head." Though taken back to the pueblo, Vargas was paralyzed on his left side, lost consciousness, and soon died. Attempting to find the cause of the melee and the identity of the participants, Martin was repeatedly thwarted; neither the "Mexicans" (who "stand together") nor the "Indians" would name those involved. Martin nonetheless concluded that while at the feast celebration, the Pueblos "drank freely of firewater" and then went to another "dance" at the home of saloonkeeper Gregorio Griego, where the fight occurred. Thus clearly linked in Martin's opinion are the "Fiesta" at Santa Barbara and the "drunken free fight" that resulted in numerous injuries and at least one death.[16]

Indian and Hispano ceremonies are thus depicted as teeming with corporeal disorder. Witness the charges leveled at the Penitente ceremony, where "the natives' backs were a mass of raw and bleeding flesh." Both the Anglo Walker Healy and Hispano "Don" Margarito Romero concurred that the Penitente "rite" was aberrant. It is Romero, in fact, who described the group as "a villainous lot of people" and "an inhuman organization." Other articles similarly describe Indian ceremonies through the lens of improperly managed bodies. The Santo Domingo corn dance included "old men singing their weird chant," while "beating their drums," and excessive alcohol consumption and fighting characterized the Santa Barbara "Fiesta."

In sharp contrast, Anglo newspaper accounts regularly praised the bodily comportment at Anglo public events and commemorations. In 1890 the *Albuquerque Morning Democrat* described the Memorial Day proceedings. The events offered the newspaper an occasion to address the wounds of the Civil War. "North and South," the paper observed, "meet in one common bond of sympathy in their sorrow for the death of their dear ones." "Let us forget that a north and south exist today," it exhorted, "but rather think that we are citizens of one common country, imbued with but one impulse and emotion—the glory of the red, white, and blue." The article notes approvingly that the Grand Army of the Republic (GAR) commemorated the day in "a quiet way." The ceremony began at nine in the morning at the GAR Hall, where members of the GAR Women's Relief Corps and the Sons of Veterans listened to a handful of speeches and "several appropriate airs" by the Albuquerque Silver Comet Band. Next, a procession made its way to the cemetery, where observers erected new headstones "furnished by the government" and covered the "graves of the dead comrades" with flowers.[17]

Five years later, the Memorial Day festivities in Albuquerque again included the GAR and the Women's Relief Corps. The most conspicuous change in the ceremony involved the addition of several prominent roles for Albuquerque schoolchildren. The commemoration began at nine in the morning, not at the GAR Hall, but in simultaneous flag-raising ceremonies at the city's four public schools. Where the 1890 celebration made no mention of Old Albuquerque, in 1895 a newspaper noted that "the program to be rendered at the First Ward High School" was to "be participated in also by the school children from Old Town."[18]

In 1905 the *Santa Fe New Mexican* reviewed Memorial Day activities in a page 1 article titled "In Honor of Dead Heroes." A smaller caption reads that the day was "observed with solemnity by the people of this ancient capital." Noting that the weather in Santa Fe justified the town's claim to "the finest climate in the world," the article describes streets "lined with evergreen," flags flying from public buildings, and bunting "drap[ing] most of the houses in the business district." During the morning, "small parties" decorated the graves of loved ones at different Santa Fe cemeteries with "beautiful blossoms." The afternoon ceremonies began at the plaza in the center of town with a parade, described by the paper as "the longest Memorial Day parade that Santa Fe has seen in many years." The article lists the order of the procession that eventually wound its way to the national cemetery. Chief Marshall William Schnepple headed the group, followed by his staff and junior aides, all of whom were named in the article. Next came the military band and local veterans, including GAR members as well as "all old soldiers."[19]

By 1910 the Memorial Day celebration in Albuquerque had grown considerably. According to the *Albuquerque Morning Journal*, the 1910 festivities covered a full day, beginning with a parade winding through New Albuquerque on its way to several cemeteries. The Learned and Lindeman boys' band led the march, followed by members of the New Mexico National Guard, the Grand Army of the Republic, the Women's Relief Corps, the Ladies of the GAR, Spanish War Veterans, Sons of Veterans, and, finally, "Citizens." After the decoration of the graves, the procession left the cemetery on its way to the Barelas Bridge. There, a "boat [was] launched" into the Rio Grande. After lunch the program began with a rendition of "Marching through Georgia" and several lectures by officials in the GAR and other veterans groups. Also addressing the crowd were Mrs. Mattie Butler and Mrs. Addie E. Mugley, "Patriotic Instructors," respectively, of the Women's Relief Corps and the Ladies of the GAR. The ceremonies ended with the band playing "America" and a benediction.[20]

In general, the order of the Memorial Day parades gave clear priority to Anglo men. While some women's groups participated in the events, the procession was always headed by men. Moreover, only very rarely did any of these male marchers have Spanish surnames. Like the military dead that the celebrations commemorated, the marchers were predominantly Anglo men. Witness also the route of the Memorial Day processions. In 1910 the parade began in New Albuquerque, wound its way through the city, and then turned to the west, toward Old Albuquerque and the Rio Grande. The marchers finally halted at the Barelas Bridge spanning the river, where "a boat [was launched]" into the spring waters. The article unfortunately does not elaborate on the contents of the boat or what, if any, meanings were attached to its voyage, but it seems clear that the

4. De Vargas Pageant Parade, Santa Fe, New Mexico, 1911. Public events like parades offered Anglo newcomers an opportunity to associate themselves with modern "American" activities like automobile driving. Photo by Jesse Nusbaum. Courtesy of the Museum of New Mexico, neg. no. 118260.

predominantly Anglo and elite participants in the parade were asserting a certain (literal) control over space in the region. Unlike Indian and Penitente processions, in other words, which were limited to particular spaces marked as racially different, the Memorial Day parade marched through New Albuquerque, Old Albuquerque, the banks of the Rio Grande, and back again to New Albuquerque. The boat launched from the Barelas Bridge, in part, thus may have represented a particular sense of spatial entitlement and freedom for Anglos in New Mexico, the literal freedom to move unfettered through the social landscapes of their choosing.

While many New Mexicans learned of the Memorial Day parades through newspaper accounts, many others attended the events in person, some, clearly, as participants, others as observers along the parade routes. For those in attendance, the emphasis on citizenship would have been inescapable. Just as lessons in bodily comportment in Indian school classrooms served to impress upon students the embodied requirements of proper citizenship, so, too, would the rows upon rows of carefully calibrated, gender-segregated marchers striding in support of soldiers past (and present) have had a significant effect on an observer. Indeed, such bodily regimentation and discipline, associated as it was with military might, would likely have made far more of an impression on the audience than any speeches or pronouncements. The finely measured body practices of current and former soldiers, civic leaders, respectable women, and even Indian school students reminded parade participants and observers alike of both the centrality of bodily integrity in American citizenship and the violence that threatened all those who challenged this emerging social order.

There is also a sense in which the layout and organization of the basic texts of the articles reinforce the depiction of the Anglo ceremonies as stable, orderly, and, in terms of gender, well divided. Unlike most accounts of Indian and Penitente celebrations, Memorial Day pieces carefully differentiated between the various participants in the day's activities. This differentiation entailed separate paragraphs or line breaks for, say, the Women's Relief Corps or the benediction by a particular minister or a rendition of "America." The resulting article as a whole thus appears neat and well organized, with clear boundaries separating marchers, speakers, and performers. In contrast, "other" events emerge as internally *un*differentiated, even jumbled and chaotic. Not only are few, if any, individual participants mentioned by name, but the structure of the articles tends to follow a standard format. The Santo Domingo corn dance, for instance, is described as a collection of events clustered one after another into the same paragraph. There is no mention of the song or songs played by the participants, only "weird chants" and drumbeats are noted. The article likewise fails to note the name of the "buck" or the "old men," or the identities of the other participants, male or female, in the rituals. Finally, a critical component of Anglos' vision of themselves as civilized and advanced was their purportedly more clear boundaries between men and women. This emphasis on gender differences emerges in the accounts of Memorial Day festivities. Article after article notes the separate activities of the Women's Relief Corps and the Ladies of the GAR. In contrast, accounts of Indian ceremonies rarely made a special note of the identities of the participants, let alone whether the event was structured along clear gender lines.

Such Anglo commemorations bore little resemblance to accounts of Indian and Penitente ceremonies. No Indian and Penitente ceremonies basked in the glow of "hallowed ground" or "solemnity." Embodied truths once again made crystal clear the embodied distance separating citizens and the improper and unfit. Public commemorations served a similar function throughout the United States. Over the course of the twentieth century, John Bodnar argues, public commemorations have increasingly served the needs of official cultures and authorities, especially the American nation-state. Like Bodnar, Benedict Anderson describes the flowering of nationalist sentiment and power, perceptively comparing nationalism not to, say, liberalism or Marxism, but to kinship and religious affiliation. For Anderson, notions of kinship are fundamental to the creation of national "imagined communities." In a modern secular age, he observes, only imagined (as in created, not as illusory or of little substance) affiliations and kin networks could inspire individuals to volunteer for potentially fatal military service or choose to send their children into battle. Mary Ryan adds the crucial component of gender to this discussion. She correctly points to the considerable investment among male authorities during parades and civic celebrations in presenting women in public as supportive of social hierarchies and as respectable, rather than disruptive, forces in public.[21] In all three cases, public commemorations appear as especially modern phenomena, marked by secularism, nationalism, and the emergence of middle-class women as political actors.

Memorial Day parades in New Mexico extend such observations, following the lead of theorist Joseph Roach, into the realm of replacement and surrogation. Replacement, the installation of a surrogate regime, such as the substitution of the rituals and rites of the Anglo social order over the remains of Indian and Hispano public affairs, was a critical component of many public events in New Mexico. Fundamental in this process of surrogation was a vision of the past devoid of the consequences of territorial expansion: military occupation, forcible seizure of land, denial of inhabitants' previously held rights and privileges.[22] Memorial Day parades celebrating the bodies of "dead comrades" with orderly processions and patriotic proclamations similarly obscured and denied the pained legacy of territorial expansion. The above Memorial Day parades and newspaper accounts studiously avoid mentioning that American military strength had been used to defeat Mexico and force the annexation of Mexican territory, including New Mexico, to the United States.

Such literal and symbolic erasures confirm the contention of many historians that the U.S. incorporation of New Mexico proceeded along rhetorical as well as political and economic fronts. A. Gabriel Meléndez argues that history and hagiographic accounts of American pioneers and settlers dominated Anglo accounts of the past. No one, according to Meléndez, was more aware of Anglo attempts to replace Spanish and Mexican heroes (Santa Fe as an "ancient capital") with an American pantheon than the Hispano writers at the center of the flourishing Spanish-language press that emerged in New Mexico in the late nineteenth century. Such writers considered history, specifically Spanish and Mexican history, fundamental to their efforts to resist Anglo incursions. Those writers would undoubtedly have viewed with considerable suspicion any parade that celebrated American military strength and made no mention of the war that brought their native land under American dominance.

Ramón Gutiérrez similarly examines Anglo efforts, in this case among boosters struggling to convince prospective migrants to move to New Mexico, to promote a particular vision of New Mexico's history. Focusing on William Ritch's 1885 book, *Aztlán: The History, Resources, and Attractions of New Mexico*, Gutiérrez argues that in the pamphlet's version of New Mexico's historical development, Anglo industriousness and individualism has replaced Hispano and Indian communal traditions.[23]

Still, Anglo writers like William Ritch walked a fine line in their discussions of Hispanos past and present. In his promotional tract, Ritch was careful not to dismiss completely the contributions of its present-day Hispano inhabitants. Ritch, according to Gutiérrez, allowed that natives of New Mexico, including Hispanos, were a "well-disposed, patriotic, and liberty-loving people who had always expressed warmth and friendship towards American immigrants." As illustration of the depth of this accommodation, compare the grudging deference paid by Anglos to Hispanos in New Mexico to the vitriol and abuse regularly directed at African Americans throughout the United States during the same time period.[24]

Like William Ritch, Anglo newspaper editors were well aware of the economic and political strength of Hispanos. An announcement from the *Albuquerque Morning Journal* points to the extent to which the Anglo press, and the Anglo business community in general, acknowledged the prominence of Hispano elites. Titled "Commercial Spanish Offered at Kiwanis," the article announced that "a course in commercial Spanish . . . was offered to the business men of Albuquerque at the Kiwanis luncheon." "If enough business men of Albuquerque will attend," the piece continues, "classes will be held at the Chamber of Commerce three times a week." While the response to the announcement, including the exact number of businessmen to sign up for the class, is unavailable, that the advertisement for improving one's ability in "commercial" Spanish appeared in 1920, some seventy years after the American occupation of New Mexico and eight years after New Mexico became a state, further underscores the continued strength and vitality of the Hispano community in New Mexico.[25]

Hispano weddings, which I will discuss in more detail in the next chapter, represented another set of public events involving notable, if not elite, Hispanos, where the Anglo press displayed evenhandedness and restraint. In 1910 the *Santa Fe New Mexican* announced a double wedding at the Santa Fe Cathedral. Juan Bautista Martinez and "Miss" Francisquita Lujan, with B. Sandoval and "Miss" Mercedes Lujan serving as their attendants, were married, as were Jack Douglas Trainor and "Miss" Antonita Romero, who had "Miss" Eloisa Delgado as bridesmaid and Fred Digneo as best man. According to the article, "the Very Rev. A. Fourchere" officiated and "a reception followed the wedding and was largely attended." Besides noting the large attendance at the event, the article signals its respect for the participants by addressing the women, all of them Hispanas, as "Miss." Furthermore, that the second marriage was an intermarriage draws little pause, further testimony to the exceptional nature of racial politics in turn-of-the-twentieth-century New Mexico. A similar wedding announcement involving a white man and an African American woman is hard to imagine in many regions of the country. Even fifteen years later, in New York, a state without laws banning intermarriage, a great scandal erupted surrounding the marriage of Leonard Rhinelander, a white socialite, and Alice Jones, a "colored" woman.[26]

The deaths of prominent Hispanos similarly drew the respectful attention of the Anglo press. According to the headline announcing her death, Anna Mary Otero was a "much beloved woman" whose "beautiful character and charitable deeds endeared her to those who knew her." Otero, the wife of Manuel Otero, an upper-level bureaucrat at the United States land office in Santa Fe, had been born in a small village south of Albuquerque and attended the Loretto Academy in Santa Fe and hailed from, in the article's estimation, "one of the most prominent Spanish families in New Mexico." In addition to mentioning surviving family members, including as in the previous marriage announcement clearly tolerated evidence of intermarriage in a daughter "Mrs. Virginia Noland" and sister "Mrs. William Lewis," the obituary observes that "Mrs. Otero was a noble woman and was beloved by many."[27]

Other less prominent, though clearly respectable, Hispanos drew similar praise. When Josefine Ortiz died suddenly in May 1905, the *Santa Fe New Mexican* described her as "Miss Josefine Ortiz, daughter of Mrs. Jesus Maria Ortiz." According to the obituary, Ortiz was "employed in the bindery of the New Mexican Printing Company." The article also notes that Ortiz "was survived by two brothers, Jesus Maria Ortiz of El Paso, Texas and Adolfo Ortiz, at home, and one sister, Miss Magdalena Ortiz," who worked with Ortiz at the bindery. Finally, the notice ends, Ortiz was "of quiet demeanor, performed her duties diligently and enjoyed the friendship of all those with whom she came in contact."[28]

Anglo newspaper accounts of Hispano public events, including Catholic ceremonies that were primarily attended by Hispanos, also highlight the respectability of Hispanos. In 1905 a Santa Fe paper noted that "members of the [Catholic] church in Santa Fe had a celebration in front of the Loretto Academy" in which the "May Queen" was crowned in "honor of the Virgin Mary." The First Calvary Band performed during the ceremony, while "incandescent electric lights in the form of a circle, formed a halo about the statue of the Virgin on the spire of the chapel, and a crescent was formed at the foot." During the entire month of May, according to the article, "these lights [would] be kept burning every night, from seven to nine o'clock."[29] Likewise, the Feast of San Felipe de Neri, the patron saint of the San Felipe Church in Old Albuquerque, drew detailed press coverage. In 1890 an Albuquerque newspaper noted that the feast at "West Albuquerque [on] Sunday attracted several hundreds of people from Albuquerque and surrounding towns." The brief article also praises the ceremonies as "interesting and impressive throughout."[30] By the first decade of the twentieth century, the press coverage of the San Felipe festival, if not the ceremony itself, had grown considerably. Sporting large headlines, articles announced, in successive years, the "San Felipe Fiesta" and the "Fiesta of San Felipe."[31] A year later, the headline "Old Town Packed with Visitors" once again announced the feast day, as "many hundreds, reaching into the thousands of people from all over the country were in Old Albuquerque." "The religious exercises," the article continues, "were, as usual, most impressive and picturesque," and "the decorations made things brilliant." The coverage emphasized the day's lectures, mentioning speeches by well-known Albuquerqueans Nestor Montoya, Tomas Werner, and Bernalillo County school superintendent A. B. Stamp, who "gave a very interesting historical sketch of Saint Philip."[32]

Few accounts are more telling of the conciliatory tone of Anglo newspapers than the summary of the 1909 "San Felipe Fiesta." The festivities began in the morning with the firing of a "salute of artillery," followed at 8:30 by an hour-long concert by the Learned and Lindeman boys' band and a high mass and sermon conducted by "Father D'Orsi of Las Vegas." After another band performance at three in the afternoon, a religious procession, including "all the sodalities and societies of the parish and two societies from Barelas [a neighboring, almost exclusively Hispano and Mexicano community]," passed though "all the principal streets of the town." The feast day ended with vespers at the church and fireworks and another band concert in the Old Albuquerque plaza. Among the selection on the program for the evening band concert were "Berry's U.S. Republic Band" march, a serenade titled "Soldier's Dream," "Belle of the West" with a trombone solo by band director F. K. Ellis, "Dance of the Pickaninnies," and "America." According to the article, the "Old Plaza [had] been decorated in gala colors in honor of the occasion."[33]

Commemorations of major historical events could elicit similarly restrained, even admiring comments in Anglo newspapers. On July 5, 1911, the Santa Fe ceremony marking a 1693 Spanish victory under Diego de Vargas over Pueblo Indians received the front-page headline "De Vargas Pageant at Santa Fe Splendid." The article describes a procession involving "descendants of Spanish settlers in the costumes of the 17th century"

5. George Armijo and four unidentified Pueblo governors, De Vargas Pageant, 1911. The presence of prominent "native" New Mexicans forced Anglos, in public events and elsewhere, to seek new strategies in the establishment of social order. Photo by Jesse Nusbaum. Courtesy of the Museum of New Mexico, neg. no. 117756.

and "Pueblo Indians of Tesuque, Taos, Ildefonso, Santa Clara, San Juan, and Santo Domingo and Cochiti, in war costume," as well as "distinguished citizens." George W. Armijo, dressed as de Vargas, reportedly read a proclamation in Spanish to the gathered crowd. Although Pueblo Indians obviously participated in the events, the article clearly distinguishes between Pueblos, on the one hand, and a merged Hispano/Anglo community, on the other. The piece ends by noting: "Indian sports and races were included in the afternoon program. The red and yellow of Spain were intertwined with the Stars and Stripes throughout the city."

Indeed, the extent of Anglo and Hispano "intertwining" here is striking. Beyond the image of the Spanish and the American flags flying proudly throughout Santa Fe, members of Theodore Roosevelt's Rough Riders, now celebrating rather than conquering Spain, were among the "military and civic organizations" joining the procession. In characteristic fashion, this alliance was marked by military personnel, members of civic groups, and "distinguished citizens." The event also overtly excluded Pueblo Indians and more subtly limited participation from those Hispanos unable to claim descendants among the original Spanish settlers or to afford to dress in the appropriate seventeenth-century costumes. Embodied distinctions here are notable as appropriate dress, recall the "war costumes" of the Pueblos, helped enforce a racialized division in a public ceremony explicitly devoted to civic membership and national belonging. The event, after all, though appearing in the newspaper on July 5, occurred on the Fourth of July and was described as a "distinctive feature of the Fourth of July celebration."[34]

Such accounts, especially juxtaposed with Memorial Day parades, are highly suggestive, pointing to a civic leadership corps comprised of both Anglo and Hispano elites. One of the most revealing examples of this shared leadership position of Anglo and Hispano elites was the parade celebrating the conclusion of the 1896 New Mexico Territorial Fair. The *Albuquerque Morning Democrat* summarized the parade's "magnificent spectacle" celebrating the end of that year's fair. At the head of the parade was the newly crowned queen of the territorial fair, "Mrs. George Harrison." According to a contemporary observer, "Mrs. George Harrison" was in fact, "Margaret Otero Harrison, the young and beautiful daughter of Mariano S. Otero [and] the wife of Dr. George W. Harrison." Margaret Otero Harrison, identified in other sources as "Margarita" Otero Harrison, was in the estimation of the newspaper account, resplendent in "white brocaded silk en train, with ornaments and a golden crown." Her brother, Frederico Otero, the "son of Hon. M. S. Otero and . . . regarded as one of the most handsome men of the city," was also a prominent participant in the festivities. Horseback, and dressed as the Duke of Albuquerque, he similarly led a procession. In both cases, the Otero sister and brother were joined by Anglos, costumed, respectively, as fashionably attired attendants to the queen and as the Duke of Albuquerque's "knights and heralds." The float ushering the queen through the streets of Albuquerque, the article notes, "provoked no end of enthusiasm and won the plaudits of the multitude."[35]

Such rousing expressions of cross-cultural public unity are exceptional indeed for turn-of-the-twentieth-century America. Recall, however, that such accounts occurred in the midst of vicious racialized attacks on the embodied acts of Indians and Penitentes. In fact, one could argue that the unifying force behind shared elite Anglo/Hispano ceremonies was the widespread denigration of Indian and Penitente bodies. Nonetheless, as the following chapter will suggest, Indians and Penitentes were not alone in enduring the slings and arrows of racialized discourse. African Americans and prostitutes, though representing a very small percentage of New Mexico's population, were similarly targeted as corporeally deviant and unfit for citizenship.

While the chapter on rape trials addressed prostitution and attempts by defense attorneys to associate rape victims with promiscuity and quasi-, if not literal, prostitution, the major symbolic role of African Americans in New Mexico's emerging racial order has yet to receive sustained treatment. I will end, then, with two examples from New Mexico newspapers that illustrate both the subtle and the not-so-subtle public denigrations of African Americans. Notice in the following accounts how African Americans, like Indians and Penitentes, serve as the negative backdrop against which respectable New Mexicans like Anglos and Hispano elites defined themselves. It is worth mentioning in this respect that vicious slandering of African Americans was not limited to newspapers associated with the Democratic Party, like the *Albuquerque Morning Democrat*, and the party's support after the Civil War of Jim Crow laws and the suppression of African American rights. As the following stories attest, Republican and Democratic newspapers alike published demeaning accounts of African Americans.

In 1918 an Albuquerque headline announced: "Grease-Painted Pueblos Dance at Rotary Lunch." As the text of the article quickly makes clear, the "series of dances which ran the gamut of everything from the tribal war dance to the corn dance" was in reality an elaborate performance put on by the Albuquerque Rotarians. The lunchtime performance began with a "grand tom-toming in the lobby," followed by the entrance of the "redskins" into the dining room. With " 'Chief' Ernest Landolfi head[ing] the band," the group of "camouflaged Pueblos—painted, feathered, and costumed by the Fred Harvey curio department—gave the Rotarians a glimpse of Pueblo pomp." The "camouflaged," "feathered," and "costumed" Rotarians appeared as "grease-painted" and "redskins." Their entrance to the dining room was announced by drumming—"a grand tom-toming"—and they eventually performed a variety of dances. The article observes that members were unrecognizable to each other, "so carefully had the veneer of civilization been concealed." The article goes on to describe a speech on German–United States diplomatic relations that followed the dancing. Again, civilization, epitomized by a public lecture and diplomatic negotiations between nation-states, is contrasted to the embodied antics of savagery.[36]

While the American tradition of "playing Indian" was well established by the time "Chief" Landolfi and others donned their fathers, such accounts are strikingly similar to descriptions of nineteenth-century minstrelsy and blackface performances, where whites painted their faces black, spoke in African American dialect, and performed public shows highlighting the supposed backwardness of African American culture. In both cases, Anglos disguised themselves as racial others in mock ceremonies that accentuated the great distance between Anglos, on the one hand, and Indians and African Americans, on the other. In stark contrast to the sensual, exuberant, unlicensed, primitive cavorting of Indians and

African Americans, white people appeared rational, calm, proper, disciplined, civilized, in full control of their bodies and emotions.[37]

Like the descriptions of Indians and Penitentes, negative depictions of the bodily comportment of African Americans helped Anglos in New Mexico assert their own contrasting bodily respectability and superiority. Such depictions also gave Anglos an opportunity to denounce the body practices of racial others without running the risk of antagonizing elite Hispanos. African Americans, in other words, as the following chapters will discuss in far greater detail, helped bear the brunt of Anglo racializing discourse. Such depictions also helped Anglos address the lingering problem of whiteness—what to do when another powerful group, like elite Hispanos, also staked, and capably defended, their own claim to privilege and respectability.

As the following story makes clear, in both New Mexico and the rest of turn-of-the-twentieth-century America, vicious attacks on African Americans provided Anglos much-needed aid and comfort in confronting the problems of whiteness. In 1894 the *Albuquerque Morning Democrat* ran the following piece:

> A crowd of Indians, whites, Mexicans, and all sorts was entertained on a vacant lot on east Railroad avenue yesterday afternoon, by a darkey. They raised a purse of $1.00 for the darkey, provided he would extricate himself without assistance after having his hands tied behind him. When a Democrat reporter arrived on the scene he had been tugging away for half an hour. His ebony skin was shining like patent leather, the cords stuck out on his neck like grape vines and the perspiration was running down his cheeks like an irrigating canal. When last heard from he was still tugging away.[38]

In the above article, the body of the African American struggling to free himself takes center stage. The "ebony skin" of the "darkey," the prominent "cords" of his neck, "perspiration . . . running down his cheeks," all are prominent features of the article. Such corporeal details are then linked, in by now a familiar racialization pattern, with more abstract notions like slavery, emancipation, wage labor, consumer culture, and modernity. In a stunning, if sinister, display of metaphorical writing, the article associates the embodied struggles of the African American with both slavery—he does after all have his hands tied behind his back—and an agrarian premodern world, with veins on his neck like "grape vines" (veins/vines), perspiration like an "irrigating canal."

Notice, in addition, the unity of "Indians, whites, Mexicans, and all sorts" in this account, their shared amusement at the struggles of the

African American. Anglos, Hispanos, and Indians, so deeply divided elsewhere in New Mexico, in this story are united, brought together by their
ridicule of the bound African American "tugging away" in a vacant lot
along Albuquerque's Railroad Avenue. This unity is especially telling in
the context of the threat African American men, in wider America and
in New Mexico, supposedly posed to the broader community. Tightly
bound, the man posed little danger; even hours later, "he was still tugging
away."

As the complicated story suggests, Anglo newspapermen, stymied by
the presence of Hispano elites from imposing racial order through the
widespread denigration of Hispanos, could turn to a distressingly wide
variety of other targets for "proof" of the excessive bodily comportment
of nonwhites. This chapter has explained how Anglo newspapers simultaneously racialized the bodily comportment of Indians and Penitentes
while at the same time announcing with considerable respect the ceremonies of elite Hispanos. But newspaper coverage of public ceremonies
and festivals were not the only spaces where elite Hispanos exerted great
power and influence in New Mexico.

As the following chapter will make clear, the homes and domestic
relations of elite Hispanos like Don Romero and the Honorable M. S.
Otero also received considerable praise in Anglo newspapers. Likewise
the domestic relations of African Americans, as well as Indians, were condemned in the New Mexico press as tumultuous, improper, and, unless
properly controlled, potentially threatening to society at large.

STRANGE BEDFELLOWS

ANGLOS AND HISPANOS IN THE REPRODUCTION OF WHITENESS

In 1882 the *Albuquerque Democrat* reported a "lively scuffle between a culled [*sic*] lady and gentleman." According to this account of domestic turmoil and public chaos, "The coon received the blows in good style, but succeeded in getting the revolver from the lady." The article ends in an attempt at humor, quoting the woman in mean-spirited dialectic, "You ain't mad, is you?" The newspaper story, describing this public dispute between an African American man and woman, links inappropriate bodily control with both racial difference and inappropriate sexuality. In the first place, the article's use of vernacular—depicted as inappropriate and incorrect acts of speech—associates the subjects of the piece with abnormal bodily comportment. The article also contrasts the actions of the African American couple with more proper romantic interactions. Unlike those engaged in a "lively scuffle" and waving revolvers, proper couples, the article suggests, would refrain from physical violence. Proper couples certainly would not argue in full view of attentive newspaper reporters, and a real "lady" would never brandish a revolver.[1]

The African American couple—like the subjects of so many articles, advertisements, and "local laconics" in New Mexico's newspapers—epitomized both the incorrect use of the body and the considerable distance separating particular racialized New Mexicans from fitness for citizenship. At the same time, the article uncannily drapes strangeness in familiarity. Recall from the introduction that African Americans never represented more than 2 percent of New Mexico's population. Nonetheless, stories like the above proliferated in New Mexico. Demographically and physically peripheral, African Americans were, as this chapter will demonstrate, central figures in newspaper discourse. Why would this be? Why would the tiny African American population come to occupy so much space in New Mexico newspapers and, one would assume, in the psyches of New Mexico newspaper readers?

The incorporation of New Mexico, bodily and otherwise, proceeded along many fronts and demanded many concessions and contrivances. It was in the domestic realm, however, where the makeshift nature of annexation and imperial expansion was laid especially bare. Nationally, according to many writers and politicians, the white, racially pure American family was the cradle of democracy and civilization. With a potent mix of white supremacy, patriarchy, and budding imperialism, Americans denounced domestic relations composed of racial mixing, non- or extramarital intimacy, non-nuclear family cohabitation, and unclear gender roles as unfit and uncivilized.[2]

In New Mexico, however, miscegenation and intermarriage could hardly be so demonized. Colonial rule for decades had depended on the land and wealth amassed through strategic intermarriages between daughters of wealthy Hispano families and Anglo men. Indeed, some of New Mexico's most prominent leaders were members of intermarried families. Moreover, attacks on non-Anglo homes as unfit and uncivilized would surely have enraged Hispanos, many of whom voted, held political office, controlled substantial wealth, and tended to view their own families with a certain pride and affection. Given the fact that disorder and violence could clearly plague Anglo families, the Hispano home could, and did, make a plausible claim to its own form of respectability.

The previous chapter demonstrated how racialization efforts in New Mexico newspapers depicted Indians, some Hispanos like Penitentes, and African Americans as corporeally disordered and unfit for citizenship, while both celebrating Anglo ceremonies like Memorial Day parades and treating the public events involving Hispano elites with respect and even admiration. In domestic matters, New Mexico newspapers once again sought a delicate balance. Anglo and Hispano homes were depicted as stable and orderly, the opposite of the tumultuous events portrayed in the article that begins this chapter, and in stark contrast to depictions of the domestic lives of African Americans, Indians, and prostitutes. Patriarchal gender relationships also characterized ideal homes. Women performing typical wifely duties like sewing, cooking, and caring for children were routinely cheered in the press. Men, by contrast, were congratulated for their business and political successes and their leadership skills within the community. In addition, the ideal home was a space of romance and the exalted sentiments of love and devotion. Relationships based on mutual admiration and respect received special praise in the press; newspapers did not announce, for instance, that certain marriages had been arranged for political purposes or point out that, say, an unplanned pregnancy, rather than elevated romantic sentiments, had spurred a couple into matrimony. Finally, the ideal home was associated, if at times subtly, with racial purity. Announcements of prominent marriages, for instance, frequently noted the names of the bride and groom's mother and father, emphasizing the clear lineage of the newly betrothed. During a period in American history when an individual's unclear ancestry could suggest miscegenation or illicit cross-cultural intimacy, such affirmations of unambiguous ancestry as in a wedding announcement were not inconsequential (moreover, that such conventions endure suggests in part their continued relevance to a society still deeply concerned with the consequences of racial crossings and cross-cultural intimacy).

How, then, did Anglo newcomers affirm the supremacy of the racially pure American home in the face of Hispanos willing and able to provide such vexing and persuasive counterevidence? Newcomers turned to the tools of modernity, primarily the newspaper, and a strategy strikingly similar to the effort to delineate, through accounts of public ceremonies, the proper bodily comportment of citizens. Anglos relied on two of America's most resilient and evocative images: the African American male rapist and the prostitute. Elsewhere in the nation, of course, newspapers focused, whether accurately or not, on crimes of sexual violence committed by African American men. Only in New Mexico, however, was the population of African Americans so small and the strength of the *non*-Anglo-American population so great. Newspaper accounts of sexual violence by African American men, drawn from sources both inside and outside New Mexico, and prostitutes, from within New Mexico, helped resolve this tension at the heart of American aspirations for empire. Before describing in more detail the attacks on the domestic lives of African Americans and prostitutes, further elaboration of the particular components of the ideal home for both Anglos and Hispanos is in order.

Wedding announcements and newspaper accounts of marriage ceremonies nicely express the Anglo conception of an ideal home. In 1910 Charles Thomas and Nellie Loomer married in an Episcopal wedding ceremony in Santa Fe. Thomas, a native of Florida, lived in Glorieta, New Mexico, and worked as a station agent for the railroad. Nellie Loomer, described as "a handsome and charming young lady, of fine character and excellent tact and business ability," was also, according to the article, a business college graduate and had moved to New Mexico from Colorado to accept a position in Glorieta as a telegraph operator. After the ceremony, the newlyweds reportedly toured the "old historic town" of Santa Fe before driving to nearby Glorieta, where the "happy couple [took] the California train amid a shower of congratulations and good wishes." After the honeymoon, Thomas and Loomer planned to make their home in Glorieta. Accentuating the couple's great promise, the article predicted that Nellie Loomer would be a "real companion and help-mate" for her husband.[3]

Announcements of engagements highlighted similar themes of romantic love and appropriately matched couples. In January 1920, according to a breathless newspaper account, Reba Conner and Horace Keenan announced that they were to be wed. Keenan, newly relocated to Albuquerque from nearly two years living in France, worked with Armour & Company, and was, in the author's estimation, "a lucky man . . . very worthy of the honor of carrying away one of the city's most popular young ladies." Conner, a graduate of the Girls' Collegiate of California, worked as a record clerk for the Santa Fe railroad and taught at a public school in Albuquerque. "In her," according to the story, "charm of personality is combined with unusual accomplishment and ability in widely varying lines." Besides describing the future bride and groom and Conner's parents, the article also notes the names of the four friends who helped organize the party. Wishing the couple "many, many happy new years," the piece ends, "may fortune ever smile on them!"[4]

New Mexico newspapers also reported the nuptials of Anglo former residents of New Mexico who had moved elsewhere. In 1905 the *Santa Fe New Mexican* announced the wedding of G. E. Meany and Nellie Drake in Prescott, Arizona. Meany, according to the article, had "spent a good deal of his boyhood in [Santa Fe] where his father for a number of years was rector of the Church of the Holy Faith." Quoting from the wedding announcement, the article notes that the church was "comfortably filled with friends of the happy couple," and that the groom was "paying teller at the Prescott National Bank, which fact alone vouches for his standing in [the] community," and the bride was a "young lady of the highest social standing."[5]

New Mexico newspapers also drew upon tales from across the country in order to address themes of romantic love and patriarchal gender relations and bolster their version of the ideal white home. In February 1895 the *Albuquerque Morning Democrat* followed the story of John Bell, who made a claim on land known as the "Cherokee strip" that had recently been "opened up" to the public near the Chiloco Indian reservation in the territory of Oklahoma. According to the story, John Bell, upon filing his claim for the apparently vacant and unimproved land, learned to his disappointment that a single woman had already filed on the same claim.

6. Wedding portrait of "Eddie" Ross and William Henry Cobb, 1891. Photo by William H. Cobb. Courtesy of the Museum of New Mexico, neg. no. 14274.

After contacting officials of the land office and registering a challenge to the woman's claim (the land, after all, appeared to have "no one in possession and no signs of improvement"), Bell discovered that the woman in fact was Sarah Bell, his ex-wife for some eight years. She apparently intended to sell her property in Illinois and take possession of her claim in Oklahoma. Although John Bell attempted to "effect" some type of settlement "through further correspondence," at first "no compromise was effected," and Sarah Bell "bought lumber and had a house built on her claim." According to the article, John Bell continued to pursue the matter, and the divorced couple eventually agreed to settle the matter in Perry (presumably a small town in Illinois). Both John and Sarah—the "two contestants"—boarded the train at Newkirk, but "before they reached their destination they were both sitting in the same seat, and John had his arm around her waist, and she was sobbing in his breast." When the train finally arrived in Perry, the re-formed couple "celebrated the anniversary of the opening of the Cherokee lands by being reunited in marriage." The article ends by noting gleefully that "both are now living happily on the new home near the Chiloco reservation."[6]

In this article, and in others like it, the restoration of proper gender roles (that is, the creation of a hierarchical family structure with the husband/father at its peak) drives much of the narrative. At first, the figure of Sarah Bell offers several challenges to predominant gender hierarchies. Not only is Bell divorced and single, but she has evidently traveled by herself to register the initial claim on the land (she was "one of the first to file" on the Cherokee strip), and the article makes no indication that she plans to marry. Furthermore, she proves adept at protecting her claim to the land. When John Bell files a contest to her claim, she does not wither from the challenge, but rather "[buys] lumber and [has] a house built on her claim." Nevertheless, when the "two contestants" board the train on their way to settle the matter, presumably through some legal agreement, the contest suddenly ends. While the observation that "they were both sitting in the same seat" suggests a degree of equality, the next two phrases paint a far more hierarchical picture. John Bell "[has] his arm around her waist" and his ex-, soon to be new, wife, is "sobbing in his breast." It is difficult to miss the proprietary implications of John Bell's arm around the waist of Sarah Bell, especially considering that the article ostensibly describes a dispute over property. John Bell now presumably has managed to secure not only a parcel of real estate but the house that Sarah Bell built on that land.

Also embedded in this tale of family reconstitution, government-inspired land grants, and the transformative presence of the railroad are allusions to white racial superiority and the structural dominance of whiteness. Land grants in the United States, for instance, never proceeded along a simple trajectory of distribution of "free land" to willing and eager—usually white—settlers. Rather, the availability of "free land" always depended on the forced expulsion of the previous—usually Indian and/or Mexican—inhabitants and was usually followed ironically by the labeling of these same groups as "landless" and "nomadic."[7] The article alludes to this profoundly racialized displacement by noting not once but twice the proximity of the Bells' land claim to the Chiloco (Indian) reservation in Oklahoma's Cherokee strip. The couple even remarries on the anniversary of the "opening of the Cherokee lands," linking the reformation of family with the loss of Native American land. Though the new home of the reunited Bell family does not literally replace the Chiloco reservation, readers could hardly avoid the implication.

According to the logic of the article, the ideal white home, characterized by marriage and romantic love between whites, solves the problem of uncertain ownership of land. After all, until the reuniting of the Bell family under the rule of John Bell, chaos seemed to reign over the land in question. Neither the land's previous Chiloco Indian inhabitants nor

Sarah Bell—both of whom are linked in the piece as inappropriate and ineffective landowners—manage any "improvements" in the land; Sarah Bell only builds a house, the article winks, when her claim is challenged. Furthermore, only a specific type of marriage appears capable of resolving the land-claim dilemma and restoring harmony. Although the incident occurs in 1895, when coverture laws in the United States and the ability of married women to control property had been in the process of changing for several decades, the article ignores such complexities and clearly advocates in favor of John Bell's undisputed control over the family and its newly acquired property.[8] There is never a hint in the article that Sarah Bell, despite her clear homesteading ability and initiative, should have any decision-making power in the relationship once her husband assumes control. The article thus openly advocates a domesticity based on a clear racial and sexual hierarchy as the best possible route toward the ordered settling of "open" land. As the article notes, with a pun that in all likelihood was fully intended, "the contest was settled" finally with a white man governing both his "improved" land, newly acquired from displaced Indians, and his contrite wife, similarly "improved," who is left sobbing at his breast.

Of course, none of this is to paint an overly simple picture of marriage and domesticity in New Mexico. Testament to the complicated nature of such stories is the final image of John and Sarah Bell. Though the story ends with John Bell's restored control, it is upon his "*breast*" that Sarah Bell weeps. Just as the disturbing (to some) possibility that white women would give freely their hand in marriage to black men, as described later in the chapter, so, too, may growing breasts, if only to provide solace for weeping women, be a newfound, and not entirely (for some) welcome, male requirement in the settling of the country. Taken a step further, Sarah Bell may have been crying because *this particular* attempt to acquire male property and privilege failed.[9] Perhaps perched beside her husband, weeping into his breast, Sarah Bell was actually designing her next move, rather than resigning herself, teary-eyed, to her drab fate.

Such anxiety about the fault lines and inconsistencies within the ideal white home were typical of broader America. Lisa Duggan has argued that the late nineteenth and early twentieth centuries brimmed with challenges to white domestic supremacy. Using Memphis, Tennessee, as an example, Duggan observes that integral to the sensationalistic, and frequently wildly inaccurate, newspaper accounts of African American male rapists and white "lesbian murderers" was their supposed threat to the sanctity and safety of the male-dominated white home. In New Mexico, the ideal white home, as defined by Anglo newcomers, faced even greater challenges. Although African Americans in the United States, like Ida B.

Wells, challenged the myth of the "black beast rapist" and white women continued to carve out space for same-sex sexual intimacies, their claims to domestic respectability were severely constrained. Wells was forced to leave Memphis, and for a time the United States, after bravely denouncing white terrorist lynchings, and same-sex families have yet to receive full societal sanction and legitimacy.[10] Hispano elites, by contrast, convincingly argued that Hispano homes were well managed, stable, and deserving of widespread acclamation. Anglo newspapers, though perhaps less than enthusiastic about the situation, were thus forced to accommodate to Hispanos, and the resulting depictions of Hispano domesticity and marital relations, like accounts of particular Hispano public ceremonies, were remarkably restrained, even at times admiring.

Testament to the mild treatment of Hispanos in Anglo newspapers is the generally approving tone adopted by the press regarding Anglo/ Hispano intermarriages. Recall from the previous chapter the marriage announcement of Jack Douglas Trainor and Antonita Romero, and the praise showered upon queen of the territorial parade, Margarita Otero Harrison, wife of Dr. George Harrison and daughter of Mariano and Filomena Otero. One of the most prominent relationships between an Anglo woman and an Hispano involved Miguel A. Otero Jr., New Mexico's territorial governor between 1897 and 1906. Otero was the son of Miguel A. Otero, a leading figure in mid-nineteenth-century New Mexico politics, and Mary Josephine Blackwood, "a belle of Charleston, South Carolina." Raised in an elite family, Otero spent much of his youth and young adulthood outside New Mexico. In December 1888 he married Caroline Virginia Emmet, whose father was a former chief justice of the Minnesota Supreme Court. The *Santa Fe Daily New Mexican* duly noted the nuptials. "The marriage of Mr. M. A. Otero and Miss Emmert [*sic*] took place in Las Vegas, at St. Paul's Episcopal church on Wednesday evening," the article observes, "and was a very brilliant affair." Evidence of the degree to which intermarriages between respectable families could draw societal sanction is another wedding announcement on the same page as the Otero-Emmet celebration. "Mr. A. W. Kimball and Miss Victoria Armijo, the beautiful daughter of Col. Perfecto Armijo," the piece reads, "were married in exquisite style at Albuquerque last evening."[11]

Less savory characters in New Mexico were similarly spared denunciations of their cross-cultural intimacies. Accounts of the 1881 death of Billy the Kid, for instance, highlight, but do not denigrate, the heterogeneity of his social world. Billy the Kid, the former Henry McCarty, alias William Bonney, is described by one historian as fluent in Spanish and the beneficiary of "an instant rapport and popularity . . . with people of Hispanic extraction." Eternally a bachelor, he was supposedly possessed of

7. Venceslao Jaramillo and Cleofas
Martinez on honeymoon trip, 1898.
Photo by Schumacher. Courtesy of
the Museum of New Mexico, neg.
no. 67224.

"a charm [that] proved unfailingly seductive" to women, "especially Hispanic young women." His last words—"Quien es? Quien es?" upon noticing a shadowed figure in a dark bedroom—speak to the extent to which
Billy the Kid traveled in, even fled to, Hispano communities and Native
American women and Hispanas in New Mexico. Minutes after his death,
"Nasaria Yerby, Abrana García, Paulita Maxwell, and the Navajo woman
Deluvina Maxwell wept, talked softly, and consoled one another," while
"a sobbing Celsa Gutierrez cursed [Pat] Garrett [his killer] and pounded
his chest." After a coroner's jury absolved Garrett of any guilt in the slay-
ing, blaming instead the Kid for the bloodshed, "the women [who] had
asked for the corpse . . . had the body carried across the parade ground to
the carpenter's shop," where, according to a witness, "it was laid out on a
workbench, [and] the women placed lighted candles around it according
to their ideas of properly conducting a 'wake' for the dead."[12]

Marriage records highlight similar cross-cultural trends in New Mexico. Intermarriages between Anglos and Hispanos were hardly a major
aberration in New Mexico. In Albuquerque, the intermarriage percentage remained fairly steady between 1890 and 1920 (between 6% and 11%).
Such percentages of intermarriage in Albuquerque are similar to intermarriage percentages in other settings in the American Southwest. The
gender dimensions of the intermarriages also mirror results from recent studies. According to one estimate, the population in Albuquerque

moved from more than four times as many men as women in 1885, to a ratio of three to two in 1910, to near parity in 1920. During periods of gender disparity, when there were more men in Albuquerque than women, intermarriages between Anglo men and Hispanas outnumbered marriages between Anglo women and Hispanos. As the gender ratio became more balanced, the gap closed considerably. In 1890, only a decade after the arrival of the railroad in Albuquerque, ten Hispanas married Anglo men, compared to only two Hispanos marrying Anglo women. In 1920 fifteen marriages involved Hispanas and Anglo men, while there were eleven marriages between Hispanos and Anglo women.[13]

Once again, notice the difference between the maintenance of racial order elsewhere in the United States and the emerging order in New Mexico, specifically the contrasting images of people of mixed heritage in broader America and within New Mexico. The contrast is especially striking between depictions of people of mixed white and African American ancestry in the United States in general, exemplified by the "tragic mulatto" figure, and the lives of New Mexicans of mixed Anglo-Hispano heritage. People of mixed heritage, whether described as "mulattos," "*coyotes*," "mixed bloods," or "half-breeds," are remarkable figures in the history in North America.[14] Earl Lewis and Heidi Ardizzone, in their analysis of the life of Alice Jones and the Rhinelander case of the 1920s, point to the convergence in the early twentieth century of two schools of thought regarding biraciality among white Americans. One version judged mulattos as less threatening than "pure-blooded" African Americans due to the supposedly civilizing and salubrious effects of their partial white blood and ancestry. The other version considered the mixture of white and African ancestry to have doomed mulattos to a desolate and destructive twilight world between black and white, polluted and polluting. Both versions share, despite their divergence, a decidedly negative assessment of biracial peoples, considering them deep threats to the supremacy of the white American home. In the early twentieth century, twenty-nine states passed or had passed laws banning intermarriage. Such laws focused primarily on prohibiting marriages between whites and African Americans, however, certain states, like California, also targeted marriages between whites and East and South Asian immigrants, Asian Americans, and Native Americans. In contrast, intermarriage and mixed heritage in New Mexico received considerable social sanction and, as the above evidence suggests, an unprecedented degree of tolerance. Indeed, it is difficult to imagine a career like that of New Mexico Governor Miguel A. Otero, the mixed-heritage son of an Anglo woman and an Hispano, occurring elsewhere in the United States.[15]

Besides descriptions of intermarriage and mixed heritage, even newspaper tales of domestic mayhem involving Hispanos were notably muted in the Anglo press. In one story from Las Vegas in northern New Mexico, Epafloridito Baca beat to death Leopoldo Montoya, whom Baca had discovered in bed with his wife. Notably absent from this narrative is any direct language of race. While the names of the participants (Epafloridito Baca, Leopoldo Montoya) are clearly of Hispano origin, nowhere in the lengthy article is there any mention of "Mexican" or "Spanish." Had the events involved African Americans, on the other hand, it is inconceivable that race would not appear as a central feature of the narrative, primarily by marking the participants as "Negro." Moreover, such stories of African American domestic disturbances frequently concluded with a sharp, even comic, comment on the incident. Recall the earlier story of the "culled" man and woman, which ends, "You ain't mad, is you?" This article from Las Vegas, by contrast, concludes not with invective but by praising the alleged murderer: "he has always borne a good reputation."[16]

As the following accounts demonstrate, domestic disorder involving racialized "others" like Indians and African Americans, both inside and outside New Mexico, were common features of New Mexico newspapers. Still, as the stories also make clear, Hispano domestic turmoil in New Mexico never drew writing as venomous or constructed danger as so urgent as did stories of prostitutes and Indian and African American domestic lives in New Mexico. Successful colonial rule in New Mexico (the war of position, as described by José Limón, carried out after open rebellions and violent resistance, the wars of maneuver, had been crushed) required constraint and caution from Anglo-dominated newspapers. The home lives of Indians, African Americans, and prostitutes may have been fair game. Hispanos and Hispanas, even those who intermarried or participated in cross-cultural intimacies, were a much different matter.[17]

Indian domestic relations drew at times harsh criticism in both newspaper stories and other sources. In March 1918 an Albuquerque judge fined Juana Chirino thirty dollars for an inopportune comment she made in court. According to the article titled "Mother-in-Law Talking in Court Convicts Self," Chirino, an Isleta Indian, was on trial for "interfering in the private life of her son Jose Chirino and his wife Louisa Padilla de Chirino," also both Isleta Indians. Apparently Chirino's daughter-in-law, "formerly a motion picture actress in Los Angeles, taking Indian parts," had filed the charge against Chirino. As the trial ended, the judge directed Jose Chirino and Louisa Padilla de Chirino, who had married only a couple of weeks earlier, to demonstrate their love for each other and their desire to "live happily ever after" by shaking hands. At this point, according to the article, Juana Chirino spoke to her son "in Indian." A translator reported to the judge that Chirino had ordered her son not to shake hands with her daughter-in-law. Furious, the judge immediately fined Juana Chirino. Although the judge eventually suspended Chirino's sentence, provided that she "discontinue making trouble between the parties," the message of the article is clear. Indian families, according to the article, required the intervention of the American court system in order to restore proper domestic relations between husband and wife.[18]

Interracial intimacies could draw similar criticism, even in sources outside of newspaper accounts. In 1905 Luella Gallup reported from Cochiti that an employee Minnie Thomas was "deeply infatuated with that young Mexican." Though promising not to write any more letters to the young man and a good employee ("I like her and her work," Gallup wrote, "and would feel sorry to have her go"), Thomas, in Gallup's words, "believes he is going to marry her." When Gallup apparently suggested to Thomas that her beloved "was only amusing himself and was flirting with other girls," Thomas replied that she had been told the same story before and refused to believe it true.[19] In another case, Dr. M. S. Murphy reported from Española that two weeks earlier he had received a note from "Miss Arnold, the ardent admirer of the Santa Clara 'brave.' " According to Murphy, "Miss Arnold" had asked him to treat "the admired" for a "sore hand." Adding that Arnold, "this man's suitor," had recently suffered a similar injury, Murphy bristled that it was hardly "her [Arnold's] business to call [Murphy] to the pueblo."[20]

Similar concerns with the consequences of interracial intimacy emerged in a 1905 letter from resident physician Edward Darns at the Zuni agency in western New Mexico. Darns noted, "It is asserted with equal positiveness by persons in a position to know" that the increased presence of Anglos ("the encroachment of the white man," Darns called it) led to "contact with the lewd careless element" and "a marked increase of immorality among the girls." "Easily susceptible to the wiles of artful men," the "poor and indigent" Zuni young women thus "sacrifice their purity for a few paltry dollars." Fearing "the disgrace of bastardy," they then "resort to artificial abortion." "A sad indictment against us," Darns concluded.[21]

Like Indians, the few African American families living in New Mexico were similarly targeted for abuse when their domestic lives became tumultuous. Newspaper accounts also often accentuated their supposedly improper bodily comportment. One story from 1905 reported that "a colored man, whose name was unobtainable," had attempted to "get a license to marry Miss Beatrice Pollard" in Santa Fe. The clerk, however, according to the article, refused to grant the license because Pollard "was only 13 years old," and the man "was 43 and at the time he had applied for the license was intoxicated." "He wanted the license," the piece ends, "because of the delicate condition in which he had placed the girl." While "Miss Beatrice Pollard's" race remains unspecified, the bodily improprieties of the African American man are made most obvious: intoxication, nonmarital, not to mention illegal, sexual intercourse (recall from chapter 3 that New Mexico's age of consent law was raised in 1897 to fourteen).[22] From Santa Fe, the *Daily New Mexican* snarled that "a half-breed colored boy and his pal, notorious little sneak thieves," had been arrested for stealing from a local store. The magistrate "Squire Martines," notably an Hispano in a position of authority, released the pair on the condition that they leave Santa Fe for "all time to come." "Good riddance," the article snaps.[23]

New Mexico newspapers surrounded such tales of African American bodily improprieties and domestic turmoil from within New Mexico with wire reports and commentary drawn from throughout America. "Of course," the *Albuquerque Morning Democrat* meanly quipped in 1895, "Frederick Douglass loved music. Was there ever a colored person who didn't?"[24] In 1895 the *Albuquerque Morning Democrat* reported from New York City the identification of the body of an unknown woman. The "mutilated corpse" was "positively identified as the remains of Mary Martin," who apparently had "lived with a negro known as William Caesar," who was under arrest for her murder.[25] In 1909 an Albuquerque paper announced: "Negro Murderer Makes Break for Freedom," describing the desperate "break for liberty" by John Junken, the "alleged slayer of Clara Rosen."[26]

Denigrating relationships involving African American men and white women from outside New Mexico was characteristic of the depictions of interracial sexual relationships in New Mexico newspapers around the turn of the century. In 1905 a Santa Fe paper reported the attempted lynching of an African American man in Columbus, Ohio. "Judge Lynch Wants Negro," the headline proclaims, "Mob Tries to Lynch George Copeland Who Murdered Miss Maranda Brieler." The article observes that Copeland had been arrested for the murder of "Miss Maranda Brieler, white," and had to be rescued by a sheriff, who "hustled him into an automobile." The "mob" was left behind, "still crying for Copeland's blood."[27] So dreadful was the 1895 tale of sex and danger from Halsey, Kentucky, that the editor of the *Albuquerque Morning Democrat* devoted four headlines, more space than the article itself, to the spectacular story. A dying man had confessed to five murders, two in Alabama, two in Tennessee, and one in Georgia. Of the five murders committed by "the Negro," three of the dead were "white women." According to the article, another man had been convicted of one of the murders on "circumstantial evidence" and had been wrongfully executed. The tale of this (as the

headline pronounces him) "Ebony 'Jack the Ripper,'" this "Colored De-
mon," ends with an especially provocative detail. Apparently, the "Negro
had carried in his pocket the skeleton of a female hand." He supposedly
"always kept" the piece around him and used it as "his luck piece for five
years in a crap game."[28]

On the surface, the above article undoubtedly belongs among the great
waves of violence and disorder that daily crashed across the front pages
of New Mexico newspapers. The same day that the "Ebony 'Jack the Ripper'" story elicited blaring headlines, two other violent crimes—one an
armed robbery, the other a murder—received large headlines on the front
page. A diamond burglary, one case of embezzlement, and two cases of
suspected arson also joined the fray, in addition to news of an earthquake,
an influenza epidemic, and two stories of "demented" men wandering the
streets.[29] And late February 1895 hardly qualified as a particularly bloody
or disastrous period. New Mexico newspapers routinely reported, even
showcased, vicious crimes, scandal-filled trials, and executions. In this respect, New Mexico was little different than much of the country, especially
the American West. Gary Hoppenstand, writing of Ambrose Bierce and
the "late-nineteenth-century macabre Gothic tale," describes "the wryly
gruesome flavor of his journalistic work." In one sense, then, the "Ebony"
Ripper article simply describes with a particular eye for graphic detail (a
woman's hand as a "luck piece," an innocent men wrongly executed) a
serial killer finally apprehended.[30]

Viewed from another angle, however, the story compels more nuanced
readings. The reference to "Jack the Ripper," for example, invokes the
original Jack the Ripper, who murdered five working-class women in
London within ten weeks in the fall of 1888. The Ripper saga incited not
one, but a multitude of competing and at times contradictory narratives
in late-nineteenth-century London. One of the most prevalent themes
coursing through the many Jack the Ripper narratives explicitly associates
the female victims with both prostitution and with more general transgressive behavior on the part of women, such as speaking in public or
walking the city streets without an escort.[31] Like the London Ripper tale,
the story of the Kentucky "Ebony" Ripper produces not one, but several
potential readings, each of which tumbles amid an array of meanings peculiar to turn-of-the-century America. One reading of the article would
view the piece as a relatively uncomplicated warning to respectable white
men and women of the supposed murderous intentions of African American men. The article appeared in 1895, a year before *Plessy v. Ferguson*,
and well into a period in American history rife with speculation about
the dangers of unchecked African American male sexuality. In the 1890s,

in both the American South and North, lynchings of African American men and women accelerated rapidly, reaching, according to one study, an average of at least two hundred lynchings a year in the border states and the states of the former Confederacy alone.[32] Thus, the article's gripping detail that the killer carried a "skeleton of a female hand" with him as a good-luck piece in crap games seemed to highlight the purported depravity of African American men. The female hand as a good-luck piece may have also strengthened the link in some readers' minds between the "Ebony" Ripper and the London Ripper, who reportedly mutilated victims and removed internal organs as trophies.

Still, the "skeleton of a female hand" detail is a complicated one. The murderer, after all, was never apprehended; rather, he confessed to the killings only on his deathbed, only *after* another man had been tried, convicted, and executed for one of the murders. What if the female hand he used as a good-luck piece represented not the murder and mutilation of "innocent" white women by African American men, but their willing alliance and eventual betrothal (i.e., "hand in marriage")? It is possible that some readers, and even the writer of the article and the newspaper's editor, associated the white women killed by the black murderer not as much with the violation of pure white womanhood as with a form of unconventional, even aberrant, consensual interracial activity between white women and African American men. Seen in this light, the article may represent a warning to both white women and African American men of the dangerous path of interracial relationships. For white women, especially, a "female hand" given freely in marriage, the article suggests, could all too easily end up a "skeleton" used for good luck in crap games. At the very least, the article manages to paint certain types of sexual relations in turn-of-the-century America—specifically those crossing racial boundaries and involving white women and men of color—as abnormal, unstable, and even potentially murderous.[33]

As mentioned, Lisa Duggan's fascinating study of newspaper accounts in 1890s Memphis usefully pairs narratives of lynching of the sort Ida B. Wells so effectively protested with spectacular accounts of homicidal lesbian lovers. Overlapping narratives of the "black beast" and the "homicidal lesbian," she says, helped "define the sanctity of the 'white home' as the central symbolic site of the nation."[34] In New Mexico newspapers, descriptions of prostitutes performed a similar function, pairing with lynching narratives to help clarify, through a productive and useful opposition, appropriate domestic relations and reputable white homes. Talk of prostitutes and prostitution, in other words, permeated discussions of bodily coherence and respectability in New Mexico, epitomizing both the absence of bodily integrity and the outer edge of citizenship, clarifying the legitimacy and propriety of a range of body practices, including sexual intercourse, healthy bodily comportment, and appropriate attire.

New Mexico newspapers went to great lengths to emphasize the threats that prostitutes and prostitution posed to respectable households. Such accounts of domestic turmoil fired by commercial sex frequently highlighted prostitutes' inability, willing or not, to maintain appropriate physical, social, and spatial boundaries. One of the most prominent features of disreputable households in New Mexico was the absence of clear and well-managed boundaries. Descriptions of the domestic lives of prostitutes, typically characterized as chaotic and grotesque, offer one of the clearest examples of such overly fluid households. In 1911 a Santa Fe newspaper celebrated the reuniting of two sisters at an orphanage in Santa Fe. The girls, both daughters of Nellie Krop, had been removed, at different times over the course of several months, from their mother's custody after raids on an "alleged disorderly house" in Albuquerque. Although the article reports that the case against Krop for operating a brothel was "largely circumstantial," she had been sentenced to twenty days in the county jail. The judge, however, suspended her sentence, and "upon a promise of further good behavior," she was released. Still, as the article makes clear, Krop's two daughters would not return to their mother's custody; rather, they "would make [their] home" at St. Vincent's Home in Santa Fe.[35]

The aberrant households of prostitutes appeared in other contexts besides newspaper accounts. There were few more prominent prostitutes, or indeed women, in New Mexico than Lizzie McGrath, who for forty years operated Albuquerque's most successful brothel. McGrath, the daughter of an Irish father and a mother born in Tennessee, had been born in 1861 and arrived in Albuquerque almost as soon as the railroad did. In 1882, at the age of twenty-one, the woman who would come to be known as the Lily of Copper Avenue moved to Albuquerque. She worked as a prostitute in several locations during those early years, including a stint in the wine room owned and operated by Gertie Oliver. By 1885, however, only three years after stepping off the train in Albuquerque, McGrath had opened her own business, the Vine Cottage, a small "clapboard house" located on 312 West Copper, in the heart of Albuquerque's bustling red-light district. In that year, 1885, the Vine Cottage was the home of five adults, three women and two men, including Joe Quang, a twenty-year-old Chinese laundryman. In 1900, at the age of thirty-eight, McGrath still lived at 312 West Copper Avenue and served as the head of a five-person household. Three other women, all white and listed as "partners," resided with McGrath in addition to Albert Henderson, an African American porter. McGrath not only owned the home on West Copper, but according to census records, owned it outright. Unlike most of her immediate female neighbors, McGrath, never married at thirty-eight, reported that she had no children, living or dead. Of her immediate female neighbors over the age of twenty-two, only McGrath had never had a child.[36]

By 1910 McGrath had moved a block to the east along Copper Avenue, settling as head of a six-woman household on 227 West Copper. McGrath, by now forty-eight, was still single, still appeared free of children, still considerably older than her housemates, and still owned outright her home and business, which was listed as a "Female Boarding House." In 1920, nearly forty years after she had first arrived in Albuquerque, fifty-eight-year-old Lizzie, now Elizabeth, McGrath appeared once again in the census living in downtown Albuquerque on West Copper Avenue. Still single, head-of-household McGrath was the keeper of a "rooming house." The four lodgers at the house included two women and two men.[37]

One striking feature of the life of Lizzie McGrath is the extent of cross-cultural, even interracial, interaction in her household. Besides violating gender boundaries, sexual boundaries, work/home boundaries, consumer/producer boundaries, McGrath lived for years, even decades, with men who were unrelated to her by blood or marriage, some of them men like African American Albert Henderson and Chinese Joe Quang. McGrath's domestic life thus epitomized the non-ideal home.

In 1911 Lizzie McGrath appealed a case to the New Mexico Territorial Supreme Court. McGrath and her lawyers attempted to persuade the justices that McGrath had been wrongfully convicted of violating the following New Mexico statute:

> That every person who shall set up or keep a brothel, bawdy house, house of assignation or prostitution, in any town, city or village in the Territory of New Mexico, within seven hundred feet of any school house, college, seminary or other institution of learning, or any church, opera house, theatre, hall of any benevolent or fraternal society, or other place of public assemblage, shall, on conviction thereof, be adjudged guilty of a misdemeanor.[38]

McGrath, according to the conviction, had established her business on West Copper Avenue in New Albuquerque, between Third and Fourth Streets. This location was within seven hundred feet of the halls of both the Masonic and the Knights of Columbus fraternal organizations and the Pastime Theater.

A basic feature of the trial was proving that McGrath in 1911 did indeed operate a brothel from her home on Copper Avenue. One witness stated that it was common knowledge that McGrath operated "a house of prostitution." He went on to claim that female customers to his saddle and harness business had complained to him about the prostitutes in the area and had voiced their reluctance to continue visiting his store. "I have been told," he said, "by women frequenting my place that they do not like to come there on account of . . . there being around there houses of prostitution, everything around there on that street." Another witness, asked if he had ever seen women standing or walking immediately outside of McGrath's, replied, "Every time I pass or walk in the vicinity, I would see somebody around there." Once again, Lizzie McGrath's domestic life as a prostitute is portrayed as aberrant and improper.[39]

Other sources similarly highlighted the supposed dangers posed by prostitutes to respectable households. An article addressing masturbation in the *New Mexico Medical Journal* abruptly turns from masturbating children to the fantastic figure of the "depraved female rapist" (or the prostitute) and the "many young boys, mere children," that she had supposedly seduced and led to "ruin." The article associates masturbating children, especially by implication those who continue to masturbate *after* learning the error of their ways, with aberrant sexuality and prostitutes ("the depraved female rapist"). This particularly dense vision of sexual abnormality could hardly contain its rhetorical excesses. While boys are only curious about autoeroticism and the mere victims of female prostitutes (and would never actually *seek* commercial sex), the two most grotesque images are female. The article bundles both masturbating girls and female prostitutes under the sign of "impure intercourse." For girls, unlike the merely curious boys, masturbation becomes a regularly indulged occurrence, a "habit." Like masturbating girls outside the scope and control of "normal" society, female prostitutes take on even greater symbolic weight. "Depraved rapists," they lie in wait for unsuspecting victims, ready to "seduce" and "ruin" them. In the rhetorical outbursts of the article, prostitutes come to represent more than even the seduction of young boys; they are the embodiment of the countless dangers "lurking" in dark city streets and sinister back alleys.[40]

At the same time that descriptions of prostitutes dominated accounts of disorderly households, stories of other white families (the absence of racial or ethnic markers in these articles suggests whiteness) gone tragically astray demonstrated the superiority of families adhering to firm boundaries and well-guarded borders. The provocatively titled "Price of Passion" article documents the shocking murder and attempted murder of three siblings in Texas. The two youngest children died, while the third managed to recover from doses of "large quantities of morphine." The murderer, the article observes, was none other than the children's mother, Mrs. Mollie Carruthers, "wife of a respectable, well-to-do farmer." Mrs.

Carruthers apparently confessed to the crime and initially claimed that "it was done to get them [presumably the children, but left unspecified] out of trouble and [that] she intended to follow." Later, the article concludes, authorities discovered that "the woman and a stranger had planned to destroy the children and then leave the country."[41]

Though the article ostensibly describes a mother's murderous attack on her children, its title ("Price of Passion") demands further interpretation. "Passion" clearly refers to Mrs. Carruthers and the "stranger" with whom she plots the crime and plans to flee the country, suggesting that at its core, the tale concerns not so much infanticide as the horrific consequences of illicit (in this case adulterous) sexuality. Carruthers's initial confession, that she planned to use morphine first to kill the children and then kill herself in order to "get them out of trouble," not only marked her as a poor mother, but also associated her subtly with prostitution and abortion. Prostitutes were more likely than middle-class women to commit suicide and also more likely to "get into trouble" and be forced to "destroy" the children.[42] Prostitutes also frequently consorted with "strangers." That Mrs. Carruthers and her partner should have planned the incident implies paradoxically, and perhaps more disturbingly for male readers uncertain about the fidelity of their wives, that cold and measured calculation, not the heat of passion, lay at the heart of this unsettling affair. Regardless, the image of Mollie Carruthers here stands in direct opposition to the proper wife demanded by the dictates of male supremacy. Like the "Ebony" Jack the Ripper, though she confesses her crime, the article makes no mention of an apology; there is no tearful act of contrition, no begging for forgiveness.

Those who pay the "price" of Mollie Carruthers's "passion" include the unfortunate Carruthers children, who "pay" with their lives, as well as Mrs. Carruthers's husband and any other close friends and relatives. Yet neither the husband (he is referred to only as "a respectable, well-to-do farmer") nor the children (identified only by their ages, 4, 11, and 14) are named in the article. This odd silence widens the circle of potential victims of this crime. Those who must "pay" for the excesses of Mrs. Carruthers's "passion," that is, are (white) Americans in general. According to the binary structure of the article, Mollie Carruthers and the "stranger" stand in direct opposition to the unnamed, prosperous, respectable farmer and his equally anonymous children. The image of the "farmer," especially a successful farmer, invokes a deeply American tradition, one intimately associated with both whiteness and masculinity. The murdered children, considering the uproar in late-nineteenth-century America surrounding "race suicide" and white women's responsibility to reproduce at a high rate, similarly represent the potentially imperiled future of the white race. Note the phrase that ends the article: "the woman and a stranger had planned to destroy the children and then leave the country." Mollie Carruthers, already deeply implicated in transgressive sexuality, appears allied with national, if not racial, treachery. She betrays both whiteness ("destroy the children") and the virtual synonym of whiteness, America (planning with a "stranger" to leave the "country"). [43]

In conclusion, marriages and domesticity based on clear social and physical boundaries in New Mexico appear the ideal of romantic love, consideration, and propriety, and as ultimately integral to the orderly functioning and welfare of the American political system. Once again, Lisa Duggan's work is instructive here. According to dominant Anglo racial hierarchies, purportedly more civilized peoples possessed more romantic, exalted sentiments of love, in contrast to the brute, purely reproductive instincts of primitive races. [44] Such a contrast appears clearly in New Mexico as well.

Nonetheless, attempts to fortify the Anglo home in New Mexico by denigrating all other domestic lives and intimate relationships faltered in the face of respectable, and powerful, Hispano elites. Forced by the colonial realities of New Mexico, where Hispanos resembled in their power and influence Cubans and Puerto Ricans more than Tejanos or Californios, to adopt new forms of social ordering, newcomers turned to body practices, racialization, and modern tools like newspapers. Such new strategies facilitated the attack on the domestic lives of African Americans and prostitutes and the reassertion of the supremacy of the white home. Those body practices appearing in newspapers as incoherent and inappropriately fluid (culturally, physically, spatially) were denounced and denigrated, condemned as unbefitting of true citizens. Geographic movement, for instance, in the "Ebony" Ripper article (the dying man who confessed to killings throughout the South) is associated with murderers and mutilation. The piece also associates sexual liaisons between white women and men of different races with sexual commerce and prostitution. Prescribed and respectable male and female behavior is typified by the end of the Bell article, as the woman sits childlike on the man's lap and weeps while the man, demonstrating no emotion, holds her firmly in his grip. Once again, the peculiar demography of New Mexico demanded novel (and imperial) strategies in the creation and maintenance of social order.

In claiming to possess respectable homes, Anglos in New Mexico announced their own whiteness, asserting a kinship with whites throughout America based on shared notions of proper bodily comportment and appropriate domestic relations. Hispano elites, however, challenged Anglo attempts to stake exclusive claims to ideal homes and home lives.

At the same time that Hispano elites played the trickster (or the *coy-ote*) to Anglo racialization projects, the similarities between Anglo and Hispano elites were difficult to ignore. Indeed, prominent Hispanos, as the introduction made clear, had for centuries claimed social superiority in New Mexico based on their own bodily comportment: "pure" blood, light skin, "civilized" habits and inclinations. Thus, while Anglos and Hispanos acknowledged the differences between the two groups (language, religion, history), certain shared notions of proper bodily comportment, respectability, and the attributes of whiteness were also unmistakable. The following two chapters, on medicine and consumer culture, will examine the creation of an embodied whiteness in New Mexico. Chapter 6 will discuss the emergence of the white body in the predominantly Anglo realm of professionalized medicine, while chapter 7 will chronicle the shared Anglo and Hispano elite white body that developed in the modern advertisements and mass consumer culture of New Mexico's English- and Spanish-language newspapers.

"PROMISCUOUS EXPECTORATION"

MEDICINE AND THE
NATURALIZATION OF WHITENESS

Indian and Hispano bodies, as I have demonstrated, were critical to Anglo racialization projects in New Mexico. Though forced by Hispano elites into certain accommodations, Anglo newspaper writers, educators, and civic leaders consistently pointed to the bodies of Indians and Hispanos as "proof" of their supposed inferiority to Anglos. Nonetheless, the emerging racial order required more than simply racializing others. Anglos would have to racialize *themselves* as well.

The following two chapters will examine the "naturalization" of whiteness from the perspective of the body. Naturalizing whiteness, recall, is a process by which the physical characteristics of the white body come to be associated with abstract qualities like superior reasoning abilities, leadership skills, respectability, advanced civilization, and fitness for citizenship. In this chapter, on medicine, the supposed bodily failures of Indians, Hispanos, African Americans, and others will appear once again with familiar and unsettling regularity. At the same time, Anglo physicians writing in the *New Mexico Medical Journal* expended considerable energy describing and evaluating the characteristics of the white body. According to physicians, the white body was characterized by the following: sex between husband and wife, good hygiene, proper ingestion of food and drink, and the avoidance of alcohol, tobacco, and public spitting. Just as embodiment was an integral component of the racialization of Indians and Hispanos, bodily comportment was fundamental to Anglo claims to whiteness in New Mexico.

Health care providers, from "orthodox" physicians to healers to water-cure practitioners, had existed in New Mexico as long as humans had. Prior to 1880, medical training in New Mexico was largely a local matter. Indian and Hispano health care providers, though well trained by older relatives and community members, bore little resemblance to the modern professional physicians trained at medical schools outside New Mexico who arrived in the territory in the late nineteenth century. According to historians, some more formally trained physicians did practice in New Mexico from the Spanish colonial period through the beginning of American occupation. Still, for most New Mexicans, the practice of medicine before 1880 relied on traditional remedies and cures administered by locally trained practitioners. While some considered such medical care to be decidedly inferior, such as Zebulon Pike, who in 1826 denounced "the deplorable state of the medical sciences" in New Mexico, many others were undoubtedly completely satisfied with their medical care and would likely have dismissed "modern" medicine with as much vehemence as Pike criticized "primitive" New Mexico medicine.[1]

Traditional medical treatments clearly endured in New Mexico well after the arrival of modern medicine. One 1905 letter, from Dr. Edward Darns at the Zuni agency in western New Mexico, addressed the frequency and methods of abortion among the Zuni. Though claiming "ignorance of much of their methods and habits," and hindered by "a universal feeling of sensitiveness among the women to having a male attendant in cases of any disease of the reproductive organs," Darns nonetheless provided one of the more detailed descriptions of reproduction and women's health available in the archives. Darns reported that one of the inducements against abortion was the Zuni fear "that the woman would dry up." Mothers of pregnant, unwed daughters, according to Darns, immediately rushed to reassure them "that it will be alright and [that] she must let it alone." Upon hearing news of a recent abortion, "the old women" also apparently "place [the woman] in warm sand for ten days hoping to forestall the wrath of nature and thus prevent her ultimately from 'Drying Up.'" Darns concluded with the following description of the Zuni method of abortion:

> The girl grasps hold of her gravid uterus though the abdominal wall and by twists and squeezes succeeds in detaching the foetal connections with the uterine wall and the foreign body is then expelled. A few days of indisposition follow and all is well.[2]

Darns also reported that based on the information he could obtain there had been no cases of infanticide in the past few years. In fact, he stated, "Zuni mothers, even of illegitimate children, [are] intensely parental in their care of the very young." In terms of "Criminal Abortion," Darns admitted receiving differing answers from those "approached on the subject." One group apparently claimed that "this practice was formerly very prevalent among the unmarried women but it had grown into disfavor." Only "a few notorious characters who cared for nothing" reportedly still practiced abortion.[3]

At the same time that traditional medical practices endured in New Mexico, some New Mexicans also selectively adopted aspects of Anglo medicine. Alice Dwire reported from Taos that the "principals of Taos Pueblo" had asked her to write a letter reaffirming their petition against the current physician Dr. Martin. According to the Taos Pueblos, Martin only distributed a "few drops at a time" of his large supply of medicine, and either did not visit the pueblo regularly or "when he comes, he drives around the Pueblo but does not stay long enough to do anything." Nonetheless, Dwire added, "they believe in both the white man's medicine and the Indian medicine and say their objection is to Dr. Martin and not to the medicine." In a subsequent letter, Dwire repeated the point, stating, "Some of the people prefer the Indian medicine and will not take ours when prescribed, some want our medicine but do not want the physician."[4]

This overlapping of traditional and modern medical practices, while occurring sporadically prior to 1880, only began in earnest when the medical profession arrived in the territory with the railroad. Up to that point, the total number of "regular" doctors, according to one historian, "probably did not exceed a couple of dozen, and only a few of them actually settled in New Mexico Territory." The first professional medical association began in 1882, but struggled mightily in its early years, reaching a "nadir of sorts . . . in June 1898, when only eight members showed up [at the annual meeting], and the society's president, first vice-president, and second vice-president were *not* among them."[5] Still, the fledgling organization had a bright future. As tuberculosis continued to ravage the country and health seekers flocked to New Mexico's clear air and reputation for healing, sanatoriums flourished, as did the physicians who operated them.

The *New Mexico Medical Journal*, first published in 1905, attempted to unite the medical profession and raise its public visibility, as well as provide timely medical information. Each issue of the journal usually spanned thirty pages, beginning with several pages of editorials and brief announcements, followed by two or three original articles and a handful of final notices and advertisements. The authors of the articles, as well as the editors, all of them physicians, were predominantly Anglo men who

had settled in New Mexico after the railroad's arrival in 1880. While Hispano doctors were rare, especially in the pages of the *NMMJ*, it is worth
noting that in one of the rape trials from chapter 3, *NM v. Bonifacio Mares*,
Dr. Felipe Romero, a physician in Las Vegas, testified that he had examined the victim Virginia Montoya. The total number of doctors in New
Mexico rose from about one hundred in 1886 to over two hundred in 1906
to 430 upon statehood in 1912. These doctors hailed from medical schools
throughout the country, with the states of Missouri and Illinois alone accounting for 20 percent of the schools, followed by Kentucky, New York,
Ohio, Pennsylvania, and Tennessee. The quality of training of New Mexico physicians ranged considerably, from graduates of some of the nation's
most prestigious medical schools like Rush Medical College in Chicago
(26 of nearly 600 physicians in New Mexico pre-statehood identified by
Jake Spidle) and Philadelphia's Jefferson Medical College (23 doctors) to
less well-regarded, even suspect, schools like the University of Louisville
Medical Department (20) and the St. Louis College of Physicians and Surgeons (17).[6]

For doctors in New Mexico, the professionalization process—joining
a medical organization like the New Mexico Medical Society; subscrib-
ing to, and even writing for, the *New Mexico Medical Journal*; attending annual medical conferences—created a vital link not simply between
doctors within New Mexico, but with physicians throughout the country.
Historians have considered professionalization to be one of the hallmarks
of modernity. Professional organizations like the American Medical Association and the American Bar Association became increasingly prominent in the nineteenth century, exerting considerable influence in a range
of political and social issues. In medicine, the AMA was instrumental in
persuading legislators across the country to criminalize abortion. At the
same time, modernity's emphasis on standardization and measurement
was evident in new forms of licensing, professional oversight, and widely
accepted accrediting procedures for the education of young professionals.
Finally, professional relationships—spanning several states, even countries, and facilitated by journals, newsletters, and annual conferences—
were fundamentally modern as national professional organizations of
exclusively doctors came to replace older, more local affiliations across
occupation, but based in the community. Doctors, in other words, in
the turn-of-the-twentieth-century professionalization process, affiliated
themselves less with lawyers and dentists down the street and more with
other physicians throughout the country.[7]

In New Mexico, modern professional organizations offered physicians
an opportunity to affiliate themselves with a nationwide American net-
work of other physicians. Such affiliations, as I will argue, were especially

8. Unidentified New Mexico doctor in office. On the periphery of the American empire, New Mexico doctors celebrated their use of modern technology and their fitness for full citizenship. Courtesy of the Museum of New Mexico, neg. no. 91143.

important in New Mexico, where physicians were painfully aware of their uncomfortable location at the far, ragged end of the American empire. Their professional organ, the *NMMJ*, while devoting itself to standard medical questions of health and illness and the treatment of the human body, simultaneously reflected the pervasive anxiety characteristic of colonizing agents. Ann Stoler's observations about the ambivalences bedeviling European colonizers is especially apt. The "racial grammar" circulating, according to Stoler, throughout Europe in the nineteenth century suspected that Europeans living in the colonies were not "truly European and fit to rule."[8] New Mexico doctors experienced a similar set of anxieties. Within, and in response to, a context of turmoil and uncertainty in New Mexico, physicians spoke often in the *NMMJ* of their credentials as Americans, differentiating themselves along a set of recognizable and interrelated, embodied axes: gender, race, national, professional, scientific. They did so, I argue, to counter the claims that New Mexicans, including themselves, were undeserving of full membership in the American polity, that they were, in fact, truly a "mongrel people" unfit for citizenship. In celebrating their own privileged relationship with medicine and science (and modernity in general), physicians cozied up to men of science and reason throughout America and, through a rhetoric of professionalism and scientific rationality, attempted to minimize the considerable distance between their own practices and the practices of their American colleagues.

At the core of this attempt by Anglo doctors to claim kinship with American doctors was an assertion of shared whiteness. This assertion of whiteness, like any racialization project, inside or outside New Mexico, was itself fundamentally about the human body. Acknowledging the centrality of bodily comportment to Anglo doctors' claims of whiteness extends Alexandra Stern's superb analysis of empire building and medical knowledge in El Paso and along the U.S.-Mexico border in the early twentieth century into New Mexico. Describing public health reforms that focused with increasing intensity on the bodies of Mexican immigrants, Stern reveals the deep linkage between medicine and the militarization of the border.[9] In illuminating such medicalization and racialization projects at the heart of modern America, this chapter suggests once again that body practices and bodily comportment proved fundamental to claims, in this case by New Mexico physicians, to whiteness and citizenship.

Articles in the *New Mexico Medical Journal* made clear distinctions between people of Mexican origin, those either born in Mexico or of Mexican descent in the United States like Hispanos, and Anglos. In a discussion of the "myxomatous degeneration of the chorionic villi," the author included several examples. The patients' race was left unspecified, except in the final example, where "Mrs. M.P." is identified as "Mexican." This rhetorical strategy was typical of the *NMMJ*. Journal articles would often mention a patient's race when discussing certain case histories. But authors only mentioned a patient's race when the patient was "Mexican," "Negro," or another racialized group. In a review of tuberculosis infection in Roswell, an author described "the consumptive" and "a patient with tuberculosis," but only notes the race of nonwhite patients. Reporting on "two cases of tuberculosis which happened in my practice," the writer added that they were "both Mexicans." In an account of postoperative treatments after abdominal surgery, the author mentioned several patients, including "a feeble old man of sixty" and "Mrs. L., aged twenty-eight, and a fine specimen of young womanhood," but only identified the race of particular patients: "a negro with a bullet-hole through the liver" and the "Mexican boy" who supposedly shot him accidentally. In a typical piece, a study of pulmonary tuberculosis, the doctor recorded the ages and dates of first examination of four patients, including the fact that two of the four were clergymen, but never mentioned their race. One can only assume, as *NMMJ* readers likely assumed, that case histories that made no mention of race were speaking of white patients. The naturalization of whiteness, where whiteness becomes the normal and the given, could hardly have been more clear.[10]

Though clearly willing to treat and write about Hispano patients, doctors were typically cautious in their descriptions of "Mexicans" in New Mexico. An overview of amoebic dysentery in the Southwest reminded readers that "it occurs not only among the Mexicans along our border, but also among the well-to-do." In fact, the writer found somewhat surprising the fact "that it is not more so there, where the hygiene of the peons is so poor."[11] Like Sheriff Dudley, from the case *NM v. Alva* from chapter 3, who carefully differentiated between "Old Mexico" Mexicans and Hispanos, notice how the author, an Anglo physician, refrained from linking Mexicans in the country of Mexico to Hispanos in New Mexico. This restraint, I argue, was typical of Anglo New Mexicans, who were hesitant to challenge the political and economic power of elite Hispanos.

Another piece, a memoir of sorts of the author's years practicing medicine in Mexico, paints a scene of American progress and Mexican backwardness. The piece begins with a romantic tale of pre-conquest Mexico, "when the Aztec retinue of Montezuma's court moved majestically, amid feathers and plumes . . . through mighty forests, bearing the Chief's daughter, a thin delicate maiden, to the warm springs" of the Topo-Chico hot springs. Upon the return of the "dark-visaged maiden [now] well, strong and vigorous," the hot springs supposedly became famous for its healing properties. The writer of the essay was stationed at the Topo-Chico hot springs, "in that strange land and still stranger tongue." In his view, Mexico was a place of "hospitality and song," with "unexplored and inexhaustible mines" and "primeval forests," and the Mexican people appeared as "patient, loyal, and with an almost idolatrous faith in medicine." Some day, the author hoped, "when her internal strifes are ended," Mexico would rise to a stage similar to that of "the nations of peace which unhappily are few" (but presumably included the United States). At that point, after the most recent round of revolutions, "her baptism in blood," the "banner of freedom will wave over [the] republic" of Mexico. In sharp contrast to the United States, Mexico is associated both with the past (witness the constant references to Aztecs, "primeval forests," and "idolatrous" Mexicans) and with an inferior stage of development—a potential for progress, but as of yet still far removed from civilization.[12]

Nonetheless, even in a space dominated by Anglos (there were, as mentioned earlier, at the time relatively few Hispano practitioners among the medical profession), discursive attacks on Hispanos in the medical journal were fairly uncommon. Indians, on the other hand, were hardly so fortunate. *NMMJ* writers consistently stressed the inferiority of Indian customs and bodily comportment. One article compares mothers who breast-fed their children to the "noble Red Man." Indians in this fascinating image are associated with extinction, the ancient past, and the "natural," while "this sweet age of advanced civilization" becomes the sole province of whites. "As in all primitive races," another piece notes, "alcohol is one of the Indian's deadliest foes." Moreover, the article reports high rates of tuberculosis, trachoma, and the number of "Indian children of school age who were not in any school." Still, the article expresses great optimism that now that "the United States government has fully recognized its obligations to the redskin," the "present policies" of the federal government would eventually "prolong his race and fit him to associate and compete with white Americans."[13]

Beyond Hispanos and Indians, doctors spoke at length of the embodied failures of a host of other racial and ethnic groups. One article responds to a proposal before the Texas medical association that prohibited African Americans, Chinese, and Japanese from membership. Such an amendment "would be an insult to science," according to the author, for it would end up excluding from the profession a host of well-trained physicians, ultimately denying professional status to "all dark skinned races, with them the Indians." The results would be unfortunate. "Some surgeons from Central America," for example, "are Indians but would shame many of us in this work," just as "Japan has produced medical men of international repute," and "China is doing so now." Still, the writer empathized with the plight of Texas doctors. Referring to F. E. Daniel, the author of the amendment, the piece observes, "We believe that Daniel, whose attainment we admire, whose mastership of the King's English we covet, had in mind the negro-pest in the South and the Mongol pest in the fruit growing district." Professional success and proper, even masterful, English here stand in direct opposition to African Americans ("negro-pest") and Asian Americans ("Mongol pest"), who are both associated with pestilence and disease.[14] Early issues of the *NMMJ* often contained jokes and brief humor pieces. One joke ridicules an "old South Carolina darky," who claimed, after having his temperature taken by a thermometer, to have already eaten. "What did you have," the doctor asks. "A lady done gimme a piece of glass ter suck, sar," the man replies, in dialect typical of medical journals.[15]

Another article, from 1913, sought to "reckon with" the influence of race on the "question of disease distribution." The author described in depth the "distinct variation in susceptibility" to disease between Jews, African Americans, and Italians, and included discussions of "the dark complexioned Creole of French or Spanish parentage," the "Southern European," the "Britisher," the "Norse races," and the "Mongolian," not to

mention a comparison of the "very extremely high type of true civilization" in Switzerland with the "older civilization[s]" of China and Egypt.
Jews, according to the article, constituted part of "the white race" and,
perhaps unsurprisingly, also emerge as particularly healthy in their care
of the body. Dismissing the notions that "inbreeding, Kosher meat theory, [or] freedom from alcohol protected Jews from tuberculosis," the
author nonetheless pointed to "sobriety" and "care in diet" as major factors in supposedly lower Jewish mortality rates. The "Jewish race," the
article adds, has also practiced "simplicity," avoided "violent labor," and
exhibited "exemplary care and training of the offspring, especially as concerns personal hygiene." In stark contrast, other "races" in the same article displayed a marked *inability* to maintain healthy habits and behaviors. Improper attention to and cultivation of the body, such as poor
personal hygiene, unsanitary living conditions, and inadequate nutrition,
characterized these groups. Arguing that "the African negro of untainted
strain" and the "true African negro" are susceptible to diseases that only
affect their "race"—"diseases of which the negro is generally an exclusive subject"—the article observes that the health of "negroes" only wors-
ened outside of Africa. In fact, diseases like tuberculosis "wreak[ed] aw-
ful havoc" in the American South. Not only did tuberculosis kill African
Americans, but in countries "into which negroes have been introduced,
they actually seem[ed] to melt away." Italians emerge as similarly marked,
suffering from "insanitary [*sic*] and overcrowded associations."[16]

In further racialized discourse, an editorial ostensibly encouraging all
physicians to join the New Mexico medical association claims that "it is
an honor to belong to the affiliated societies . . . a sign of good standing." A physician who chooses not to join the association, however, who
"has no desire to improve himself," is described as having "a nigger in the
woodpile somewhere." "As a rule," the editorial continues, "the nigger is
in the very man's heart." In 1910, two years before New Mexico would
finally be admitted as a state, Dr. Francis Fest, the editor of the *NMMJ*,
spoke of venereal disease. Amid impassioned commentary on the manifold threats of sexual incontinence and misbehavior arose discussions
of the sexual customs of foreign peoples. In Japan, the doctor wrote, "the
host will offer you his servant maid when you stop as his guest over night,"
while "the Brahmin was moral [*sic*] to deflorate the brides of others," and
"the barren Chinese woman finds it moral for her husband to have a con-
cubine."[17]

Another, more subtle, form of racialized discourse focused on bodily
incoherence and a racialized propensity for crossing social boundaries.
Notice, for instance, the phrase "promiscuous expectorators." In proposing public health measures deemed necessary to protect New Mexico

from the spread of tuberculosis, physician Robert McBride used "promiscuous expectoration" to describe the coughing and sputum associated with tuberculosis. The phrase also nicely encapsulates several of the threats from contagious diseases in New Mexico. "Promiscuous" suggests transit and transgression, the multiple crossing and recrossing of significant boundaries. This constant shuttling between locations is of course deeply sexual, implying multiple sexual partners as well as prostitution, but also contains a sense of general movement, of passing from one locale or community or individual to another, with little in the way of hindrance or deterrence. Such mobility, as the rape trial of Prudencio Martinez from chapter 3 and the discussions of prostitution and the home from chapter 5 suggest, had racial meanings as well. White people supposedly maintained proper spatial boundaries, while racialized others passed "promiscuously" from location to location. "Expectoration"—essentially the act of spitting or discharging a substance, usually mucus, from one's throat or lungs—similarly evokes boundary crossing, this time the crossing of a poorly maintained border between one's body and the outside. Sexuality again emerges here, in that expectorators and spitters, like the reputation of prostitutes and the sexually incontinent, exhibited little control over bodily exits and entrances.

I have lingered at this phrase because critical to the identification of the infected and potentially contagious person in New Mexico, and elsewhere in turn-of-the-century America, was an evaluation of that individual's capacity to move, their ability to infect across boundaries, to carry sickness and even death into the homes and hearths of the previously healthy. "Promiscuous expectoration" nicely summarizes two of the body practices at the heart of this identification process: the physical movement across social borders and a porous boundary around one's own body. In other words, the phrase brings together fears about both a porous social body and a porous individual body.

Consider, for instance, the frequency of articles denouncing spitting. One author of a piece on municipal hygiene suggested the passage and enforcement of "strict anti-spitting ordinances" and argued that "all public buildings, including places of worship and amusement, should be liberally supplied with cuspidors" in order that "careless expectorating be eliminated." In a short list of questions titled "Do You Know That," the last question reads, "The careless spitter is a public danger?" Like spitting, coughing and sneezing could also trigger alarm. In light of evidence that measles was transferred from "the mucous membranes by sneezing and probably coughing," another article suggests that "personal hygiene with nose and throat disinfection affords a more rational preventive measure."[18] Advocating certain precautions to limit the spread of contagious disease, another doctor also warned that "the army of tubercular invalids should be brought under some sort of control." "Promiscuous expectoration should be stopped," he blustered, "and every possible means taken to prevent these unfortunates from becoming a danger to the population." This mention of a threat to "the population" is a thinly veiled invocation of whiteness. As historians like Alexandra Stern and Nayan Shah point out, public health measures like the above were all too frequently directed at communities like Mexican and Asian immigrants and tended to mask broader concerns about racial purity and white privilege. Likewise, in New Mexico, attacks on careless coughing and spitting carried significant racial meanings.[19]

Taken together, the above racialized accounts suggest a familiar set of embodied features: lack of proper hygiene, poorly controlled bodily boundaries, excessive alcohol consumption, "promiscuous expectoration," and nonmarital sexual intercourse. While clearly participating in modern scientific forms of racial differentiation, it bears repeating that such typically American racialization projects emerged in New Mexico, a putatively American possession filled with powerful entrenched groups like elite Hispanos, where the precise features of "American" and "white" had yet to be settled. For no one was this more true than for New Mexico physicians tapping sadly at America's window. Much was at stake in seemingly innocuous comments about "Mexico" or "primitive races," or "Mongol pests," or "South Carolina darkeys." Physicians, in proclaiming their own whiteness and fitness for American citizenship, needed to differentiate themselves from racialized others in New Mexico. Evidence drawn from the systematic and measured medical treatment of human bodies was ideally suited to such a project.

The bodies of Indians, Hispanos, and African Americans were therefore not the only objects of scrutiny and racialization in the pages of the *New Mexico Medical Journal*. In naturalizing whiteness, Anglo physicians also turned their medical gaze to the embodied characteristics of whiteness. In stark contrast to the bodies of other New Mexicans, white bodies were characterized by the following: marital sexual intercourse, cleanliness, and proper consumption (appropriate food and drink, but not alcohol or patent medicines). One author, stressing the immediate dangers of disease and immorality, exhorted readers to support sex education, "the only hope for improvement of present conditions." Noting, like the rhetoric of some rape trials in New Mexico, that "sexual intercourse is moral only between man and wife," the author suggested that "sexual activity [be] restricted to the married." Sex education, according to the author, would separate correct medical information from "wrong knowledge instilled by venial vendors of nostrums, by quacks and charlatans."

The next paragraph specifies some of the potential beneficiaries of sex education, namely, female and male masturbating children. Asking, "How many girls do not masturbate without knowing what they are doing," the article contends that improved information on sex would convince girls that masturbation was an unhealthy, even potentially dangerous, activity and encourage them to "stop the habit." Likewise, sex education would discourage boys, "victims because their curiosity led them to it," from masturbating. Girls and boys who continued to masturbate in spite of the wise counsel of educators, of course, could expect few rewards and many horrors. Only proper sexual education, it suggests, could rescue boys from the "danger lurking in impure intercourse."[20]

Articles on the diagnosis and treatment of syphilis, which figured prominently in New Mexico medical discourse, similarly celebrated those individuals engaging in marital sexual intercourse.[21] One short article, with the provocative title "Innocent Victims of the Black Plague," calls for a national law compelling all young men to "furnish a certificate of some reputable physician that he is free from all infectious or communicable disease" before being allowed to marry. Such a law, according to the article, would "make for a stronger and healthier race" and "add immensely to the sum total of human happiness." To illustrate the dangers of this "social cancer," the author painted a vivid picture. Regardless of social standing or "how carefully you have given your family all moral and religious training," the article warns, "you may wake up some morning and find that this hydraheaded monster has crept into the sacred family circle over night." What is the use, the author added, of "adorning the daughters of this fair land with a beautiful christian character, with the accomplishments of a modern education and refinement, if they are to be handed over to masculine brutes to become the victims of the great black plague."[22] As another writer noted, "The bulk of all organic nervous disease," not to mention everything from eye problems to stomach trouble were attributed to syphilis.[23] "Its importance," another asserted, "cannot be exaggerated!"[24] An editorial otherwise addressed to the causes of cancer could not help but note that cancer of the tongue was more likely to attack "syphilitic subjects with bad teeth who were confirmed smokers," while a book review illustrates the need for "underlying principles of eugenics" with the lurid, quasi-biblical example of forty women "known to have had syphilis" who "syphilized over four hundred men, forty of whom, in turn, syphilized their own wives."[25] Once again, healthy sexual intercourse, unlike sexual practices linked to "infectious or communicable disease," is associated with racial purity and whiteness, morality, and Christianity.

Closely related to marital sexual intercourse as a characteristic of the white body was cleanliness. One piece encouraging improved instruction in hygiene reports that Wellesley College had begun to emphasize issues of hygiene far beyond the scope of mere physical education. The article goes on to describe in great detail the potential benefits for New Mexico of more detailed instruction on general hygiene, making explicit the link between hygiene and the creation of good citizens. With improved guidance in hygiene, girls especially, the author noted, would "develop and conserve . . . the health and strength of their bodies." Without such guidance, that is, "without suitable restrictions," girls could all too easily engage in "exhausting competitive games at a time when the whole body, especially the nervous system and pelvic organs, are crying out for all possible easement of even ordinary demands on her energy." Not only exercise, but "faulty carriage and posture" could cause harm to young girls, especially those who "readily and slavishly follow fashions." The "debutante slouch," the author warned, "cannot help having a most injurious effect on pelvic health in women and on their ability to bear children." The "forward tilting of the pelvis and the inevitable downward displacement of the abdominal viscera" and the "underdevelopment and disuse of the spinal muscles" could lead to dangerously ill health and nervous disorders in womanhood. The article in this way conflates lack of "suitable restrictions," excessive competition, and "slavish" attention to fashion with abnormal and faulty use of the body. The woman who replicates such physical habits thus potentially harms not simply her own ability to bear children, but commits a possible crime "against oneself and one's community." Slouching debutantes and exhaustingly competitive girls, thus, at least according to this article, represent not only sick people, but are identified as potential criminals as well, with the potential to bring harm to "our children, our community, our state and our nation." Good posture and physical comportment, on the other hand, are depicted as integral to "self support and for good citizenship." [26]

Attacks in the *NMMJ* on alcohol consumption and other supposedly intemperate bodily actions similarly highlighted the characteristics required of proper, and white, citizens. One article, on alcoholism and the Prohibition movement, opens by placing the issue squarely within a nationalistic framework. "America is a young nation," the essay begins, "what Americans take up shows the fire of youth. This fire leads to extremes. Intemperance is a factor of national loss, an economic detriment." The article goes on to link alcohol consumption with "the low barroom, the breeding place of vice and crime," "drunken excesses, crimes and murder," and prostitution. At the same time, the piece celebrates "respectable localities in which the free man and woman can enjoy God's gift openly and without sights of depravity." [27] The article clearly links abstinence from alcohol with "the free man and woman," "God's gift," and "respectable localities." Another article calls attention to a case where a prisoner had been pardoned after supposedly successful surgery designed to release the pressure on his brain and cure his "criminal tendencies." Unfortunately, according to the editorial, the paroled prisoner had been recently arrested on a burglary charge, suggesting either that "the improvement was only temporary, or that the operation and his subsequent good conduct were steps in a scheme to secure his release from prison." While refuting the link between moral character and pressure on the brain, the editorial also differentiates the prisoner's pre-surgery behavior—"sullen and morose"—from his post-operative transformation. No longer a "criminal," the man was now a "useful citizen." He was "bright and cheerful, walked with a firmer step, [and] held his head erect."[28]

Talk of genetics offered another well-lit stage for the exhibition of the physical characteristics of the white body. One book review has only words of praise for a recently published (1913) study of marriage and genetic theory. Only through the "application of the principles of eugenics," the reviewer claimed, could the "future welfare of the race" be assured. Simple "ignorance," the article asserts, "keeps many innocent victims from protecting themselves and their offspring from disease and degeneracy." Only vigorous education, the "constant and continued effort of the medical profession" to assume the responsibility of "telling the people and teaching them to appreciate [the] 'causes and effects'" of their actions, could address this predicament. To illustrate, the review quotes at length from the book's introduction, a detailed comparison of the "contrasting history of two families," the pseudonymous "Jukes" and the relatives of one "Elizabeth Tuttle."[29]

In a language deeply indebted to modern scientific forms of classification and measurement, the article documents the respective transgressions and achievements of each family. The "original progenitor" of the "notorious" Jukes family was a "hard-drinker" from the "forest-clad hills" of upstate New York. The article, thus, makes deeply racialized distinctions, centered on images of out-of-control and excessive behavior. The "stamp" of the Jukes family begins with a "hard-drinker" from the "forest-clad hills," invoking not simply intemperance, but barbarity and primitive, nonwhite bloodlines. Racialization, however, is not limited to the nonwhite. Elizabeth Tuttle, the progenitor of the other family, was born with "the stamp of physical and mental superiority" and, naturally, married a lawyer from Connecticut. In the Jukes family, "one hundred and forty were criminal offenders," "sixty were habitual thieves," and "forty of the women were known to have had syphilis and estimated to have syphilized over four hundred men," costing society at large a total bill of $1.3 million. Elizabeth Tuttle, on the other hand, could claim, among others, "three hundred college graduates," "sixty-five authors of 135 books," and "a large number of leaders of industries" as her direct descendants. Abstinence from alcohol, "physical superiority," proper sexual relations ("marrying a lawyer" rather than "syphilizing" a host of unwitting victims), all are celebrated as superior, and implicitly white, embodied acts. Just as racial purity required clear boundaries separating the races, little overlap (such as a thieving Tuttle or a respectable Juke), let alone intermarriage, occurred between the two mutually exclusive families.[30]

Taken together, the articles thus merge particular body practices with criminality, on the one hand, and citizenship and whiteness, on the other, clustering alcohol consumption and "sullen and morose" demeanor among the characteristics of criminals, and turning sobriety, a head held high, direct, purposeful walk, and good cheer into features typical of "free" and "respectable" American citizens. Embodied gender distinctions similarly underwrote physicians' descriptions of white bodies. Recall that clear gender differentiation was frequently cited by Anglos as a characteristic of "higher," that is, more white, forms of civilization. Indian school students, for instance, were constantly forced, in their instructions in civilization, to obey strict gender divisions.[31] Likewise, in medical discourse, women and men were painstakingly differentiated, particular maladies were said to strike women far more than men, and certain types of illness were peculiar to one sex and not the other. Typically, from childbirth to child rearing to diseases of the female reproductive system, each volume of the *NMMJ* included at least one major article referring to the treatment of female patients. Due to a more nervous condition, for example, women supposedly suffered more headaches than men, with a rate of "twenty-five per cent of men and fifty per cent of women." The author blamed headaches in men on "hav[ing] spent the night at a banquet and indulged too freely," while constipation, "perhaps the most fruitful of all causes of headaches," is linked to head pain in women and is apparently "all the more insidious because women become so habituated to the condition of sluggish bowels that they fail to realize the importance of its bearing upon their general health." Describing a new surgical technique for infected lymph nodes, another author noted, "We desire (especially in the case of female patients) to have the scar so placed that it will be least noticeable and . . . particularly hidden from an observer looking from the front." One of the clear advantages of the new technique is that "it permits ladies to wear a moderately low necked gown, without uncovering the scar." Unlike depictions of women as particularly concerned with revealing unsightly surgical scars during parties, men apparently have no such cosmetic worries.[32]

Another article, noting that in the incidence of gallbladder diseases "about 75 per cent . . . have been females and of these 90 per cent have borne children," also emphasizes the link between illness and women's fashion concerns. "The majority of our cases have occurred," the author reported, "in short, stout women . . . [who are] subject to greater pressure during pregnancy and are more given to tight lacing than their slender sisters." A 1913 editorial entitled "Women Motorists" describes the "weaker sex" as "naturally quick of eye and deft of wrist," "in general more excitable and of less steady judgment than men," and more prone to "introspection." Such gender differences, according to the article, "could lead to speeding and to the fear of accidents," resulting in a range of ailments including "auto-eye . . . a spasm of the ciliary muscles" (from viewing constantly changing objects while traveling at high speeds), cramping or "auto-leg," and "nerve strain and nerve exhaustion followed by hysteria and neurasthenia."[33]

Fundamental to this project of gender differentiation was the identification of women with marriage and reproduction.[34] Readers of the *NMMJ* would have found marriage and reproduction fundamental to a woman's identity, in sharp contrast to the far more varied components of a man's identity. Writers frequently depicted marriage as the normal status of every woman. An essay on salpingitis, a pelvic inflammatory disease, begins by noting that it was "one of the most common diseases of women." "Women," however, quickly metastasizes into "married women." The next sentence explains that "the reasons for its being so frequently met with in married women is that it is nearly always secondary to an infection of the uterus." Furthermore, salpingitis supposedly occurs "at some point in the life of a large per cent of married women." "All women," the writer suggested, emphasizing again the conflation of women in general with married women in particular, "should be examined carefully for the, possible, existence of salpingitis."[35]

In terms of reproduction, one article puts it plainly, "Motherhood is the highest, noblest and best of all Divinely instituted privileges." As such, in the view of another author, pregnancy demanded a detailed regimen, beginning with conception and lasting throughout the pregnancy. The pregnant woman "should at once notify her physician" and "receive advice and instruction as to the conduct and dangers of pregnancy," while the physician should "learn the patient's personal and family history, with all previous diseases, and all difficulties of previous labors, all family peculiarities, etc." Recommendations included what food to eat and how to prepare it, how and when to bathe, proper clothing, as well as advice "as to the dangers of constipation, and how prevented; as to the bad effects of sexual intercourse, and the necessity of its control; as to the proper care of the breasts; and of the frequent examinations of the urine." Pregnancy thus demanded far more of both the patient and the doctor than any other medical condition. [36]

Articles also spoke frequently of the need to preserve, at all costs, a woman's ability to bear children. "Ventro-fixation," for instance, was recommended for women past the age of child bearing, but "should never, under any circumstances, be resorted to in one who is likely to ever become pregnant, because . . . abortion would be the most favorable thing that could happen." Surgeons, another writer warned, "should be guarded in advising surgical measures which . . . would prevent future conception; particularly should we be doubly careful when the woman is young and without children." [37]

Women's reproductive responsibilities extended into child raising as well. Mothers were advised to "form the habit of frequent, interested, open-minded visiting" of their children's schools. Another characteristic of good mothers was the supervision of their children's food preparation and feeding. "No intelligent mother," one piece reads, "will leave to an ordinary servant the task of caring for or preparing the milk for her baby." The "average mother," according to another article, "does not realize the importance of care in feeding her child." A doctor "might as well ask her to fly as tell her to combine" the proper ingredients in a milk formula. Another writer was more blunt, arguing that "the natural and only real food for the infant is from the mother's breast." While an essay on alcoholism sought to refute the "venerable and deeply rooted fact" that the mental state of a pregnant woman was "a most potent cause of malformations" in the fetus, the article still manages to blame mothers for their children's problems. "It must be admitted," the author claimed, "that the mental state of the mother may indirectly influence the development of the offspring." [38]

Few articles sketched a more clear distinction between good and bad mothers than the provocatively titled "Human Waste, and the Children of the Needy," by Dr. C. E. Lukens of Albuquerque. On the one hand, Lukens paints the picture of a proper home, musing poetically (and not incidentally reinforcing the image of physicians as upright members of society), "For most of you [fellow doctors] were raised within the sweet and beautiful surroundings of mother love and home." Needy children, on the other hand, emerge from "the surroundings of darkest immorality." While Lukens appears to blame equally the fathers and mothers of such poor children—"in one family the father and mother, a pimp and a prostitute, in the other, the mother dead, the father a worthless individual"—the article goes on to associate the plight of children primarily with female neglect and deviance. One young woman, "too far advanced in years and criminality" to be saved by the efforts of the Children's Home Society, had her three children taken by the court, thus "saving [her children] from the contamination of a prostitute mother." In another case, "the Society came into the possession of a little girl from a criminal mother." In stark contrast to depictions of children from "good family homes" as "strong and gracious characters" and "in every way normal and right minded children," the little girl appeared "physically demoralized, with a disposition as ugly as her poor face." Besides the failure to feed their children properly and "a poor mental state," sexual deviance, communicable disease ("contamination of a prostitute mother"), and physical unattractiveness thus come to characterize the behavior of bad mothers.[39]

The illustrations in the journal similarly focused on female patients and female sexuality. Just as many articles were addressed to female patients and their ailments, the earliest photographic illustrations focused on the proper treatment of women. In 1913, long before photographs were a common feature of the journal, an article on breast cancer includes seven photographs, five of the patient and two of the excised tumor. The photographic sequence begins with three pictures of the woman, naked to the waist, in profile, her right arm raised above her head. The fourth photo is a frontal view of the woman with both hands above her head. The fifth is a picture of ostensibly the same woman, her head and most of her body now covered by a large dark shawl, revealing only the scar of a radical mastectomy. Later photographic illustrations similarly display the female body. One, for instance, chronicles the repair of a perineum damaged during childbirth. At the same time, during this period in the journal's history, there is never a naked *male* body or a photographic display devoted to prostate surgery or testicular carcinoma.[40]

Male reproductive functions, in fact, only surfaced in discussions of male sexual dysfunction and were never considered as basic a component in the creation of male identity. In "Impotence," the author carefully divided the loss of "the power of copulation, or ability to properly perform the sexual act," into "two varieties of sexual incapacity": the pathologic condition or complete absence of spermatozoa ("impotentia generandi") and the inability to "consummate cohabitation" ("impotentia coudeni"). Physicians, the author notes, are rarely consulted for impotence of the first category, except "where there is a desire, or cause, for offspring"; the second, *impotentia coudeni*, receives far more attention. So, too, suitably, does *impotentia coudeni* draw the article's most dazzling rhetorical firepower. Far worse than "the fruitlessness of marriage or sterility" is the "psychic state of these poor pitiable patients," driven into "the arms of despair and suicide" by a "psychic depression" of which even medical doctors "have no conception." After this outburst of emotion (impotence sufferers as "poor pitiable" victims of a "despair" and "depression" beyond the comprehension of even trained professionals), the article quickly regains its composure, hastily identifying four classes of *impotentia coudeni* ("organic," "psychical," "relative," and "irritable") and their etiologies. Even this rhetoric bubbles with the fantastic and uncontrolled. Cases of "relative impotence," for example, "are to be found [in] those unfortunates who are bordering on, or have crossed the line into perverted sexual desires and acts."[41]

Even articles critical of male behavior nonetheless tended to clearly differentiate men from women. Some like the following distinctly associated masculinity with American citizenship. In 1912 Dr. Evelyn Fisher-Frisbie addressed the subject of "Gonorrhea in the Female." Dr. Fisher-Frisbie opened the address with a remarkable statement. "When 'His Majesty,' the American citizen," the doctor began, "once enters his palace—the female genital tract, he has usually come to stay until he and his hosts have reduced the wonderful and intricate abode to ruins." Continuing, Fisher-Frisbie noted, "It behooves us to guard with more zeal his original entrance into the palace." Here again, amid talk of sexual hygiene and education is talk of citizen, nation, and the reinforcing of critical gender distinctions. Like other descriptions of diverse national sexual habits, a notable feature of Fisher-Frisbie's address is citizenship, most vividly in identifying men as " 'His Majesty,' the American citizen."[42]

The above set of bodily distinctions offered sustenance to New Mexico doctors seeking to affirm their fitness for American citizenship. Based on their white bodies, doctors could assert, from their location on the periphery of America, their fitness for full inclusion in the American national citizenry. Carroll Smith-Rosenberg has observed that white middle-class men in nineteenth-century America initially constituted themselves as bourgeois by defining themselves in opposition to middle-class women.[43] New Mexico doctors followed a similar course, though importantly, within the context of a colonial setting. Like their jittery European colonial counterparts described by Ann Stoler, doctors materialized here as modern, professional, scientific, progressive, masculine, and fully qualified for citizenship in spite of their residence in New Mexico.[44] An obituary for Dr. William Burr typifies the profession's ideals for itself. The son of a doctor, Burr graduated from medical school at the University of Maryland and moved to New Mexico at the age of fifty-five, where he eventually became a surgeon for the Santa Fe railroad. According to the announcement of his death, Burr's "genial disposition, sincerity of purpose and faithful discharge of his duties made his many friends value him both as a *citizen* and as a physician" (emphasis mine).[45]

Self-descriptions and advice on the appropriate behavior for physicians often occurred in the midst of more technical descriptions. In an elaborate essay addressing the tearing of the perineum during childbirth, Dr. William Howe of East Last Vegas, New Mexico (notice the careful use of *East* Las Vegas, the newer Anglo-dominated section of the town), devoted a considerable portion of the article to the relationship between doctors and their patients. He alternated between criticizing physicians for their hasty and at times reckless surgical techniques and advising readers, presumably all in the medical profession, on the correct way to interact with patients. Howe remembered, for instance, "the horror of seeing a splendid man, one whom I have held and still hold in the highest regard as a teacher of obstetrics, hastily doing a podalic version through a[n] incompletely dilated os in a case of eclampsia, produce a transverse tear of the cervix." Howe noted that the ideal practitioner "should assume 'the never get in a hurry' attitude and be willing to spend ample time at the bedside of his patient, who deserves his most thoughtful, inspiring, sympathetic, and encouraging attention."[46]

Other articles spoke more broadly of the profession and its leadership role in society. Dr. Robert E. McBride of Las Cruces, the new president of the New Mexico Medical Society, welcomed the audience to the 27th annual meeting of the organization and greeted them "in the name of organized medicine." McBride's speech surveyed the past achievements of the association and sketched the many challenges that lay ahead. Membership, he congratulated the audience, in 1908 had risen to 158 physicians, and two counties had recently "been organized," each contributing eleven new members to the territorial association. McBride noted with pride that medical licensing laws in the territory even surpassed those of some of "the more thickly settled eastern states." He also cautioned that "the rapidly growing population of the territory [was] creating problems." Specifically, he recommended the creation of a territorial Board of Health with the capacity to ensure proper fumigation, disinfection, and registration of infected regions, and called for a renewed effort to purge the association of poorly trained and self-interested physicians. He concluded on an optimistic, if modest note, encouraging his fellow practitioners to "become more capable and honorable as well as more useful to the public."[47]

McBride's speech is typical. Sober and measured, even at times humble and self-effacing, the speech scrupulously reproduces the reasoned, restrained rhetoric of medicine and scientific rationality. McBride carefully listed all five of the current requirements for medical licensing in the territory. He also detailed a proposed separation of the Medical Examiners Board from the Board of Health, outlining the specific and distinct duties of each. Emblematic of the well-controlled tone that McBride, and the medical community at large, sought to cultivate was the response

McBride claimed that often met physician-inspired public health measures. In direct contrast to the studied and proper speech of doctors, a "good 'cussing' [was] usually," according to the author, "the reward for an attempt to perform conscientious duty." That is, not only did physicians in New Mexico regularly "organize" and "register" and "perform conscientious duty," they did so in the face of direct opposition from nonphysicians whose distinguishing features included lack of conscientiousness, vulgar, offensive language, and "cussing." In describing the impediments to "the material advancement of the physician," McBride directed a particularly accusing jab at physicians themselves. "Many men," he noted, "are too zealous of their own interests." Greedy and unethical physicians, he charged, "rise to heights of fancied greatness on the prostrate bodies of their abused fellow practitioner." Thus, like so many articles in the *NMMJ*, McBride's presidential address, in measured tones and with little fanfare (remember his concluding modesty, "more capable . . . honorable . . . useful"), distinguished between the actions of physicians and the ribald, unhealthy, often ungrateful behavior ("too zealous," "fancied greatness," "cussing" often the only "reward" given to the healers) of both errant physicians and the diseased.[48]

Public health issues were a particular concern among physicians, both on a general level (articles comparing disease susceptibility among different races or tuberculosis rates nationwide) and on a more practical side (extolling the virtues of increased regulation of spitting in public or warning of the dangers of improperly packaged specimens). An editorial calls a carelessly wrapped set of cotton swabs mailed from Atlanta and laced with diphtheria "as deadly as dynamite or an infernal machine." Another article addresses the prevention of communicable diseases in Santa Fe. The article attempts to enact a clear and unambiguous distinction between healthy and unhealthy practices. The author recommended a twofold approach to sanitation, the *elimination* of all "menaces to public health" and the *dissemination* "among the people" of knowledge about the "origin and nature of contagious disease." Doctors in the article are depicted as those engaged in "constant observation" and regular "inspection." Physicians attend an "enlightened Board of Health" and issue written certificates of sanitation for public funerals and school absences. Thus, doctors are advised both to remove disease and actively disseminate valuable information to the public, while the diseased and the ill (whether sick individuals or entire diseased towns) are simply to wait passively to be cured of illness and to receive health education.[49]

While the above articles speak of "menaces to public health" and "the people," and thus subtly allude to race and racial difference, there are more direct examples of the racialized and embodied contrast between the identities of physicians and "others." Take one writer's chronicle of a trip to Rochester, Minnesota, and that exemplar of medical innovation, the Mayo Clinic. Though not addressed to the treatment of a certain disease or the use of a particular operative technique, the article surveys the hospital and its various carefully delineated departments. One paragraph documents the "magnificent organization for the treatment of disease," consisting of "rooms of microphotographs . . . freezing microtones, batteries of microscope, projectoscopes, [and] illuminating boxes." Another describes the painstaking diagnosis of a patient, where the "ureters are catheterized, the feces are examined, the stomach contents are analyzed, [and] the lungs, heart, throat, and in fact every part of the body is examined," until "the condition of every organ of the body has been carefully determined." In addition to a detailed summary of the preparation of patients for surgery, the author mapped with great precision the actual physical layout of the surgical wing of the hospital ("the five operating rooms at St. Mary's are in the form of a letter T, at the right top is room 1, Charles Mayo, to the left W.J.'s with sterilizing room between"). The article concludes, "The hospital is very orderly, very clean, very quiet, and very much crowded," appropriate for the "mecca of modern surgery."[50]

In contrast to the article's assessments of physicians catheterizing, examining, analyzing, and categorizing, several paragraphs, all near the beginning of the piece, describe the area surrounding the Mayo Clinic. After a brief note on the best route into Rochester, the author embarked on a curious tour of the town and its history. The governing image is a familiar one, the backward small town ushered into modernity by the business sense and unwavering will of talented leaders. On one side rests "an old town," through which a "sluggish" stream meanders. In the past, the author noted, Rochester was "semi-conscious of its existence," its manufacturing and farming interests making "barely enough noise to keep it partly awake." The article proposes a complicated metaphor for this period in the town's history. On the banks of a "lagoon . . . back water . . . overgrown with willows," beside the "murky depths" stirred only occasionally by "mud feeding catfish" and "emit[ting] here and there a bubble of marsh gas," sits a boy fishing. He is barefoot, "doz[ing] on the bank" with a "crooked pole" and "stealthily play[ing] hookey." Later, the author added a couple of "dead old churches" to this depiction of Rochester in the past, "her somnambulism" and "lethargy." In contrast, of course, stands Rochester of the present (and implicitly Rochester of the future), a "thriving city of bright homes, modern ideas, commercial importance," a "quiet, moral, enterprising, businesslike, substantial little city."[51]

I suggest that we read these passages not simply as extraneous jottings of a physician with a knack for hyperbole and a penchant for waxing nostalgic, but as significant markers of racialized identity and difference. Descriptions of modern progress and ever-improving knowledge inevitably invoked associations with "civilization" and white racial supremacy. As Eric Lott, Gail Bederman, Philip Deloria, and others argue, there is an American tradition that finds great pleasure in explicitly racist forms of nostalgia, especially in the association of racialized "others" with "arrested development" and a near permanent stage of childhood. The Mayo Clinic, thus, on the one hand, "embod[ies] the accumulated knowledge of past ages of research," where ultra-modern physicians spend their days engaged in categorizing, examining, and sterilizing. On the other hand, the author described the "dead old churches" and "somnambulism" of the "sleepy little town" of "semi-conscious" Rochester, with its "sluggish" ways and "murky depths." Basic to the identity of the physician in the article, therefore, is progress, civilization, and whiteness.[52]

In discussions of the disease susceptibility of various races and the poor hygiene of certain "populations," writers thus bolstered their essays with detailed references to science and technology. Such discussions strived for, and frequently achieved, a tone of scientific observation and reasoned inquiry, all the while highlighting the physical characteristics and attributes of sexually and racially different individuals and communities. For New Mexico physicians, located on the margins of America, this melding of exalted modern science and professional aspirations with crass racialization served an important purpose. In denigrating the bodies of racial others and celebrating their own white bodies, doctors positioned themselves as fully American and fit for inclusion in the American polity.

Still, for all its aspirations to rational, measured scientific discourse, the *New Mexico Medical Journal* was hardly seamless or free of contradiction. Racial and sexual "others," no more orderly and manageable than newly racialized and colonized peoples elsewhere in the nation and world, constantly burst into medical discourses in New Mexico at unexpected and unsettling moments. For instance, New Mexico physicians depended deeply on the presence of women, especially elite women, in their waiting rooms and on their operating tables. Though they may have cursed their misfortune, most doctors in New Mexico sorely needed the reliable income that could come from treating "female complaints," attending to healthy childbirths, and performing surgery on women.[53]

Articles in the *NMMJ* reflected the dependence of physicians on female patients. Rare was an issue that did not make some comment, usually in a snide aside, about women who refused to pay their bills or patients taking their business elsewhere. Such articles also pointed to the dangers to the white race of unruly female patients. A poem titled simply

"The Hypochondriac" is a remarkable testament to the anxiety that educated elite women could produce in the medical profession. Unambiguously female (nearly every line manages to mention "her" supposed ailments or what outrages "she" commits), the hypochondriac is also clearly coded as bourgeois. Not only does "she [have] doctors by the score" and "can fluently converse" on "the workings of her spleen" and "her temperature mean," but she has the material means to "live on asafoetida / Valerian, bromidia / And hibernate in rooms that are air tight." Still, the hypochondriac flagrantly violates all the norms of respectable femininity. Like an animal, she "hibernates" in her unventilated room, and, the poem notes, "the blood flies to her head / 'Quite naturally,' we said / Since a vacuum by nature's abhorred." Moreover, she has "no interest . . . in mountain, plain or lake," but focuses instead on microbes and the "history of her case." Preferring hibernation, self-diagnosis, and studying microbes to scenic vistas and picnics, the hypochondriac, in other words, is hardly the ideal bourgeois woman. Buried within the charge of self-absorption is a hint of anxiety about self-sufficient (self-pleasuring?) and nonreproducing white women. The hypochondriac, after all, "hibernates in rooms that are air tight." She is self-sufficient, "living on" a handful of drugs and bromides, and she even locks the windows that would "allow the deadly draught / To meander thru the sleeping room at night," hardly an image of "normal" marital sexual intercourse. The hypochondriac is so focused on her own well-being, on her own body, in fact, that no one can please her. "True sympathy she ne'er expects to find," and "grown people" she considers 'too exacting.'" She even refuses motherhood, finding "children 'so distracting.'" Finally, in an image bathed in the iconography of commercialized sexuality, the hypochondriac, like a prostitute, "has doctors by the score / But shows them all the door." The hypochondriac, here associated with images of self-reliant "New Women" and female prostitutes, is thus overly concerned with and overly knowledgeable about her own body. For Anglos, especially those in New Mexico, concerned about disproportionate numbers of nonwhites making claims on citizenship and social power, a wealthy white woman who refused to bear children was hardly reassuring.[54]

In another article New Mexico doctors, like physicians throughout the country, appear to find "twilight sleep," the inducement through the use of narcotics of a painless sleeplike condition for a woman during childbirth, somewhat disconcerting.[55] At first glance, the editorial, entitled "'Twilight Sleep' in the Light of Day," appears like so many others, carefully reasoned and judicious. The author duly noted the arguments supporting both defenders and opponents of twilight sleep and cited famous advocates on each side. At first, the article associates twilight sleep with only a select, easily identified group. "Some women of neurotic tendencies—pampered, petted, unaccustomed to the hardnesses of life," it observes, welcome the technique. As the article progresses, however, the rhetorical volume rises. The author soon bemoaned the fact that "most of the doses of narcotics we give are given, not because we think the patient needs the narcotic, but because *he* will promptly go to another doctor if we refuse" (emphasis mine). Noting that this "craze for pain-stopping" must cease and that "we are becoming soft," the article asserts that "part of a doctor's job" is to save "many a man and woman from themselves." By the end of the article, the calm, reasoned approach toward twilight sleep, seeking to expose it to rational thought, has given way almost completely to thundering denunciations of "softening moral fiber," "the narcotism of alcohol and tobacco in excess," and the need for "sex patriotism" and "moral heroism." "The ultra-modern fear of pain and the craze for narcotics," the author warned, "is a matter of the well-being of the race at large." Thus, the use of narcotics during childbirth potentially threatens men as well as women, and even imperils the future of "the race." The very title of the piece, exposing a "dark" secret to the "light" of science and reason, hints at the unsettling metaphorical resonance to doctors of the unknown and the mysterious, especially when it was associated with female bodies and racial order.[56]

Finally, proper New Mexicans, at least according to the *NMMJ*, avoided the consumption of patent medicine cures, turning instead to a proper diet and the professional advice of physicians. Tuberculosis sufferers, for instance, are advised that "cathartics and laxatives are to be avoided as much as possible, and where there is constipation it can usually be overcome by a modification of the diet." Another article complains of patients "taking the whole gamut of respiratory stimulants, expectorants and heart tonics before there is any real indication." Echoing the charge that improper female patients tended to move from doctor to doctor, an article on constipation recommends against "a change from one cathartic pill to another." One author noted with frustration "the impossibility of persuading John Jones, who has used Dr. Rogue's Ready Relief . . . that Ready Relief is only pink hydrant water, but he still insists that as he was sick before taking it and recovered after taking, there can be no doubt Ready Relief cured him."[57]

Another article, assailing the "alleged efficacy" of certain tuberculosis cures, is typical. Claiming that "proprietary remedies . . . immodestly and incorrectly advertised" their worth, the author argued that tuberculosis nostrums prove especially popular, and lucrative. By treating consumption only through the "outdoor treatment" ("therapeutic nihilism," it claims), physicians permitted, even encouraged, according to the article, "the advertising quack and patent medicine vendor" to deceive and swindle patients by promising "unfailing panaceas" that inevitably failed. Here, the association between patent medicine and bodies out of control, especially female bodies out of control, stands out. Implied in the above comments was the supposed emotional vulnerability of the unhealthy patent medicine user. Driven, according to doctors, by fear and ignorance, the sick actively seek out ineffective, even dangerous, "nostrums." Not only do consumptives "flock" to physician-recommended "climatic resorts" (like so many birds responding blindly to instinct), but they are guileless and easily fooled. They "fall readily into the hands of quacks" and are "only too ready to grasp at any straw." Consumers of patent medicine—in sharp contrast to reasonable and self-controlled physicians—become associated with out-of-control individuals, with people that "immodestly and incorrectly" display themselves, that "fall readily" and "grasp" indiscriminately "at any straw," "flocking" to the closest hope of a cure. To people behaving recklessly, already coded as sexually different, this article adds "immodesty," clearly a gendered, if not deeply class- and race-based, term. Though short (less than half a page), the article manages to project a vivid set of sexualized actions against which medical discourse in New Mexico established its claims to authority and status. In a rhetoric marked by images of sexual difference and female disloyalty, criticisms of patent-medicine (ab)users thus also helped draw the outlines of civic respectability in New Mexico.[58]

Such articles offer primers on the authors' expectations of their patients, male *or* female. According to the pieces, patients should be, in the first place, loyal, exactly the opposite of the hypochondriac who "shows the door" to doctor after doctor. That is, the body of the patient should be the exclusive province of only one physician at a time, with the physician, not the patient, making the decision to consult another doctor or change treatment regimens. The essays also confirm the deep ambivalence among physicians about their reliance on female patients, and the attendant fears many doctors may have felt about their ability to maintain independent, free, manly social status under such circumstances. For instance, despite the fact that each purports to describe physically weak, "pampered" women, female patients appear quite powerful and assertive, even masculine, in these articles. Perhaps it was only a typographic error or a harmless miscue, but it seems all too telling that the author of the twilight sleep essay, while describing the tendency for patients (who up to this point have been identified exclusively as women) to move from doctor to doctor until one finally prescribes a painkiller, complained that "*he* will promptly go to another doctor if we refuse."

Medical literature like the *NMMJ* that clearly focused on questions of healthy and unhealthy bodies was thus also a space of racial and gender differentiation. As the preceding examples suggest, discursive attacks on unhygienic conditions and improper childhood nutrition, not to mention professional malfeasance, excessive drinking, and the evils of crowded tenements, often focused on particular body practices, defining some practices as especially characteristic of racialized individuals and groups (the sick, the diseased, the agents of contamination, the racially inferior) and others as the exclusive province of physicians, citizens, and good mothers. As in Indian schools, courtrooms, and newspapers, Anglo newcomers denounced the bodily comportment of Indians, Hispanos, and African Americans. At the same time, physicians described the normal white body as engaging in marital sexual intercourse, abstaining from alcohol, hygienic, and in control of what enters and exits the body. In the process of naturalizing whiteness, this white body helped support physicians' claims to social leadership and citizenship.

Nonetheless, doctors' attempts to claim social superiority based on their whiteness was always contested. The above articles illustrate the incomplete and fractured nature of medical authority in New Mexico, where physicians' carefully tended reputations for exclusive knowledge and authority over the human body could, and did, appear to wilt a bit. As the halting growth of the New Mexico Medical Society suggests, modern medicine in early-twentieth-century New Mexico had risen to prominence, but hardly to dominance, especially in the deeply contested area of caring for women's health and treating "female complaints." Medically sexualized and racialized, the patients, the sick, and the diseased, though often demonized and excluded, continued to haunt doctors in New Mexico, driving many physicians/writers to stunning displays of rhetorical excess. The repressed and the denied, that is, never completely disappeared. Hydra-headed monsters, unfaithful patients, masturbating girls, and even promiscuous expectorators inevitably lurked at the edges, if not within the rafters, of bourgeois order and respectability. In fact, such discursive phantoms may have proved more endemic to the creation of the New Mexico's social order than even the most level-headed and sober doctor would have wanted to admit.[59]

"JUST GAUZY ENOUGH"

CONSUMER CULTURE AND THE SHARED WHITE BODY OF ANGLOS AND HISPANOS

Notions, hats, caps, boots, and shoes. Plaster, lime, and cement. *Ropa para el hombre más grande y el muchacho más chico.* Drugs, medicines, paints, and oils. Pianos, organs, sewing machines, wallpaper, window shades. Fresh fish, oysters, poultry. *Zapatos de todos tamaños.* Winter suits, overcoats, underwear, and good flannel shirts. *Ropa de señoras y caballeros.*[1]

Such were the goods and services hawked in New Mexico's newspapers, Anglo and Hispano alike, in the late nineteenth and early twentieth centuries. Mass consumer culture, as central to American modernity as the most professional of doctors or the most scientific of managers, would prove through its notions and hats, *ropa de señoras* and *zapatos de todos tamaños*, critical to the embodied nature of New Mexico's emerging racialization projects.

The rise of mass consumer culture signaled an important turning point in modernizing America. Older goals of improving production through increased innovation and efficiency shifted during this period. Rather than cut back on production when demand for goods faltered, producers increasingly emphasized product distribution and marketing, seeking through a variety of means to create greater demand for their products. Advertising, the stimulation of desire for consumer goods, rapidly rose to prominence. New enticements emerged to attract consumers to purchase the products rapidly pouring from America's factories and warehouses.[2]

Besides its fundamental role in modernity, advertising and mass consumer culture also proved critical to colonial and imperial rule. In British colonizing efforts in Africa, for instance, advertising helped legitimate empire by depicting Africans in advertisements as racially inferior, uncivilized, and childlike. Moreover, Africans, especially African women, rarely appeared as consumers of mass-produced goods. Their discursive and physical exclusion from such central spaces of modernity and civic legitimacy helped to justify the British civilizing mission.[3]

In New Mexico, where American imperial aspirations converged with modernity, similar embodied and racialized distinctions developed in mass consumer culture, dividing those fit for citizenship (usually Anglo and Hispano elites) from those undeserving of full civic participation. As advertising for consumer products amply demonstrated, the racialized border between those with legitimate access to consumer goods and public space and those excluded from citizenship often depended on bodily comportment. Talk of bodily comportment in consumer arenas—principally in newspaper advertisements, national and international news, crime reports, and local society pieces—paid particular attention to the surfaces, entrances, and exits of the body, carefully delineating what was to be placed *on the body*, *in the body*, and how things were to be eliminated *from the body*. Orifices and openings, according to the advertisements and articles, were to be scrupulously guarded, and unsightly protrusions on the body's surface and other bodily anomalies (corns, bunions, warts, etc.) were to be effectively and speedily excised. In both Spanish and English newspapers, bodies that appeared too old, too fat, too sloppy, or too unruly (to name only a few of the numerous unacceptable bodily practices and excesses) were denigrated and cruelly mocked.

At the same time that bodily comportment helped differentiate respectable New Mexicans from the indecorous and the unfit, the emergence of mass consumer culture in New Mexico, viewed from the perspective of racialization and the naturalization of whiteness, offered Anglos and Hispanos a space for the articulation of a shared white body. Strikingly, in advertisements in English- and Spanish-language newspapers, the bodies of elite Anglos and Hispanos were virtually identical; both shared claims to the "white" body. Advertisements for a wide variety of consumer goods represented respectable Anglos and Hispanos as actively controlling their bodies. At the same time, only the wealthiest of New Mexicans could afford such products. Recall from chapter 1 that New Mexico's Hispano elites represented only a small percentage, between 5 and 10 percent, of Hispanos. As economic data from Albuquerque demonstrate, the vast majority of Hispanos earned less than $300 annually. With a monthly income of $25, it is unlikely that the average Hispano could afford, say, a "Gent's solid silver, stem wind Waltham watch,"

9. Rosenwald Bros. store, Albuquerque, New Mexico, ca. 1915–20. Participation in mass consumer culture differentiated respectable New Mexicans from the unfit and the improper. Photo by William R. Walton. Courtesy of the Museum of New Mexico, neg. no. 8646.

on sale for $12.50, or half a month's wages, at Everitt's Jewelry Store in Albuquerque.[4] Anglos in New Mexico, though wealthier on average than Hispanos, according to Albuquerque statistics, were also limited by economic constraints from purchasing such items. Thus, engagement with mass consumer culture offered wealthy Anglos and Hispanos alike the opportunity to participate in a relatively exclusive, though still quite public arena, one nicely suited to the specific demands of New Mexico's racialized social order.

As the following examples of consumer body practices from New Mexico's newspapers suggest, the construction of respectable Anglo/Hispano community in post-1880 New Mexico emerged along two intertwined fronts. Elite Anglos and Hispanos in New Mexico defined themselves simultaneously by what they *were* and what they *were not*, what they did with their bodies and what they did not do. Turned inward, in advertisements and newspaper articles, Anglos and Hispanos celebrated their managed, well-controlled white bodies. Turned outward, in other, often literally adjacent articles, elites in New Mexico denounced sexual and racial "others" as excessive, unruly, and dangerous. Still, as the anxiety in newspaper articles reveals, and our understanding of projects of order and control as riddled with missteps and unevenness confirms, the achievement of social order may have proved to be a seductive, and all too elusive, enticement for aspiring elite New Mexicans after the arrival of the railroad in 1880.

Women's bodies were especially integral to this assertion of whiteness in New Mexico. As Carroll Smith-Rosenberg has observed, the regulation and control of bourgeois Anglo female bodies underwrote the formation of bourgeois Anglo society in the United States. Only after regulating the bodies of bourgeois women and later working-class women, Smith-Rosenberg argues, did bourgeois men "seek to control the bodies and the sexuality of other men."[5] Consumer practices proved indispensable to this process, as the clothing, jewelry, hairstyles, and public presentation of bourgeois women marked the status and wealth of their husbands, fathers, and sons. Bourgeois women thus increasingly carried the responsibility of entering public space and purchasing consumer goods for their families. Likewise, well-appointed and properly consuming wives marked the boundary between proper marital sexual activity and illicit sexuality. Married or soon-to-be married bourgeois women displayed themselves publicly in only the most ladylike and appropriate fashions, while prostitutes, the exemplars of illicit sexuality, purportedly draped themselves in gaudy, colorful clothing. Well-regulated and effectively maintained bourgeois female bodies, in control of various surfaces and orifices, served as analogies for and valued companions to a well-ordered social body.

In New Mexico, women's public acts of consumption were similarly linked to Anglo and Hispano displays of racial legitimacy and whiteness. While male bodies received some attention in advertisements, the bodies of women dominated advertising discourse. In advertisements, elite Hispana and Anglo women's bodies emerged as well-tended, carefully compartmentalized domains and both English- and Spanish-language newspapers depicted women buying and wearing the proper clothing as expected and normal behavior. Claiming "rafts of clothing," an ad for L. Washburn and Company advises the reader, "You cannot afford to go poorly dressed," and goes on to describe suits "cut in the latest style" that are "marvels of beauty."[6] Ilfeld Brothers announced "ladies dressing sacques" in "delicate tints" and "made in the latest fashion."[7] Advertisements targeted all aspects of the female, and occasionally male, body. Spiegelberg Brothers claimed that they had a "fine display of Ladies, Misses and Children's Hats."[8] An ad for Jaffa Brothers notes that the underwear in their establishment are "just gauzy enough" (creating a distinction that I will address later in this chapter).[9] Ads for nonclothing products reinforced this emphasis on adorning one's body in the proper clothing. An advertisement for dining-room supplies combines a claim of "the largest and only exclusive stock in the Southwest" with a picture of an elegant light-skinned young woman seated at a well-appointed table, cleaning her dinnerware.[10] Another ad depicts a long-skirted matron, also light-skinned, seated before an elegant piano, and notes that a "Chickering Bros. piano is none to [sic] good for anybody, and is good enough for everybody."[11]

Humor sections similarly offered primers on the accoutrements of wealth and status, as in a cartoon, titled "Cynical," where a well-dressed, cigar-smoking man ("The Husband") stands before a spectacled woman ("The Wife") seated in a plush chair in a well-furnished house. The husband declares to his wife, "Well, say what you will, my dear, you'll find worse men than me in the world." Undoubtedly frightened of the prospect of a world filled with characters even more nefarious than her husband, the wife replies tartly, "Oh, Tom, how can you be so bitter?"[12] At the same time that women often appeared as the exemplars of consumer culture, men could, and did, act as shoppers as well. In one piece, a "Customer" asks the "Tailor" for a "material that won't show the dust" because he is "going to the races a good bit in the spring." The tailor answers, "I presume you have no objections in paying cash down." The male customer, concerned about his clothes appearing dusty, seeks a tailor for a specific type of material. The cartoon accentuates this potential link between shopping and masculine identity by having the customer be an aficionado of "the races," a habit more identified with men than with women. In "Making Sure," a butcher asks the clerk if a certain customer had been charged for his steak, telling the clerk to bill the man a second time. "Charge it again and be sure," the butcher directs the clerk. "I'd rather charge it twice than forget it once."[13] The piece similarly contains a male shopper, although in the careful gender distinctions typical of advertisements, the joke never hints that buying steaks could constitute the same type of consumer behavior as wearing a pompadour.

Although historians have only begun to address the impact of United States mass consumer culture on the nearly half-million Mexican-origin inhabitants of the American Southwest around the turn of the twentieth century, it is clear that elite Hispanos in New Mexico were active participants in the emerging consumer realm. A large nearly quarter-page advertisement in the Spanish-language La Opinión Pública for the Casa de Rosenwald in Albuquerque exhorts "the whole town" to visit the store and "check out their prices."[14] Although the ad mentions men's clothes, female shoppers are the obvious targets, both as purchasers for men and as consumers for themselves. One of the two illustrations presents a fancy decorated woman's boot in profile. Another ad, for a clothing store and covering a complete page in La Bandera Americana, pictures an American flag and an illustration of another fashionable light-skinned young woman, announcing incredible bargains on men's and women's clothing.[15] And another advertisement, for a dealer in home furnishings, shows a well-dressed light-skinned lady amidst stacks of elegant rugs and tapestries.[16] In addition to selling consumer goods, these ads thus recommended certain types of behavior as appropriate for shoppers, including wearing elegant clothes both at home and while shopping.

Even Hispanos uncomfortable with the emergence of mass consumer culture nonetheless acknowledged its impact. One Hispano writer, José Escobar, in an 1897 article from Albuquerque's *El Nuevo Mundo*, made the connection all too clear between the desire of Hispanos to enter consumer society and social, if not marital, strife and disorder:

> The youth of Latin background, born for the most part under the American flag, have had to adopt Anglo Saxon habits. . . . But among this youth, unfortunately, there is a certain element of "slick boys" and "crank girls" who, despite their "tanned" complexion, have gotten it into their heads that they are "true Americans" and they want nothing in the world to do with conversing in the lovely language of Valera and Nuñez de Arce. It is not unusual for "Miss Jacinta" or "Mister Mulehead" to make a slang or patois of the two languages which is more than a little difficult to understand.
>
> In our customs, as in our language, the styles of the North have been imitated, and now we have "ladies" who smoke and ride bicycles, and naturally the number of marriages listed in the Civil Register has declined, because to marry a "modern" woman is the same as taking a rope and hanging oneself . . . quite simply.
>
> If the "mamas" of these modern girls gave them the benefit of some sophistication in sewing and cooking they would do them much more good than by letting them spend their "pennies" on outlandish hats costing a king's ransom, which pleases the shopkeepers while the fathers and husbands "uncongratulate" each other.[17]

In speaking of consumer society, the article also speaks directly to bodily comportment. The dangerous "slick boys" and "crank girls" engage in a range of, for the author, scandalous behaviors. While noting that both young men and women speak a "patois" of English and Spanish, the author reserves special scorn for the "Miss Jacintas." These "ladies" ride bicycles and smoke cigarettes, activities that apparently seriously jeopardize their chances to find a respectable husband. Not learning to cook or sew, the young women also "spend their 'pennies'" wantonly and buy "outlandish hats." In contrast to normal practices, such as speaking Spanish, marrying a good husband, cooking, and sewing, such "ladies" choose to speak incorrectly, smoke, ride bicycles, go shopping, and wear expensive clothes.

Through this focus on bodily comportment, the article nicely illustrates the attempts by elite Hispanos to assert for themselves a degree of whiteness, an elevated social standing based on supposedly superior bodily habits and tendencies. As class differences helped divide the Hispano community into a small elite cadre and a much larger non-elite group, few Hispanos could afford the multitude of goods advertised in New Mexico newspapers. In belittling the lavish spending habits of young Hispanos, Hispano writers subtly depicted themselves as those New Mexicans who practiced the superior bodily acts ("conversing in the lovely language of Valera and Nuñez de Arce") and who best appreciated "the benefit of some sophistication."

Active participants in mass consumer culture, wealthy Hispanos and Anglos shared a particular form of bodily comportment, one that emphasized well-tended bodily surfaces and careful attention to what entered and exited the body. The respectable white body deserving of social status and privilege required smooth, unblemished surfaces. Accordingly, New Mexico papers advertised a variety of remedies to allow one to rid the surface of one's body from unsightly, and socially unacceptable, impurities. For example, William Chaplin exhorted readers who wanted to "get rid of corns or bunions" to visit his establishment, where he promised to "cure [their] feet with a pair of his celebrated shoes or boots."[18] Women especially received encouragement to cultivate smooth bodily surfaces. An ad for Dr. Pierce's Favorite Prescription advises women "just entering the doors of society or womanhood" that their aspirations for beauty and health require "clear skin, rosy cheeks, [and] bright eyes," all attributes of a proper bourgeois bodily surface.[19] An illustration of these "society buds" accompanies the advertisement, depicting the faces of two fair-skinned young women intertwined with the petals of a rosebush. Advertisements for Burdock Blood Bitters claim that a "woman loves a clear, rosy complexion," and that their product "purifies the blood, clears the skin, [and] restores ruddy, sound health."[20] Such ads, and many more like them, emphasized the role of clear, unblemished, smooth bodily surfaces in the creation of middle-class female identity. A respectable woman in New Mexico, the ads hinted, needed at least to aspire to, if not literally to achieve, clear and unblemished skin.

In addition to the cultivation of the surface of one's body, newspaper advertisements in New Mexico recommended placing the proper products into the body. Appropriate food and drink, of course, received special attention, as did medicine and various forms of patent cures (products of dubious effectiveness promising to cure a multitude of ailments). Like the ads championing clean skin and unblemished complexion, announcements for food and beverages highlighted the purity and unsullied nature of their products. FG Pratt and Company generously proclaimed, "The store would like to reduce the number of badly-fed people in this town," noting that a "badly-fed person [is not] getting out of life half that's in it." A well-fed person, on the other hand, one who properly monitors what enters their body, "bid[s] for good health and take[s] long strides toward personal efficiency in [their] life's work."[21] In terms of drink, a liquor dealer guaranteed all wine products to be "the *pure* juice of the grape."[22] Another ad states the point even more clearly, asking readers rhetorically, "Who would drink the trash put on the market as beverages when one can get the St. Louis ABC Bohemian bottled beer?" The ad continues, observing that bottled beer "quenches your thirst and builds your system."[23]

Advertisements recommended other products besides food and beverages that readers striving for legitimacy could properly admit into their bodies. Claims of purity and cleanliness similarly predominated in ads for medicine and all-purpose products. An ad for Dr. Price's Cream Baking Powder, for instance, announces that the chief chemist of the U.S. Department of Agriculture had recently awarded "highest honors" to Dr. Price's baking powder for its "leavening power, keeping properties, purity and excellence." Furthermore, the ad notes that the chief chemist "rejected" Alum baking powders (undoubtedly a major competitor of Dr. Price's) for being "unwholesome."[24] A large picture of a classical white female angel accompanying the article reinforces the product's claims of purity and "wholesomeness." Another ad for Pierce's Pleasant Pellets promises to cure headaches. Unlike "the offending matter which deranges the stomach and causes the headache," the pills, composed of the "purest" materials, are "easily swallowed" and "worth more than their weight in gold."[25] The ad includes testimony from "Mr. E. Vargason, Esq.," whose professional standing ("Esq." signifying his occupation as an attorney) is confirmed by a head and shoulder drawing of a well-groomed gentleman. Once again, the ad distinguishes its product ("pure" materials, safely ingested, comparable to precious metal) and its users (professional, well educated) from impure and dangerous materials ("offending matter" that causes "derangement" of the body's interior).

Another ad for Dr. Pierce's medical miracles appeared in a Las Vegas, New Mexico, newspaper in 1908. "A Lazy Liver," the ad proclaims, "may be only a tired liver or a starved liver," a sign of "an ill-nourished, enfeebled body whose organs are weary with overwork." Attempting to treat the "lagging, torpid liver" with certain medicines, by "lashing it" with "strong, drastic drugs" would be, the ad suggests, akin to "beat[ing] a weary or starved man because he lagged in his work." Such action would be "stupid as well as savage." Instead, the use of Dr. Pierce's pills promises to "restore the normal activity of the stomach," cleaning the body of "poisonous accumulations." The elaborate imagery that surrounds the liver in this ad highlights several behaviors and characteristics. First, there is the conflation of an unhealthy liver with hunger (starved, ill-nourished), fatigue (tired, weary with overwork), and the absence of necessary motivation (lazy, torpid, lagging). Second, the ad clusters together the ingestion of "strong, drastic drugs" with violent punishment like "lashing" and "beating." The ad describes such actions as "stupid" and "savage." This description identifies the potential purchaser of the product as not merely unhealthy and ailing, but as empowered and proactive. In the ad, the person who treats their "lazy liver" emerges as intelligent and civilized, the opposite of stupid and savage. Furthermore, he—it is difficult to imagine a woman in this role—is capable of wielding a whip, presumably unlike the weary or starved man, but chooses a different course.[26]

Finally, newspaper ads focused on elimination and bodily exits, what emerged from the body. New Mexico newspapers remained relatively silent when it came to the human body's most notable removal functions, the elimination of excrement and urine. One exception was ads for patent medicine products. One ad lists among the multiple uses of their pills the cure of "all derangements of the liver, stomach, and bowels." In another, Curtis Fleck of Anaheim, California, testified that he found Chamberlain's Colic, Cholera, and Diarrhea Remedy so effective he became "as enthusiastic over its wonderful work as any one can be."[27] Candy Cathartic Cascarets likewise pledged to "regulate the liver" and "cure constipation."[28] Other related functions involving the emergence from the body of particular materials appeared occasionally in newspaper advertisements. For instance, ads at times praised only a particular form and manner of speech, producing a slew of correct words and phrases that should exit the body. Proper speakers, for example, did not ask for charity or handouts. An ad for a hardware store claims an "old and established reputation," pointing to the names of satisfied customers, all prominent community members, as evidence of their reliability. The advertisement begins, however, with a different claim, that the establishment "does not have to beg or borrow tools and pipe."[29] Pleading for assistance or aid obviously did not qualify as the appropriate types of words to escape the body. For women, according to other ads, correct speech should include discussions of shopping and consumer goods. One store noted that "the general topic of conversation among the ladies of Santa Fe is the beautiful carpets at Z. Staab and Brothers."[30] Schools of foreign language also advertised tutorials in French, not, significantly, in Spanish or one of the several Pueblo Indian languages. That is, in addition to speaking correct and respectable English, proper New Mexicans practiced a civilized foreign "tongue" such as French.

Questions of appropriate sexual behavior underwrote much of this advertising discourse. Control of the body's entrances obviously required a certain degree of sexual control. Take, for instance, the previously mentioned "just gauzy enough" ad for women's underwear, an ad that exemplifies the complex relationship between sexuality and control of the body. The ad reads in full: "Misses and ladies' underwear, not too gauzy, but just gauzy enough, at Jaffa Bros."[31] It reveals an important distinction between acceptable expressions of sexual desire ("just gauzy enough") and improper sexuality ("too gauzy"). Female consumers, according to the ad, must appear sexually responsive and available, yet respectable and proper. That is, respectable women must establish along their bodies a critical barrier between appropriate sexual access to their bodies and inappropriate sexual advances. Bourgeois bodies, especially female bourgeois bodies, therefore, not only must allow the proper food, drink, and medicine to enter their bodies; they must encourage the appropriate ("just gauzy enough") sexual activity as well.

Other advertisements in New Mexico newspapers concerning sexual behavior also addressed bodily elimination and emergence. An advertisement for Dr. Pierce's Favorite Prescription is titled "It isn't in the ordinary way." The ad begins with an illustration of a horse running backward pulling a woman in a carriage. Dr. Pierce, of course, promised a remedy *in* the ordinary way, curing "female complaint of every kind," including "internal inflammation or ulceration, bearing-down sensations, and all chronic weaknesses and irregularities." In one sense, the ad suggests that women should control their bodies literally through the proper adoption of consumer medical products. In another sense, as women's historians have noted, such ads, and similar advertisements for constipation cures, frequently masked the sale of abortifacients. Proper women, according to the ad, should not consult midwives or concoct their own remedies for "female ills."[32] Such a choice would "not be in the ordinary way," akin to a horse pulling a carriage backward. At the same time, the ad may consider pregnancy *itself* to be out of the ordinary. Leslie Reagan has pointed out that abortion was often described as a "restoration" of a regular female cycle.[33] The pills, therefore, may restore a woman's "ordinary"—that is, her nonpregnant—condition. The ad may also signal some concern about the consequences of women in public. Transportation and mobility were important issues in New Mexico and the broader American West.[34] Recall the demonized image from chapter 3 of two Hispanos wandering drunk through the streets of Las Vegas. Recall also the story of the "transit of Venus" and the "streetcar" accident involving the unfortunate Navajo woman. Later in this chapter, I will discuss some examples of the anxiety surrounding women in public.[35]

Women were not the only newspaper readers with sexual "dysfunction" targeted by advertisers. One ad announces boldly, "Manhood Restored" and includes a dramatic before-and-after sketch of the faces of a "Cupidene" user. The "before" drawing depicts a gaunt, tired-looking man with disheveled and thin hair, lines on his forehead and cheek, bags under his eyes, a poorly trimmed mustache, and a despondent frown. In stark contrast, the man after he has subscribed to the benefits of Cupidene appears well fed and full cheeked, with eyebrows raised attentively, mustache trimmed, and turned-up, thick, bushy hair. The text of the ad promises men a rapid cure to ailments of "the generative organs" as diverse as "Lost Manhood, Insomnia, Pains in the Back, Seminal Emulation, Nervous Debility, Pimples, Unfitness to Marry, Exhausting Drains, Varicocele, and Constipation." It further claims to cure "quickness of discharge, which if not checked leads to Spermatorrhea and all the horrors of impotency." A critical word in the ad is "restored." The "after" picture of the healthy, apparently vigorous man illustrates "normal" manhood, a man not afflicted with such disabling illnesses as pimples, constipation, unfitness to marry, and premature ejaculation. Expected male body practices, the ad suggests, would include those behaviors demonstrated by the man whose use of Cupidene has restored his manhood: appearing alert, without thin hair or lines on one's face; trimming one's mustache to stand at attention and not to droop; ridding one's face of pimples; ejaculating in a timely, not overly "quick" manner; desire, or at least "fitness," to marry; and the ability to reproduce.[36]

Newspaper advertisements also marked off clear distinctions between men and women, carefully defining the accepted roles and behavior of each group. One ad claims that because "the modern man [does] not admire the fainting woman," modern women need desperately the strength and vigor promised by Dr. Pierce's Favorite Prescription pill. A woman testifies in the ad that with the pills she could "walk a mile and do all [her] own housework." The drawing accompanying the ad depicts a man in a three-piece suit holding aloft a woman in a long dress who has clearly fainted. Although "modern" men, according to the ad, hardly admired fainting women, they still stood ready and able to protect them from danger. No ad for Dr. Pierce's pills ever showed a woman carrying a fainting man, despite the fact that the pills were often advertised for men as well as women. Furthermore, "modern" women still needed to do housework. The ad notes pointedly *not* that Dr. Pierce's pills could help women become better workers or bank presidents or politicians, but that "it fits for wifehood and motherhood."[37] Other ads sounded similar notes of clear gender distinction. Men almost invariably appeared engaged in physical labor, as carpenters, dentists, or butchers, while women either stood alone modeling the latest fashions or followed typically "female" pursuits, such as playing the piano or baking at a stove, in the home.

This array of body practices in advertising discourse in New Mexico newspapers was critical to both racialization projects in New Mexico and the creation of whiteness. The ads, for instance, suggesting a strict division between body practices associated with men and those defined as feminine are reminiscent of New Mexico Indian schools, where educators claimed that clear gender boundaries were fundamental to civilization and whiteness. Similar, though perhaps a bit more subtle, racialization projects informed newspaper advertisements such as those promising to cure either female constipation or male constipation, not the ability to cure *both*. Likewise, men did not faint or use stoves at home or polish dinnerware or speak of beautiful carpets. Women did not build houses or sell meat or extract teeth. Class status and wealth, of course, were required if one hoped to purchase such products and make such claims of gender division and whiteness. Ads counseled readers in English- and Spanish-language newspapers alike to devote a large portion of their available resources—including not just material resources, but time and energy— to buying clothes. As one ad bluntly states, one "could not afford" not to engage in the act of buying and dressing in the expected clothes. Other expected bodily comportment that emerged from the consumer arena included a clear expectation that those with diseases or ailments ranging from coughs, colds, constipation, pimples, and diarrhea to "irregularity," impotence, and "quickness of discharge" would seek help for their "impurities."

Advertisements, however, were not alone in drawing racial distinctions from bodily comportment in New Mexico's developing consumer culture. Both out-of-town and local news portrayed legitimate civic participation in large measure as a matter of the correct use of the body. These descriptions, and prescriptions, of proper bodily behavior appeared in several types of articles. First, New Mexico newspapers usually contained at least a page devoted to national and international news. In addition to political and economic reports, these sections included numerous chronicles of the high society doings of American and European elites. Second, newspapers concentrated on local New Mexican elites, sketching similarly laudatory accounts of social outings, parties, and respectable civic activities. Third, newspapers contained brief notices, "local laconics" according to one weekly, celebrating various examples of a well-ordered social world. Articles showered words of praise and congratulation on everything from amicable divorces to men behaving admirably. As in the newspaper advertisements, newspaper articles (whether long or short, local or international, serious or in jest) frequently rested their symbolic narrative weight on concerns about the surfaces, entrances, and exits of particular male and female bodies in turn-of-the-century New Mexico.

Attention to the body's, typically the female body's, well-maintained surfaces emerges most frequently in announcements of prominent engagements and wedding ceremonies. Impressive marriage ceremonies and the tasteful presentation of gifts emphasized the consumer patterns integral to the proper display of the body. In the nuptial announcements and celebrations of American and European elites, as well as for members of New Mexico's high society, the most common bodily practices concerned the clothing of the body: the elaborate wedding and bridesmaids' dresses, the bride's hair and jewelry, the groom's tuxedo and tails. One article recounted in great detail the dresses of both the bride, "a pink mesaline gown with an under drop of silver lace," and her mother, "a gown of blue net over rose."[38] Descriptions of other weddings followed a similar pattern. The article reporting the nuptials of Lizzie Preissner and William Brittenstine in Albuquerque in the spring of 1895 includes the location of the ceremony and the names of the parents and wedding officiants, and ends by wishing the newlyweds "happiness, prosperity and long life." "The bride and bridesmaid," the article notes, "were attired in white, and the beauty of the bride attracted universal attention and was the subject of general remark," while the groom "[is] a fireman on the Santa Fe Road, and one of our best young men."[39] While the article identifies the bride and bridesmaids according to their physical attributes and attire, the groom is associated almost exclusively with his job.

Like marriage announcements, more general news also emphasized both the purchase of commodities and the effective bodily control required to be considered respectable. One article recommends in great detail the proper dress and comportment for women. Titled "For the Ladies," the article reviews current fashion trends, noting that "Polish caps with tassels are now worn" and that "plush roses form the favorite garnitures of many lovely evening dresses." The piece also includes explicit advice for bourgeois women, observing that "the most fastidiously fashionable women" match "their bonnets, muffs and costumes," and that "imported evening dresses have very long trains."[40] Clearly, only *non*bourgeois women would fail to match their bonnets and muffs or try to declare their evening dress "imported" if it did not have a very long train. Only proper ladies would "fastidiously" monitor the surface appearances of their bodies.

Naturalizing whiteness, the creation of a shared elite Anglo/Hispano white body, thus appeared with a certain clarity in New Mexico's developing consumer culture. As occurred elsewhere in New Mexico, the bodily comportment of racialized others helped nurture this fledgling Anglo/Hispano alliance. In direct, and productive, contrast to the image of well-controlled surfaces and orifices of bodies behaving normally, the most salient features of abnormal, and socially unacceptable, body practices was the loss or outright absence of bodily control. The story of the Navajo "squaw" from chapter 4 is typical in that respect. Not only does the Navajo woman literally lose control of her body and fall from a streetcar, but the reference to a planetary eclipse (the "transit of Venus") suggests abnormal bodily excess, that the Navajo woman in effect blotted out the sun when she fell. The article also manages to note that the poor woman fell because she had positioned her body incorrectly while exiting the streetcar, "exhibit[ing] the bad sense of stepping off a moving streetcar this morning with her back to the driver."[41]

In what is by now a familiar pattern, Anglo and Hispano elites also aggressively denounced the bodily comportment of a host of other New Mexicans. Newspaper crime reports emphasized the linkage between improper consumer activity, criminality, and race. In issue after issue, newspaper reports of crime focused on the racially marked characteristics of the criminal or accused criminal. As Anne McClintock has observed, commodity culture and imperial projects devoted to the creation and maintenance of racial difference often walked hand in hand. She notes, for instance, that in the nineteenth century, Africans constantly challenged European attempts to destabilize and replace indigenous economies through the use of commodities. McClintock reads the African habit—in the eyes of Europeans—of "making off with property that did not belong to them," not as theft, but as a deliberate "refusal of European notions of property ownership and exchange value."[42] In turn-of-the-century New Mexico, the repeated association of racialized others with the theft of consumer commodities and other crimes like prostitution points to traces of imperialism embedded in the reporting of criminal activities. The articles imply, once again, that racial otherness was incompatible with proper modern consumer behavior.

Crimes involving African Americans were frequent targets of newspaper reports. Although African Americans comprised a minute percentage of New Mexico's population between 1880 and 1920, "Negro" men and women were disproportionately the subject of newspaper articles.[43] In fact, according to the skewed newspaper coverage of criminal activity, African Americans supposedly committed the majority of crimes, ranging from rape and murder to public intoxication and vagrancy, in both New Mexico and the nation. One typical piece from Hannibal, Missouri, notes that "Chas. Bohon, colored[,] has been sentenced to . . . five years in the penitentiary on a charge of grand larceny and burglary," while "Sam Wellington, another negro, received two years for robbing a peddler."[44] A story from Elizabethtown, New Mexico, describes the theft of several barrels of whiskey from a distillery. In addition to naming the two "colored whiskey thieves," the article notes ominously that the theft occurred several months ago. Since then, according to the article, "the colored population of the town have been having a general picnic by feasting upon the fiery fluid."[45] Vagrancy charges, one paper observed, had been "preferred against four colored people," after one had been accused of theft.[46] Linking individual African American criminal activity to community-wide law breaking, such articles depicted African Americans in general as a dangerous, racially marked criminal population.

Like reports on crime, small jokes and tongue-in-cheek newspaper articles commonly associated certain body practices with racialized deviance. One extraordinary article from 1918 in Albuquerque pictures a caricatured smiling African American domestic, complete with bandanna tied around her head, and the title "Gwineter Make a Hoe-Cake." The piece was actually a recipe for corn bread, but executed in the style of a minstrel tune, complete with absurd verses like "De hoe-cake's got a sol inside an' doesn't need no yeas'," and "you mix 'em up tergedder." The use of vernacular speech, of course, creates a clear boundary between the perception of the speech habits of African Americans and the manner in which other groups and individuals, defined by contrast as grammatically correct and proper, supposedly talked. The piece also slyly advocates for the use of modern cooking technology. The absurdly speaking cook advises against using corn like "de fine and yalluh kin' dat's grinded in de town." She complains that cornmeal bought in the city cannot compare to "country meal" because the "swizzlin' city steam-mill . . . don't know how to grind the cohn and not grind out de sweet." Likewise, the recipe recommends patting the corn into cakes "des like de chillun make mud pies," a far cry from the advertisements celebrating the newest stoves and ovens. Taken together, the behavior of the African American cook described in the article links irregular vernacular speech with premodern country living and childhood. Buying corn bread at the store and making bread from wheat flour thus emerge as especially regular and normalized activities.[47] Other articles spoke more directly to the link between consumer culture and particular racialized body practices. One article notes that the "Zulu hat" was supposedly quite fashionable among "New York Ladies." In mock earnestness, the article describes the "entire Zulu costume," which it claims consisted in its entirety of "a ring in the nose" and "one slender string of blue beads."[48] An improper African American female body (unclothed, adorned only with a string of beads and a nose ring) once again represents excess and abnormality, the discursive opposite of the properly clothed white body.

African Americans, however, were not the sole targets of elite Anglo and Hispano discourses of whiteness. In New Mexico, prostitutes, as we have seen in previous chapters, especially represented disordered, socially dangerous, excessive sexual and racial bodies. Descriptions of Hispana prostitutes are especially telling. Anglos and Hispano elites could both depict themselves as white in contrast to Hispana prostitutes. Anglos denounced Hispana prostitutes in what is by now a familiar racialization process. At the same time, such depictions also helped shore up elite Hispano claims to whiteness by emphasizing the improper consumer behavior practiced by prostitutes, epitomized of course by the exchange of sexual intercourse for money. Just as Hispano critiques of spendthrift "crank girls" helped clarify the proper consumer habits of respectable Hispanos, criticism of prostitutes allowed elite Hispanos to accentuate the distance separating themselves, and their whiteness and superior leadership skills, from the mass of non-elite Hispanos. Both Anglos and elite Hispanos therefore had much to gain from condemning the bodily comportment and improper consumer practices of prostitutes.

One piece, for example, observing a fight between "two Mexican girls" at a dance hall, a space commonly associated with prostitution, reports that "the only damage done was to clothes." Both women, according to the report, were rendered naked by the brawl, "one, after the struggle, appeared as Lady Godiva, the other could have passed as Mother Eve, but the fig leaf was lacking."[49] The comparison of "two Mexican girls" with "Lady Godiva" and "Mother Eve" accentuates their racial differences. Lady Godiva and Mother Eve (significantly *lacking* the sexual modesty and discretion of a fig leaf) are rendered similar to the prostitutes in their shared sexual impropriety. In an attempt at humor, however, the article juxtaposes the traditional images of Eve and Lady Godiva with the image of two "Mexican girls" tearing at each other's clothes outside a dance hall. Similar in terms of sexual deviance, the women stand in direct racial opposition. Only bodily excess, the women's brazen—and, the article suggests, deliberate—public display of their own unclothed bodies unites the two discourses. In this newspaper article and others like it, the improper space of bodily excess (brawling soon-to-be-naked women) brings together the discourses of sexual deviance and racial difference.

In another newspaper account, a large dance sponsored by "one of the leaders of the demimonde" apparently attracted countless "abandoned women." Despite the fact that "the women were, in many cases, handsomely dressed" and "would easily pass in a ballroom which claimed more pretensions," their facial expressions, "the blasé look which had possession of their faces," betrayed their debased standing. The article goes on to describe the raucous party. Noting that "the 'young ladies' gradually became excited with the wine and beer they drank," the article observes that during "the blow out" that evening "money flowed over the bar one way, while whiskey and wine went over it the other." Opposing powerful "flows" (money one way, liquor the other) soon led to "the stomachs of the rioters . . . being gradually filled with spirits" while their pockets "were becoming empty and those of the venturesome madam correspondingly full." A parody of proper consumer behavior (the exchange of money and product becomes a "blow out," "riotous" and "flowing over"), the report explicitly weds prostitution and its "venturesome madams" with bodily excess, massive consumption of alcohol, grotesquely bulging stomachs, and the loss of ability to control one's spending.[50]

Another newspaper article notes that several prostitutes had "fallen into the habit of exhibiting their ugly mugs about the city in a hack." "Their obscene actions" supposedly drew the "disgust of respectable citizens" and warranted official "suppression." Another article, describing a stabbing in a dance hall, observes that the two women accused of the crime, "Marinda and Minnie," were "hard citizens." Accentuating their distance from respectable society, the article continues, "They have become so debauched in crime that the merciful creator has removed from their visages all traces of womanly beauty." Instead, the women carried "the stamp of vagrant and outcast indelibly on their features."[51]

A notice from one of Albuquerque's Spanish-language newspapers exemplifies the relationship between prostitution, excessive bodily practices, and disrepute. Apparently, two "beautiful young women," walking along the street in front of the notorious "el Portal de Murphy" saloon, were attacked by "a fearless dog." Fleeing from the dog, the "shy doves" tripped and fell to the ground. Upon rising, according to the article, "they left on the ground a lukewarm liquid, as if to demonstrate the great terror they had suffered." The article ends by advising the dog's owner in the future to tie up the "brave animal" and avoid a repetition of an event that both "infuriates and makes one laugh at the same time." Literally "soiled doves," the prostitutes in the article cannot control their own bodies; terrified by the dog, they not only urinate on themselves, but fantastically leave a pool of "lukewarm liquid" on the ground when they rise. The snug relationship in turn-of-the-century New Mexico between bodily excess (specifically, the failure to control adequately one's orifices) and disreputable public behavior could hardly be more clear.[52]

Discourses of prostitution thus emphasized the grotesque nature of prostitutes' bodily appearance, just as newspaper advertisements and

10. Bank Saloon, Las Vegas, New Mexico, 1915. In the contorted racial and sexual politics of New Mexico, alcohol consumption was frequently a marker of bodily incoherence and social inferiority. Courtesy of the Museum of New Mexico, neg. no. 49225.

news reports highlighted the unblemished, well-tended surfaces of re-spectable women's bodies. Attacks on prostitutes in New Mexico in this respect mirror broader America, where, as Nancy Cott observes, prosti-tutes exemplified the opposite of respectable married women, especially in the association of prostitution with improper economic and consumer activity. "Where marriage," she says, "implied mutual love and consent, legality and formality, willing bonds for a good bargain, prostitution sig-nified sordid monetary exchange and desperation or coercion on the part of the woman involved."[53]

In discussing prostitutes, newspapers also provided a narrative space for implicit as well as explicit talk of citizenship and the embodied charac-teristics of those unfit for inclusion in the American polity. Such articles emphasized the considerable, even insurmountable, distance separating respectable citizens from prostitutes. One article, from a Santa Fe news-paper, describes the capital city's own efforts to eliminate prostitution: "The city authorities are to be commended for their firm stand against the spread of the moral evil in this city. Street running is not only prohib-ited by ordinance but the police are enforcing the ordinance rigidly. The arrest yesterday of five girls and their summary punishment should serve as an example. Santa Fe has so many evils to contend with that it must be spared this, the most demoralizing of them."[54] In 1911, after the announcement of a new effort to attack prostitution in Albuquerque, an article titled "Denizens of the Half World Leave" describes the exodus from the city of prostitutes: "Yesterday was the first day of July and in accordance with the orders of the city council and urged by the police, denizens of the 3rd Street tenderloin district began leaving for other fields, many leaving yesterday for El Paso. It is understood that the saloons in the reservation which have relied chiefly for their business on the disorderly houses will probably not renew their licenses."[55]

One man's recollections of the red-light district from his childhood in Albuquerque similarly reveal the significance of bodily comportment in distinguishing prostitutes from respectable New Mexicans. The district, or "glamorous area" and mysterious "world set apart," in Kenneth Balcomb's memory centered on the intersection of Third Street and Copper Avenue and extended north on Third and east and west on Copper and Tijeras for several blocks. Balcomb also remembered the vivid sight of prostitutes strolling through the streets of Albuquerque on shopping excursions. "These painted ladies," he recalls, were a sight to behold, "their rouged cheeks, painted lips, darkened eyelashes, huge hats, bustles, and highly colored dresses made them stand out." More than dress and makeup, however, differentiated prostitutes from respectable shoppers in Albuquerque for Balcomb. Prostitutes were not allowed to walk together in public, but were required to keep a distance of at least four paces between them while walking. Thus could respectable men and women, and boys like Balcomb, easily tell the difference between prostitutes and proper women.[56]

The 1911 trial of Lizzie McGrath for operating a brothel, discussed in chapter 5, strikes a similar chord. In testimony regarding the residents of the building that McGrath owned and lived in, one witness was directed to describe "what were these women doing; how were they dressed, and what made you think they belonged at that house." "Well," he replied, "I suppose from the general reputation of the house, what they were there for." He went on to describe the women's clothing. Asked how they were dressed, he answered, "Oh, several different ways, some with Kimonos, and some in full dress."[57]

As with all ordering projects, this shared Anglo and Hispano effort to impose a seamless colonial blanket upon New Mexico hardly proceeded without snags, embarrassing slippages, and the occasional untucked edge. The contradictions at the heart of modernity and imperial expansion could at times burst into view. Bourgeois women throughout the United States, for instance, educated by newspaper and magazine advertisements, gaudy window displays, and luxurious store interiors to desire consumer goods, often exceeded the proper limits and expectations placed upon them. While not exactly the back alleys and mean streets of urban reformers, the promenades, department stores, and storefront windows of modernity produced their fair share of bourgeois male trepidation, as respectable, and married, women flirted with handsome clerks, shoplifted small items, and stretched the available credit and credibility of their concerned husbands. Rita Felski, among others, has noted the vexatious position of female consumers in the rise of turn-of-the-century mass consumer culture. Consuming women, she argues, though crucial to the marking of bourgeois identity, were "portrayed as buying machines, driven by impulses beyond their control to squander money on the accumulation of ever more possessions." In belittling consuming women, bourgeois men also asserted their own masculine identity. Carroll Smith-Rosenberg has observed that bourgeois men in the late nineteenth century initially consolidated their identity by contrasting themselves with women of their own class and race. As the opposite of excessive, spendthrift, irrational women, men appeared in venues like newspaper accounts as measured, practical, and financially prudent.[58]

New Mexico in this respect differed little from New York or London. Anxiety about women in public was common in New Mexico newspapers. At the same time, such expressions of anxiety may have helped men in New Mexico, Anglo and Hispano, portray themselves as emotionally stable and fiscally continent. For example, one lengthy newspaper piece followed a reporter through the opening day festivities of an Albuquerque department store. The article recounts in some detail the various departments, from dress goods and hosiery to hats and cloaks, and includes a lively conversation between the reporter and the store's manager. The placid contents of the article, however, contrast dramatically with the article's headline and opening sentences. The headline reads in large print "Where Were the Police?" and in smaller print, "A large crowd forcing its way into the Cyclone grocery house." Before his amiable conversation with the store manager, the reporter had to force his way, "by dint of hard work and a good deal of pushing," past a "large number of ladies congregated" in front of the store.[59] The carefully compartmentalized store interior is contradicted in the article by the nearly riotous women ("where were the police?") "forcing" their way into the store.

Nearly forty years later, another Albuquerque establishment experienced a similar burst of female consumer activity. In March 1918 a headline announced that "Bargain Hunters Tied Up Traffic" and "Several Women Fainted." Apparently the Wright Clothing Company of No. 110 West Central Ave. advertised a large sale to begin at 9:30 in the morning.

As the store opened, according to the article, a "concerted attack made by several thousands of Albuquerque citizens" overwhelmed the store's employees, who "did what they could to handle the crowd, but their numbers were not equal to the task." The store was forced to call off the sale and notify police, who discovered that the "whole street was a struggling, squirming mass of humanity." Wading into the affray, officers managed to disperse the mostly female crowd and engineer a more orderly opening of the store. One officer noted that some of "these women didn't know any better than to try to carry children in their arms or push baby buggies into the crush. It's a wonder they weren't killed." Despite the chaos, the only casualties were several female fainting spells and one woman who was "badly handled by the crowd." The article ends on a positive note. After police reopened the store, the piece observes, customers claimed that "it was well worth their time because they found the goods to be just as advertised." The doors would open again that morning, the paper announced, and readers were advised "to inspect these bargains while you have this opportunity."[60]

Despite the large headlines and identical typeface, the "article" appears to have been a fairly elaborate ruse. In retrospect, one clue may have been the careful mention of the name and address of the clothing store, or the reiteration of the store's sales, clearances, and great bargains. "Several Thousands of Albuquerque Citizens" also may have overstated the case a bit, considering the town's total 1920 population of less than twenty thousand. Still, like the previous announcement of riotous female shoppers, the article reveals some anxious moments. As the police officer reported, women—respectable and proper, one would assume, since few advertisers would seek penniless, disreputable shoppers—supposedly put their children and infants at risk of death or serious injury in their rush for bargain merchandise. An entire city street was likewise transformed into a "squirming mass of humanity." In an age of child welfare laws and considerable labor unrest, including the active participation and leadership of women in consumer boycotts of the sort described by historian Dana Frank in Seattle, riotous women shoppers ignoring the safety of their children posed a certain realistic threat to stable, well-ordered society.[61]

Descriptions of other public women in New Mexico, even those not associated with shopping, revealed similar intonations of the perils of women in public. Take, for instance, an article describing a meeting of the female members of the Albuquerque Library Association in 1883. The text of the piece goes to great lengths to demonstrate the efficiency and capability of the "forty prominent ladies," noting their "marked interest in the organization," their "self-sacrificing disposition," and the notable absence of "bickering" during the meeting. The headline of the article, however, promises a far different event. "Feminine Flurry," it announces in bold print, followed by "How the fair sex were persuaded to serve as officers of the A.L.A."[62] According to the article, and the smaller headline, the ladies' meeting resembled a teacup far more than a tempest. Nevertheless, a meeting of forty of Albuquerque's leading society ladies somehow managed to solicit comparisons to stormy weather and chaotic, flurried activity. The "fair sex" of one headline contrasts sharply, and significantly, with the "feminine flurry" of the other. Once again, bourgeois women in public could provoke contradictory, anxious moments.

Such anxiety could work in the opposite direction as well, as accounts of respectable women behaving badly competed with depictions of commercially successfully and upwardly aspiring "disorderly" women. Lizzie McGrath, for instance, was not only a brothel owner; she was a very successful brothel owner. During her four decades in Albuquerque, McGrath, as several sources make clear, was an outstanding entrepreneur. Evidence about her ability to amass significant wealth appears in this newspaper report from 1883: "Miss Lizzie McGarth [sic], the lily of Copper Avenue, had $140 in coin stolen from her room yesterday. She was absent from her room at that time . . . and she credits a gentleman who wore eyeglasses with being the thief."[63] Lizzie McGrath—a notorious prostitute, leading "denizen of the half world," and clearly one of the most prominent "loose" and abandoned women and soiled doves of early Albuquerque—managed nonetheless to claim for herself several of the key components of middle-class respectability. She was, in a period of great mobility in America, remarkably stable and immobile. She lived in Albuquerque some forty years in roughly the same downtown neighborhood. She was a home owner and ran her own, quite profitable business. She was an employer and in census schedule after census schedule, the head of her own household. Moreover, she clearly felt entitled to use the legal system, so entitled in fact that she was one of the very few women, or men, to be able to afford, considering lawyer fees and the like, to appeal a case to the New Mexico Supreme Court.

Finally, take the tale of Carrie Swain, another humor piece linking body practices associated with consumer culture with deviance. In a likely fictitious article entitled "Brave Carrie Swain," two well-known society ladies are saved from drowning by the actress Carrie Swain. Hearing their calls for help, Swain "hastily divest[ed] herself of her garments" and "plunged into the water," saving the women from certain death by supporting their bodies until "a boat was manned and put out from the shore." According to the article, the rescue of the two women brought to a total of seven lives that Carrie Swain had saved over the summer, not to mention her rescue three years earlier of the daughter of a prominent San Francisco publisher. The high number of rescues, Swain's occupation as an actress, and the careful wording of the article ("divested herself of her garments" and "a boat was *manned*") suggest a bit of a send-up. Even as a lark, though, the article is telling. The piece explicitly associates abnormal gender roles, exemplified by Carrie Swain, the heroic woman and the female public performer, with acts of (female) bodily excess: stripping off one's clothes, plunging into the ocean, and supporting the bodies of two women. Certain body practices, in this case excessive and spectacular ones, like those of the actress Carrie Swain, thus are discursively linked with sexual difference and abnormal gender roles. Moreover, in a period of transforming gender roles, and concern on the part of men over the continued power and potency of white masculinity, Carrie Swain's heroism, even in jest, speaks to the fears as well as the jeers of a world turned upside down.[64]

Anxiety emerged in humor sections of the newspaper as well. Humor pieces frequently addressed the often-strained relationship between customers and retail merchants and clerks. One joke, titled "Almost Compulsory," finds "Esmeralda" noting to her friend, "You seem to be acquainted with that shopgirl who nodded to you." "Gwendolen" then replies, "Yes, I don't dare to snub her. She sold me most of my pompadour I'm wearing and she remembers it."[65] The joke is especially interesting, for it confirms Susan Porter Benson's contention that great tension existed between women shoppers and the mostly female clerks in department stores.[66] The joke recognizes the power that certain "shopgirls" wielded over their customers, forcing them (with the threat of exposing the sources of their beauty—"she sold me most of my pompadour I'm wearing and she remembers it") to acknowledge a certain social standing and not to "snub" the clerks.

The anxiety over such consuming women, and the contradictions of consumer culture exposed in their descriptions, was minor compared to the anxiety in newspaper articles about disorderly racial bodies. Another imperial setting around the turn of the twentieth century offers a useful comparison: Puerto Rico. Eileen Suárez Findlay has recently described overlapping systems of sexual and racial control in Ponce, Puerto Rico, during the decades immediately preceding and following U.S. occupation in 1898. Focusing on anti-prostitution campaigns, attempts to reform marriage, and radical sexual politics, Findlay argues that working-class (or plebian, as she says) Afro–Puerto Rican women, though often targeted as particular threats to social order, consistently turned to both Spanish and American courts to defend their rights.[67]

In polyglot New Mexico, a similarly visible heterogeneous population (recall the Indian woman on the streetcar or the comments about Hispanos and consumer culture) also made claims to public respectability. Likewise, those defined as sexually and racially "other" often proved difficult to control. Nonbourgeois women often purchased consumer products like dresses and hats, and even paraded themselves in public with such "incorrect" goods. Navajo "squaws" may have occasionally fallen off streetcars, but one must assume that many more managed to negotiate with ease the streetcars of urban New Mexico.

One article titled "Loud Language" reads as follows:

> Dolores Garcia y Savedra was brought before Judge Sullivan yesterday morning on complaint of Manuel Greening, charging her with abusive language. The heart of the judge was touched by the sight of one of the gentler sex, and he bade the woman go her way, after advising her to put a check to her tongue.[68]

This article illustrates the enduring ambiguity within the racialized order in New Mexico. Demonized as lacking bodily control ("abusive language," a tongue in need of "checking"), Dolores, a member of the "gentler sex," still managed to transgress certain boundaries of bourgeois New Mexico. After all, though arrested for "abusive language," Dolores Garcia y Savedra nevertheless used that same language, the same "unchecked" tongue, to talk her way out of a fine. Whether speaking abusively or talking sweet, "public" women like Dolores Garcia y Savedra were disruptive forces in the emerging New Mexico order. Sexual and racialized bodies, though discursively excluded from respectability, still inspired a fair share of anxious moments.

Another article, from February 1882, illustrates the explicitly racial and sexual tenor of this anxiety. "A Lost Confidence" reads:

> An Old Town merchant keeps, or rather kept, a clerk. Tuesday he told the young man that he intended to go to the new town and would return in three to four hours. He did not go to new town but went away a safe distance and watched for developments. Soon a handsome young señorita on whom the gay and frisky counter hopper had made a match entered the establishment. Shortly afterward the front door was closed, it is presumed for the reason that the young man did not care to have his billing and cooing open to public gaze. The enraged employer interrupted the proceedings and gave the clerk his walking papers. Another case of loving not wisely but too well.[69]

The article paints a familiar scene of overlapping sexual passion ("gay and frisky," "loving not wisely but too well") and racialization (a "young señorita"). The piece even includes the wonderful image of the clerk hopping over a store counter to court his lover, literally vaulting through a critical boundary between producer and consumer in the emerging consumer order. The title of the article, "A Lost Confidence," however, betrays this easy interpretation. The suspicious owner of the store returns to fire the clerk, but is left without an employee and, worse, unable to leave subsequent workers alone in the store. As the bittersweet headline suggests, the owner, like respectable New Mexicans throughout the era, depended on (or had "confidence" in) the limited and well-monitored presence of racial and sexualized bodies as well as their discursive exclusion. The tension between the headline and the text of the article suggests the anxiety and contradiction inherent in such a vexed relationship.

In fact, the anxiety generated by consumer culture—in the advertisements, mass-produced consumer goods, retail sales jobs, even the potentially dangerous rides aboard streetcars—exposed deeper anxieties in New Mexico. The quilt work of conquest and incorporation produced great tension as well as well-ordered bodies. Even under the most stable of conditions, the emerging Anglo/Hispano order in New Mexico, exemplified by the shared white bodies of elite Hispanos and Anglos, took a great deal of work to maintain. Unruly folks (bourgeois women, poor Hispanos, Indians, African Americans, prostitutes) at times proved far more excessive, far more dangerous, indeed far more "gauzy," than New Mexico's colonial order could fully contain or adequately tuck in. Physical bodies, the foundation of the search for racialized order, served simultaneously as the focus of anxiety as well as the stage for occasional small acts of resistance.

CONCLUSION

BIRTH OF A *COYOTE* NATION

For newcomers and natives alike facing the unexpected in an imperfectly translated land, unsettling encounters occurred throughout turn-of-the-century New Mexico, stretching beyond the train depot, into courtrooms and hospitals, stores and households, schools and processions. Human bodies were at the center of these encounters. As the preceding chapters have demonstrated, New Mexicans routinely described, evaluated, debated, and condemned a range of body practices. One of the major arguments of *Coyote Nation* is that the actions of human bodies, the bodily comportments of a dizzying assortment of New Mexicans, became fundamental to an emerging racial order.

In New Mexico, the power of settled groups like Hispano elites dampened the utility of traditional forms of social ordering based on racial binaries. The importance of bodily comportment to the formation of racial order was therefore amplified in New Mexico. Descriptions of human bodies tended to condense around, and were fundamental to the creation of, particular racialized groups: Indians, Hispanos, African Americans, "whites." Pueblo children found their bodily habits to be the subject of special concern, as educators focused intently on speech, type of clothing, length of hair, proper consumption, dancing, and medical treatment. In rape trials, women's physical acts of self-defense came under scrutiny, as did vaginal intercourse, the consumption of alcohol, and genital examination. Public body practices also came to the forefront in New Mexico, with detailed descriptions of the bodies of New Mexicans as they danced, chanted, and marched in public events. In the realm of marriage and domesticity, newspapers contrasted marital sexual intercourse with commercial sex like prostitution, and described aberrant acts such as the excessive consumption of alcohol, public nudity, and interracial sexual intimacy. In medical journals, particular embodied actions, like spitting or walking with stooped shoulders or tilting forward one's pelvis, helped determine racial identity, including, importantly, the whiteness of New Mexico physicians. Likewise, newspaper advertisements and articles championed wearing proper clothes and consuming the right food and drink as requisite to whiteness, while simultaneously condemning awkward tumbles and unsightly faces.

In certain respects, the sculpting of a social order from the stuff of body practices in New Mexico appears little different from the same process in broader turn-of-the-century America. In both New Mexico and the wider United States, physicians were treated with deference and allowed unprecedented access to the bodies of their (mostly female) patients. Identifying a woman as a prostitute or a quasi-prostitute likewise barred that woman from the full protection of the law and the ability to bring rape charges. The reputation of a New Mexican as a drunkard would, as in America in general, limit that individual's credibility before a judge or a jury. Furthermore, the ability, especially for a woman, to consume properly (wear the appropriate clothes and manage one's body effectively) permitted her to walk city streets throughout the United States without fear of arrest or ridicule.

In many cases, the particular attributes of racialized and sexualized individuals and groups in New Mexico will also appear familiar to observers of turn-of-the-twentieth-century America. Take, for instance, the images of the supposedly uncivilized Indian children, or the infectious prostitute, or the outsize dialect of African Americans, or the dangerous consuming women. Or notice that whiteness and masculinity in both New Mexico and post-Reconstruction America appeared as the provinces of well-regulated, temperate, and proper body movements and habits.

At the same time, other aspects of New Mexico may not appear so familiar to readers, just as New Mexico appeared odd and disquieting to contemporary observers. Indeed, the racialization process in particular proceeded far differently in New Mexico. New Mexico's Hispano elites, though representing a small percentage of the population, exerted considerable power in New Mexico. Elite Hispano men and women were not ridiculed in the press nor disallowed from bringing rape charges nor forbidden from participating in Memorial Day parades. The emerging New Mexico social order appeared flexible enough to permit the entrance of select "native" New Mexicans. Those individuals displaying correct body practices (consuming the right products, celebrating the right holidays, wearing the right fashions and hairstyles, and consorting with the right men and women), even if their first language was Spanish or last names were Otero or Perea or Armijo, could claim civic legitimacy in New Mexico.

In another difference, masculinity in New Mexico—and civilization and whiteness—emphasized length of hair and type of clothing to an extent uncommon in the rest of the country. While becoming a man in the United States in general required certain hair and clothes, in New Mexico long hair and "Indian" styles immediately marked a male individual as racially and sexually different, making one vulnerable to a variety of material dangers and disadvantages including the inability to vote and less protection from the courts. Thus, although New Mexico faithfully mirrored broader America in many ways, in critical other respects the Land of Enchantment, as New Mexico would come to be known, remained a territory different.

In proposing the centrality of bodily comportment to the developing racial order of modernizing New Mexico, *Coyote Nation* calls for a revised approach to commonly understood topics in American history like modernity, imperialism, whiteness, and Chicano history. In the first place, American modernity (defined, recall, in the introduction as the collapsing of time and space into new sets of measurable relationships), and the attendant emergence of mass consumer culture, new forms of sexual and racial classification and control, scientific and medical discourses and technologies, political transformations, and professionalization were unmistakable in New Mexico. The elevation in status and authority of the medical profession, for instance, is for several scholars integral to modernity. Carroll Smith-Rosenberg, Lisa Duggan, Leslie Reagan, Alexandra Stern, and others have correctly noted the increasing prominence of physicians in creating and dispersing sexual knowledge in America during the turn of the twentieth century.[1] Similarly, in New Mexico arenas such as rape trials, the physician and the special role of the invariably male medical expert in gathering and dispensing for the court his specialized medical knowledge of sexuality proved especially significant. Recall from chapter 3 the deference and respect afforded Dr. McClanahan during his description of his physical examination, including a vaginal examination, of Margaret Carling.

The link between modernity and sexuality has also been fruitfully examined by several writers. John D'Emilio and Estelle Freedman in *Intimate Matters*, their invaluable survey of the history of American sexualities, pinpoint the years between 1880 and 1930 as the beginnings of American sexual modernity. D'Emilio and Freedman highlight two transformations in particular: (1) an acknowledgment that for women, as well as men, sexuality was a fundamental component of one's individual identity; and (2) the increasing public visibility of sexuality, in commercial sex like prostitution, medical discourses, newspaper accounts, film, and mass-circulation periodicals. As the preceding chapters attest, sexual discourses in New Mexico circulated widely between 1880 and 1920, almost precisely the same period described by D'Emilio and Freedman.[2] Likewise, *Coyote Nation* confirms the notion that a focus on the individual body was basic to modern America. Recall from the Indian schools the focus on individual grooming and care of the body and the emphasis on each student's personal cultivation of civilized bodily comportment; or the expressions of individual sexual desire in rape trials, as when Geronimo Pino's lawyer asked him if he had ever "wanted to" rape Andrea Cordova; or the proliferation of advertisements promising consumers, as individuals, everything from abortifacients to "gauzy" underwear to restored "manhood."

At the same time that it supports the above contentions about American sexual modernity, *Coyote Nation* calls attention to a major gap in the existing scholarship on the rise of modern America. The relationship between race and modernity, especially in studies of the emergence of sexual modernity, continues to vex scholars. Even those historians committed to addressing race and racial formation nonetheless frequently only do so within a distressingly narrow framework of white and black. Lisa Duggan, for example, argues that American modernity is at its core fundamentally racialized. Yet Duggan is silent on racial matters beyond the binary of black and white. By highlighting the process of racialization in a region of profound cultural heterogeneity, where, in addition to Anglos and African Americans, Indians and Hispanos were prominent, *Coyote Nation* has pointed to the great rewards available to scholars willing to engage racial heterogeneity rather than racial binaries in their study of modern sexuality. It is significant, for instance, that the presence of Hispano elites heightened the importance of bodily comportment and sexuality in the process of racialization. Likewise, note the pivotal role of African Americans, though small in terms of population, in discourses on race and racial difference.[3]

This study has also located New Mexico at the muddy mouth of American imperialism, where the fresh water of nineteenth-century territorial expansion empties into the twentieth-century ocean of empire. *Coyote Nation* is a response to recent calls by scholars for a reinvigorated analysis of the "cultures of U.S. imperialism." Such calls, and the first-rate scholarship that accompanies them, have much to offer. In comparing, for instance, the anti-colonial writings of California novelist María

Amparo Ruiz de Burton with Cuban nationalist writer José Martí, literary scholars Rosaura Sánchez and José David Saldívar have bridged an important theoretical gap in the study of American imperialism, bringing into conversation historians and theorists of the U.S.-Mexico borderlands with scholars of the Latino Caribbean. Likewise, José Limón aptly notes the broader imperial tones struck by soldier/anthropologist John Gregory Burke's comparison, in his 1894 essay "The America Congo," of the Rio Grande to the Congo River in Africa.[4] At the same time, Vicente Rafael's stunning juxtaposition of census enumerations and theatrical performances as twin sites of imperial interrogation and resistance in the Philippines relocates culture and cultural production to the center of the study of American imperialism. So, too, do Amy Kaplan, in her essay on Theodore Roosevelt and the anxieties gnawing at white masculinity during the Spanish-American War, and Kristin Hoganson—who argues that domestic gender politics played formative roles in the decision to enter the war—demand that the racial and gender turmoil engulfing turn-of-the-twentieth-century America be understood as integral to American overseas expansion.[5]

Nonetheless, these works remain limited, either by privileging literary sources or by focusing, however brilliantly, on more traditional spaces of American imperialism like Puerto Rico, Cuba, and the Philippines. It is telling for instance, that Amy Kaplan's recent treatment of U.S. imperialism barely mentions the process of conquest and colonial incorporation occurring *at the same time* in New Mexico. *Coyote Nation*, by contrast, offers a historically grounded account of U.S. imperial aspirations drawn from *within* the confines of the continental United States.[6] In doing so, this project confirms and extends the pathbreaking work of Alexandra Stern and John Nieto-Phillips, who have focused, respectively, on public health and militarization along the U.S.-Mexico border and similarities in Puerto Rican and New Mexican educational policies. Other writers have made similar observations. Richard Rodriguez has recently noted that Richard Henry Dana viewed California in *Two Years Before the Mast* as "an extension of Latin America." Dana would hardly be surprised, Rodriguez says, to find that contemporary California "has become what it already was in the 1830s," that is, once again an extension of Latin America.[7]

I maintain that in parts of the Southwest, and in New Mexico in particular, Latin America may have actually endured well beyond the 1830s. In fact, turn-of-the-century New Mexico perhaps is better understood as one of the earliest "modern" extensions of the United States into Latin America. Indeed, a defining feature of modern America, its imperialistic adventure with Latin America, may have roots in New Mexico. It was in New Mexico, after all, that for the first time in modern American history, a univocal world was forced to come to terms with a settled, well-financed, polyglot population, one that would not easily be moved. Unlike California or Texas, where Californios and Tejanos rapidly lost land, political power, and status in the nineteenth century and Native Americans were alternately massacred or further displaced, New Mexico's "native" population, with Hispano elites being the most notable, managed to retain some measure of power. In this sense, New Mexico begins to look much more like Panama or Cuba or Puerto Rico.[8]

The pivotal role of New Mexico Hispanos, especially elite Hispanos, in the history of American imperialism was indebted in large measure to wealthy Hispanos' ability to assert, and defend, their claim to whiteness. *Coyote Nation* thus speaks also to the history of whiteness and whiteness studies. Historians of whiteness like David Roediger, Gail Bederman, George Lipsitz, Tomás Almaguer, Neil Foley, Matthew Frey Jacobson, and Lisa Duggan have made invaluable contributions to our understanding of race relations, power, and the creation and maintenance of social inequality. This project confirms many of their most significant arguments about the development and sustenance of white racialization projects. Besides his pioneering proposal that the history of whiteness in the United States is a deserving, indeed politically necessary, field of study, David Roediger's analysis of the role of whiteness in class formation demonstrates the pervasiveness of discourses of whiteness in nineteenth-century America. In newspapers, magazines, musical and theatrical performances, speeches, books, and pamphlets, talk of whiteness, according to Roediger, proliferated. So, too, was talk of whiteness, from newspaper articles and advertisements to medical journals, common in New Mexico. Similarly Gail Bederman's argument that supporters of white superiority in America relied upon claims that more "civilized" whites erected clear boundaries differentiating between men and women, and, conversely, that less civilized peoples tolerated, even encouraged, gender ambiguity, receives ample supporting evidence in New Mexico. Recall, for instance, the emphasis placed within U.S. Indian schools on clear boundaries between Indian boys and girls.[9]

Likewise, George Lipsitz's brave admonition against individuals of color who benefit from, and wittingly or not help support, white privilege in twentieth-century America, finds historical precedent in New Mexico. Note especially the ruling alliances formed by wealthy Hispanos with Anglo newcomers based largely on shared notions of whiteness, the superiority of white bodies, and the often vicious denunciations of the bodily comportment of non-elite Hispanos, Indians, and African Americans. Tomás Almaguer's and Neil Foley's depictions of the inner workings of white supremacy in California and Texas, respectively, where whites occupied the top rung of a racial hierarchy while a range of racialized others battled each for position along the lower rungs, is echoed in New Mexico, with the elevated position of wealthy Hispanos, in contrast to Indians and African Americans, again providing powerful historical support. Matthew Frey Jacobson usefully points out that significant divisions occurred within whiteness, that whiteness was not static nor monolithic, but dynamic and shifting according to historical context and setting. The shared claims of whiteness by Hispano elites and Anglos in New Mexico provides further evidence of such a multifaceted view of whiteness. Finally, Lisa Duggan's observation that celebrations of white domesticity and white homes were critical components of white supremacy applies nicely to New Mexico, where newspaper accounts of the supposed threats to the white home posed by African Americans and prostitutes helped solidify racial and social order.[10]

At the same time, *Coyote Nation* has been inspired by such authors' provocative, if at times all too brief, discussions of the role of sexuality in racial formation. Overlooked in such comments and the works in general, is the extent to which bodily comportment helped determine whiteness. *Coyote Nation* has demonstrated the centrality of bodily actions to many forms of racialization, including the racialization of elite Anglos and Hispanos. Indeed, the shared white body was integral to the naturalization of whiteness in New Mexico. Both through intermarriage and mass consumer culture, bodily actions proved fundamental to the development of a leadership cadre of Anglo and Hispano elites in New Mexico. Furthermore, this project has repeatedly highlighted the "productive effects" of sexual discourse within whiteness. That is, discourses of sexuality, whether denunciations of the deviant bodies of prostitutes or critiques of Pueblo domestic lives or medical accounts of masturbating girls or advertisements promising to cure sexual dysfunction, helped produce whiteness and sustain claims to white privilege. Ann Stoler is indeed correct when she insists that Michel Foucault's writings on the productive effects of sexual discourses can be of use to historians of race and imperialism. In fact, viewed from the perspective of New Mexico, it is quite clear that sexuality has been a critical factor not just in the history of whiteness, but in the broader history of U.S. racial formation.[11]

Finally, *Coyote Nation* adds to a growing, yet still relatively small body of work in Chicano history on the period 1880–1920. Chicano history, a vibrant field examining the history of Mexican-origin peoples in the United States, has focused on two time periods in particular: (1) the Spanish colonial period beginning roughly in 1600 and stretching to the aftermath of the Mexican-American War in 1848, and (2) from the beginning of large-scale Mexican immigration to the United States after 1910 and the Mexican Revolution to the Chicano movement of the 1960s. The turn of the twentieth century, by contrast, has received comparatively little attention. Nonetheless, a handful of recent studies have offered invaluable points of comparison to this project's concentration on the decades between 1880 and 1920. The racialization projects that Tomás Almaguer establishes for nineteenth-century California, where Anglos inserted themselves atop a complicated racial hierarchy, occurred in New Mexico as well. Neil Foley's examination of the establishment of white supremacy in Texas similarly resembles the New Mexico experience. Martha Menchaca has likewise documented the profound losses in land, political power, and social status that plagued Chicanos in the second half of the nineteenth century in the Southwest.[12]

While supporting such authors' well-placed emphasis on the late nineteenth and early twentieth centuries as critical decades in Chicano history, *Coyote Nation* speaks directly to two themes (modernity and sexuality) largely overlooked in their influential works. Hispanos in New Mexico were, like a great many Americans, a profoundly forward-looking people, engaged at multiple levels with the forces of modernity. Drawn to and by the modern world, Hispanos climbed aboard railroads, bought the latest consumer goods, depended on modern science and medicine, and in numerous other ways adapted to and adopted American modernity. Take, for example, the role of advertising and mass consumer culture in Hispano New Mexico. While historians like Vicki Ruiz have brilliantly described the impact of American popular culture, in the form of movie magazines and beauty products, on the daughters of Mexican immigrants in the middle decades of the twentieth century, such profound engagements with mass consumer culture, one of the hallmarks of modernity, clearly has far deeper roots in Chicana/o history. Indeed, historians of the American West interested in the region's modernization would be well served by looking at the role of nineteenth- and early-twentieth-century "consuming" Chicanos in the making of a modern West.[13]

Coyote Nation also demonstrates that the insidious racialization projects erected throughout the Southwest were directed fundamentally at the bodies and sexual practices of Chicanos and Indians. Thus, besides accounting more precisely for the currents of race and racialization animating social order in New Mexico, this study also calls attention to the various and varied body practices, coherent and incontinent, in the Chicano past. My work in this sense is deeply indebted to, and hopes to extend, the groundbreaking work in Chicano history by María Montoya, Sarah Deutsch, Deena González, and Antonia Castañeda. Like such authors, I argue that we need to investigate sexuality and embodiment to understand fully the racialization of Chicanos and the course of U.S. expansion.[14]

In conclusion, I have argued that the description, evaluation, and categorization of human bodies, through the use of modern materials like governmental institutions, medical discourse, and consumer culture, were fundamental to the racialized incorporation of New Mexico. This contention highlights New Mexico as a valuable case study in the constitution of modern racial and imperial order during a period of national instability and dislocation. To accentuate New Mexico's significant place in broader America, notice that Anglo and Hispano elites were hardly monolithic; they coexisted and interacted with a host of other discourses. Modernizing societies, after all, by their nature are heterogeneous and polyglot; a cacophony of divergent voices marks their emergence. As we have seen, the emerging New Mexico body politic (composed of Americans of predominantly northern European ancestry and a handful of Hispanos, Jews, and German and Italian immigrants) defined itself in two ways: (1) by depicting acceptable body practices as orderly and well controlled; and (2) by contrasting those practices and their resulting identities to a variety of poorly managed, excessive, inappropriate body practices.

Peter Stallybrass and Allon White have argued that bourgeois identity in general was based on precisely this process of exclusion. Stallybrass and White also note, however, that the disgust so central to elite projects of exclusion (the designation of certain peoples and their bodily practices as "low, dirty, repulsive, noisy, [and] contaminating") inevitably returned as "the object of nostalgia, longing and fascination." Disgust, in other words, "always [bore] the imprint of desire."[15] Eric Lott has described a like phenomenon in nineteenth-century America. Black minstrelsy, he notes, represented more than the exploitation of African American performers and the theft of their material and cultural productions. Minstrel performances also produced and were produced by deep feelings of fascination and "love" for African Americans among whites. In particular, Lott argues, "white male desire for black men was everywhere to be found in minstrel acts."[16] Ann Stoler makes a similar observation in her analysis of the complicated relationship between various "projects" of European colonial domination and Michel Foucault's notion of bourgeois identity formation. Stoler observes that the same "colonial discourses on moral reform and sexual regulation . . . that spoke incessantly of the subversive dangers of [colonized peoples] and their moral perversions," also managed to "create spaces" for the incitement of inappropriate sexual desire.[17] In the works of the above authors, as well as in recent scholarship in a number of fields, disgust (whether colonial attention to sexual perversion or the vulgar caricatures of African Americans in minstrel shows) always accompanies and is accompanied by desire. Dread, to paraphrase Judith Walkowitz, never strayed too far from Delight.[18]

The anxiety and contradictions bursting forth from New Mexico trial transcripts, medical journals, newspaper articles, and government documents suggest a similar tension in turn-of-the-century New Mexico between disgust (exclusion, demonization, cruel parody) and desire (fascination, obsessive scrutiny, symbolic centrality). How else to explain the hydra-headed monsters, female rapists, masturbating girls, and promiscuous expectorators lurking at the edges of even the most level-headed and measured medical discourses? Or hyperbolic attacks on New Mexico's tiny African American community? Or the nervous snickers accompanying newspaper articles about "feminine flurries," stains of "lukewarm liquid," and Navajo "squaws" on streetcars?

Such accounts from the turn of the twentieth century may seem far removed from the turn of the twenty-first. Yet, I would argue, just as American imperial incursions into New Mexico offered a preview of U.S. foreign interventions in Latin America and elsewhere for a century to come, so, too, does the significance of bodily comportment in New Mexico resonate deeply with contemporary race relations. After all, twenty-first-century American race relations have much in common with New Mexico a century ago. As in New Mexico, racial heterogeneity, not racial binaries, predominate in the United States, especially in the wake of recent large-scale immigration from Latin America and Asia. Likewise, the economic and political power of a small percentage of African Americans, Latinos, and Asian Americans has precluded the widespread denigration of entire racialized groups, a process resembling that which occurred as a result of the power of elite Hispanos in New Mexico. In this context, bodily comportment is of great significance in determining social status, respectability, and citizenship in contemporary America.

A final conclusion of *Coyote Nation* therefore is that contemporary America may have much to learn from borderlands regions such as turn-of-the-twentieth-century New Mexico. Indeed, postmodern America—unsettled, polyglot, brimming with the mongrel and hybrid—should heed the modern howls of a *coyote* New Mexico.

NOTES

CHAPTER ONE

1. Richard White has noted that by 1900 the American West "depended on out-side markets, outside capital, and, most often, skills and technologies im-ported from the outside," and New Mexico was certainly no exception. Richard White, *"It's Your Misfortune and None of My Own": A New History of the American West* (Norman: University of Oklahoma Press, 1991), 267. See also the work of María E. Montoya on southeastern New Mexico, *Translating Property: The Maxwell Land Grant and the Conflict over Land in the American West, 1840–1900* (Berkeley: University of California Press, 2002).

2. U.S. Bureau of the Census, *Fourteenth Census of the United States* (Washington, DC, 1920).

3. Polingaysi Qoyawayma, *No Turning Back: A True Account of a Hopi Indian Girl's Struggle to Bridge the Gap between the World of Her People and the World of the White Man* (Albuquerque: University of New Mexico Press, 1964), 55; Charles Brown, quoted in Lillian Schlissel, Byrd Gibbons, and Elizabeth Hampsten, eds., *Far from Home: Families of the Westward Journey* (New York: Schocken Books, 1989), 142; Ernest Peixotto, *Our Hispanic Southwest* (New York: Charles Scribner's Sons, 1916), 162.

4. "Expansion Continental and Overseas," in Eric Foner and John A. Garraty, eds., *The Reader's Companion to American History* (Boston: Houghton Mifflin Co., 1991), 368.

5. Myron P. Gutmann et al., "The Demographic Impact of the Mexican Revo-lution in the United States" (translation of "Los efectos demográficos de la

revolución Mexicana en Estados Unidos," *Historica Mexicana* 50 [2000]), 6; Tomás Almaguer, *Racial Fault Lines: The Historical Origins of White Supremacy in California* (Berkeley: University of California Press, 1994), 130.

6. John Mack Faragher et al., eds., *Out of Many, Volume One, Brief 4th Edition* (New York: Prentice Hall, 2003), 353–54.

7. Gutmann et al., "The Demographic Impact," 6. Between 1880 and 1920, unlike California or Texas, relatively few Mexican immigrants arrived in New Mexico. Richard L. Nostrand, *The Hispano Homeland* (Norman: University of Oklahoma Press, 1992), 164. Such immigrants to the American Southwest are often credited with revitalizing Chicano culture in the region, with strengthening a sense of Mexican identity. New Mexico, however, remained in relative terms only a "minor destination" for immigrants from Mexico throughout the twentieth century. For a recent discussion of the role of immigration in the creation of identity, see David G. Gutiérrez, "Migration, Emergent Ethnicity, and the 'Third Space': The Shifting Politics of Nationalism in Greater Mexico," *Journal of American History* 86 (September 1999): 481–517.

8. U.S. Census, 1920.

9. David R. Roediger, *The Wages of Whiteness: Race and the Making of the American Working Class* (London: Verso, 1991); George Lipsitz, *The Possessive Investment in Whiteness: How White People Profit from Identity Politics* (Philadelphia: Temple University Press, 1998), vii. Other recent studies of whiteness are Eric Lott, *Love and Theft: Blackface Minstrelsy and the American Working Class* (New York: Oxford University Press, 1995); Ruth Frankenberg, *White Women, Race Matters: The Social Construction of Whiteness* (Minneapolis: University of Minnesota Press, 1993); and Matthew Frye Jacobson, *Whiteness of a Different Color: European Immigrants and the Alchemy of Race* (Cambridge: Harvard University Press, 1998).

10. U.S. Census, 1920.

11. For some notable interpretations of American history during this period, see Almaguer, *Racial Fault Lines*; Gail Bederman, *Manliness and Civilization: A Cultural History of Gender and Race in the United States, 1880–1917* (Chicago: University of Chicago Press, 1995); John D'Emilio and Estelle Freedman, *Intimate Matters: A History of Sexuality in America* (New York: Harper and Row, 1988); Lisa Duggan, *Sapphic Slashers: Sex, Violence, and American Modernity* (Durham, NC: Duke University Press, 2000); Neil Foley, *The White Scourge: Mexicans, Blacks, and Poor Whites in Texas Cotton Culture* (Berkeley: University of California Press, 1997); Glenda Gilmore, *Gender and Jim Crow: Women and the Politics of White Supremacy in North Carolina, 1896–1920* (Chapel Hill: University of North Carolina Press, 1996); Grace Elizabeth Hale, *Making Whiteness: The Culture of Segregation in the South* (New York: Pantheon Press, 1998); Martha Hodes, *White Women, Black Men: Illicit Sex in the Nineteenth-Century South* (New Haven: Yale University Press, 1997); Amy Kaplan and

Donald E. Pease, eds., *Cultures of United States Imperialism* (Durham, NC: Duke University Press, 1993); Nina Silber, *The Romance of Reunion: Northerners and the South, 1865–1900* (Chapel Hill: University of North Carolina Press, 1994); Carroll Smith-Rosenberg, *Disorderly Conduct: Visions of Gender in Victorian America* (New York: Oxford University Press, 1985); Alan Trachtenberg, *The Incorporation of America: Culture and Society in the Gilded Age* (New York: Hill and Wang, 1982); Robert H. Wiebe, *The Search for Order, 1877–1920* (New York: Hill and Wang, 1967); and C. Vann Woodward, *Origins of the New South, 1877–1913* (Baton Rouge: Louisiana State University Press, 1951).

12. Marc Simmons, *New Mexico: An Interpretive History* (Albuquerque: University of New Mexico Press, 1977), 164; Ramón A. Gutiérrez, *When Jesus Came, the Corn Mothers Went Away: Marriage, Sexuality, and Power in New Mexico, 1500–1846* (Stanford: Stanford University Press, 1991). See also Judith B. De-Mark, "The Immigrant Experience in Albuquerque, 1880–1920" (Ph.D. diss., University of New Mexico, 1984); Sarah Deutsch, *No Separate Refuge: Culture, Class, and Gender on an Anglo-Hispanic Frontier in the American Southwest, 1880–1940* (New York: Oxford University Press, 1987); Deena J. González, "The Spanish-Mexican Women of Santa Fé: Patterns of Their Resistance and Accommodation, 1820–1880" (Ph.D. diss., University of California, Berkeley, 1985); Howard R. Lamar, *The Far Southwest, 1846–1912* (New York: W. W. Norton, 1970); Robert W. Larson, *New Mexico's Quest for Statehood, 1846–1912* (Albuquerque: University of New Mexico Press, 1968); Terry Jon Lehman, "Santa Fé and Albuquerque 1870–1900: Contrast and Conflict in the Development of Two Southwestern Towns" (Ph.D. diss., Indiana University, 1974); Montoya, *Translating Property*; Charles H. Montgomery, *The Spanish Redemption: Heritage, Power, and Loss on New Mexico's Upper Rio Grande* (Berkeley: University of California Press, 2002); John M. Nieto-Phillips, " 'No Other Blood': History, Language, and 'Spanish American' Ethnic Identity in New Mexico, 1880s–1920s" (Ph.D. diss., University of California, Los Angeles, 1997); Nostrand, *The Hispano Homeland*; Estévan Rael-Gálvez, "Identifying Captivity and Capturing Identity: Narratives of American Indian Slavery, Colorado and New Mexico, 1776–1934" (Ph.D. diss., University of Michigan, 2002); and David A. Reichard, " 'Justice is God's law': The Struggle to Control Social Conflict and United States Colonization of New Mexico, 1846–1912" (Ph.D. diss., Temple University, 1996).

13. Gutiérrez, *When Jesus Came*, 46.

14. Nostrand, *The Hispano Homeland*, 50; Gutiérrez, *When Jesus Came*, chap. 1.

15. Gutiérrez, *When Jesus Came*, chap. 4.

16. Ibid.

17. Martha Menchaca, *Recovering History, Constructing Race: The Indian, Black, and White Roots of Mexican Americans* (Austin: University of Texas Press, 2001), 96.

18. While I will use more specific designations when at all possible (such as Navajo or Pueblo Indian or Laguna Pueblo), "Indian" will appear here as a general term to cover the various Native American cultural and ethnic groups in the broader New Mexico region.

19. Margaret D. Jacobs, *Engendered Encounters: Feminism and Pueblo Cultures, 1879–1934* (Lincoln: University of Nebraska Press, 1999), 11; David Wallace Adams, *Education for Extinction: American Indians and the Boarding School Experience, 1875–1928* (Lawrence: University of Kansas Press, 1995), 56, 58.

20. Joe S. Sando, *Pueblo Nations: Eight Centuries of Pueblo Indian History* (Santa Fe: Clear Light Publishers, 1998), 88, 107–10; Jacobs, *Engendered Encounters*, 9, 12; see also Rael-Gálvez, "Identifying Captivity." Other Indian groups in New Mexico, like the Navajo, Apache, and Ute, were forced onto official reservations where they were treated as dependents of the U.S. government. It is also worth noting that despite their "civilized" nature, Pueblo Indians were still denied voting rights and full legal American citizenship until 1948.

21. Nostrand, *The Hispano Homeland*, 61, 65, 67. New Mexico's "nomad" Indian population of 4,341 was determined by subtracting the 968 Ute Indians living in Colorado from the total 5,309 "nomad" Indians living in New Mexico Territory and southwestern Colorado.

22. Gutmann et al., "The Demographic Impact," 6.

23. Regrettably, discerning the precise influence of Pueblo Indian, and other Indian, heritage within post-1880 Hispano culture is beyond the scope of this study. Surname alone is often not sufficient as New Mexican Indians frequently had Spanish first and last names. Individuals of mixed Anglo and Hispano heritage are similarly difficult to identify with great precision. Considering the disproportionate number of intermarriages involving Anglo men and Hispanas, and resulting people of mixed heritage with English surnames, however, it is unlikely that the category Hispano contained a large number of mixed-heritage individuals with Spanish surnames.

24. Montgomery, *The Spanish Redemption*, 8; Deutsch, *No Separate Refuge*, 29.

25. DeMark, "The Immigrant Experience," 115, 118, 120, 124; Nostrand, *The Hispano Homeland*; Deutsch, *No Separate Refuge*.

26. Nostrand, *The Hispano Homeland*, 20, 45, 97; Deutsch, *No Separate Refuge*, 31; DeMark, "The Immigrant Experience," 160; McKinney, "History of the Albuquerque Indian School," 133.

27. Nostrand, *The Hispano Homeland*, 19–20, 45, 97, 71, 145, 169–71. See also Deutsch, *No Separate Refuge*; and Montoya, *Translating Property*.

28. U.S. Bureau of the Census, *Tenth Census of the United States* (Washington, DC, 1880); U.S. Bureau of the Census, *Twelfth Census of the United States* (Washington, DC, 1900); U.S. Census, 1920. Following are statistics on birthplaces of New Mexico newcomers. In 1880: Texas (1,027), California (1,131), Missouri (883), Ohio (826), Mexico (5,173), Ireland (795), and "the German

empire" (729). In 1900: Texas (8,724), Missouri (3,458), Colorado (2,721), Illinois (2,531), Mexico (6,649), Germany (1,360), Ireland (692), and Italy (661). In 1920: Texas (34,936), Missouri (9,837), Oklahoma (7,551), Mexico (20,272), Germany (1,178), Ireland (434), and Italy (1,678). Nostrand, *The Hispano Homeland*, 105, 107.

29. Nostrand, *The Hispano Homeland*, 110, 112, 116, 118; DeMark, "The Immigrant Experience," 124, 160.

30. U.S. Census, 1880, 1900, 1910, 1920; DeMark, "The Immigrant Experience," 124. See Jacobson, *Whiteness of a Different Color*, for similar patterns in the creation of whiteness in broader America. Peter Stallybrass and Allon White, *The Politics and Poetics of Transgression* (Ithaca: Cornell University Press, 1986), 5–6.

31. Montoya, *Translating Property*, 85, 91.

32. Reichard, " 'Justice is God's law,' " 290–91.

33. Ibid., 253, 251.

34. Ibid., 271.

35. Throughout the territorial period, women in New Mexico could not vote in territorial elections and, as mentioned, Pueblo Indians were denied suffrage in territorial, state, and national elections until 1948.

36. Howard R. Lamar, ed., *The New Encyclopedia of the American West* (New Haven: Yale University Press, 1998), 929, 1101, 1227.

37. Larson, *New Mexico's Quest for Statehood*.

38. U.S. Census, 1920.

39. Quoted in Nieto-Phillips, " 'No Other Blood,' " 88, 108.

40. Vicente L. Rafael, "White Love: Surveillance and Nationalist Resistance in the U.S. Colonization of the Philippines," in *Cultures of United States Imperialism*, ed. Amy Kaplan and Donald E. Pease (Durham, NC: Duke University Press, 1993), 185–218. See also Pedro A. Cabán, *Constructing a Colonial People: Puerto Rico and the United States, 1898–1932* (New York: Westview Press, 1999); Eileen J. Suarez Findlay, *Imposing Decency: The Politics of Sexuality and Race in Puerto Rico, 1870–1920* (Durham, NC: Duke University Press, 2000); Kelvin A. Santiago-Valles, *"Subject People" and Colonial Discourses: Economic Transformation and Social Disorder in Puerto Rico, 1898–1947* (Albany: State University of New York Press, 1994); and Ann L. Stoler, *Race and the Education of Desire: Foucault's History of Sexuality and the Colonial Order of Things* (Durham, NC: Duke University Press, 1996).

41. See Jacobs, *Engendered Encounters*; Rael-Gálvez, "Identifying Captivity"; and Montoya, *Translating Property*.

42. Anselmo Arellano, "The People's Movement: Las Gorras Blancas," in *The Contested Homeland: A Chicano History of New Mexico*, ed. Erlinda Gonzales-Berry and David Maciel (Albuquerque: University of New Mexico Press, 2000), 59–82; *Laws of the State of New Mexico* (Albuquerque: Albright & Anderson, 1912); *Laws of the State of New Mexico* (Albuquerque: Central Printing, 1921). See also

A. Gabriel Meléndez, *"So All Is Not Lost": The Poetics of Print in Nuevomexi-cano Communities, 1834–1958* (Albuquerque: University of New Mexico Press, 1997); Doris Meyer, *Speaking for Themselves: Neomexicano Cultural Identity and the Spanish-Language Press, 1880–1920* (Albuquerque: University of New Mexico Press, 1996); Montgomery, *The Spanish Redemption*; Montoya, *Translating Property*; and Nieto-Phillips, " 'No Other Blood.' "

43. See, for instance, Ramón A. Gutiérrez, "Decolonizing the Body: Kinship and the Nation," *American Archivist* 57 (Winter 1994): 86–99.

44. *Albuquerque Daily Citizen*, March 19, 1895, 2.

45. Mary Douglas, *Natural Symbols: Explorations in Cosmology* (New York: Rout-ledge, 1970), 74, 77; Stallybrass and White, *Politics and Poetics of Transgression*, 22–23. See also William Miller, *The Anatomy of Disgust* (Cambridge: Harvard University Press, 1997); and Alan Hyde, *Bodies of Law* (Princeton: Princeton University Press, 1997).

46. For recent examples, see Charles Montgomery, "The Trap of Race and Mem-ory: The Language of Spanish Civility on the Upper Rio Grande," *American Quarterly* 52 (September 2000): 478–513; and John Nieto-Phillips, "Spanish American Ethnic Identity and New Mexico's Statehood Struggle," in *Contested Homeland: A Chicano History of New Mexico*, ed. Erlinda Gonzales-Berry and David R. Maciel (Albuquerque: University of New Mexico Press, 2000), 97–142. Studies of this era in New Mexico history that address gender and sexuality more directly include Deutsch, *No Separate Refuge*; Meyer, *Speaking for Them-selves*; Jacobs, *Engendered Encounters*; and Montoya, *Translating Property*.

47. Nancy Leys Stepan, "Race, Gender, Science, and Citizenship," *Gender and His-tory* 10 (April 1998): 30.

48. Michael Omi and Howard Winant define race as "a concept which signifies and symbolizes social conflicts and interests by referring to different types of human bodies." See Michael Omi and Howard Winant, *Racial Formation in the United States: From the 1960's to the 1990's* (New York: Routledge, 1994); 55. See also Almaguer, *Racial Fault Lines*, for an innovative application of theories of racialization to a specific historical context.

49. Estelle Freedman and John D'Emilio consider "sexuality" to encompass far more than procreative sex, covering "the procreation of children, the attain-ment of physical pleasure (eroticism), recreation or sport, personal intimacy, spiritual transcendence, [and] power over others." Such a broad definition of sexuality includes masculinity and femininity, gendered images and dis-courses, as well as legal and illegal uses of the body. The inclusiveness of the definition of sexuality also nicely approximates the wide range of sexual acts, sexual actors, and sexual bodies that are defined as abnormal and deviant. D'Emilio and Freedman, *Intimate Matters*, xv.

50. This is one of the more famous lines from the movie *Usual Suspects* (1995).

51. José Limón, *Dancing with the Devil: Society and Cultural Poetics in Mexican-American South Texas* (Madison: University of Wisconsin Press, 1994), 26.

52. Record Group 75, entry 40, Santa Fe, 1903, Pueblo Records, National Archives and Records Administration, Rocky Mountain Branch, Denver, Colorado (hereafter RG 75).

53. Ibid.

54. I borrow here from the title of Judith R. Walkowitz, *City of Dreadful Delight: Narratives of Sexual Danger in Late-Victorian London* (Chicago: University of Chicago Press, 1991).

CHAPTER TWO

1. RG 75, entry 83, subheading 806.

2. Ibid.

3. Qoyawayma, *No Turning Back*, 160.

4. Thanks to Beth McLaughlin for making this valuable observation.

5. Douglas, *Natural Symbols*; Stallybrass and White, *The Politics and Poetics of Transgression*; Anne McClintock, *Imperial Leather: Race, Gender, and Sexuality in the Colonial Contest* (London: Routledge, 1995).

6. Adams, *Education for Extinction*, ix, 14. Adams's *Education for Extinction* focuses on the boarding-school experience for Native Americans, analyzing policy formation, the specific goals and practices of policy makers and reformers, and the varied responses to such actions by students and their families. While Adams provides many valuable examples of conflicts over sexual norms and expectations in the context of the schools, his study does not directly address the intersecting threads of race and sexuality in the Anglo–Native American educational experience.

7. Adams, *Education for Extinction*, 56–58; Edward H. Spicer, *Cycles of Conquest: The Impact of Spain, Mexico, and the United States on the Indians of the Southwest, 1533–1960* (Tucson: University of Arizona Press, 1962), 438.

8. Sando, *Pueblo Nations*, 133; Spicer, *Cycles of Conquest*, 174, 438.

9. McKinney, "History of the Albuquerque Indian School," 121.

10. Ibid., 118; Adams, *Education for Extinction*, 83–84, 90.

11. Jacobs, *Engendered Encounters*.

12. Cabán, *Constructing a Colonial People*, 4, 129.

13. For a discussion of colonial anxieties, see Stoler, *Race and the Education of Desire*, 191.

14. RG 75, entry 42, folder G.

15. RG 75, entry 83, subheading 820.3.

16. RG 75, entry 42, folder G.

17. RG 75, entry 40, Picuris, 1913.

18. Ibid., Peñasco, 1914.

19. RG 75, entry 83, subheading 806.

20. Cabán, *Constructing a Colonial People*, 129.

21. Adams, *Education for Extinction*, 141, 108, 110.

22. Mrs. Walter K. Marmon, Pueblo Oral History Collection, roll 9, tape 514, p. 8,

Center for Southwest Research (CSWR); Mrs. Walter K. Marmon, ibid., roll 8, tape 1, p. 25; Clemente Vigil, ibid., roll 9, tape 753, p. 21.

23. RG 75, entry 40, Santo Domingo, 1914. For discussions of the racial politics embedded in public health reforms, see Alexandra Minna Stern, "Buildings, Boundaries, and Blood: Medicalization and Nation-Building on the U.S.-Mexico Border, 1910–1930," *Hispanic American Historical Review* 79, no. 1 (February 1999): 41–81; and Nayan Shah, *Contagious Divides: Epidemics and Race in San Francisco's Chinatown* (Berkeley: University of California Press, 2001).

24. RG 75, entry 40, Santo Domingo, 1914.

25. RG 75, entry 40, Sandoval, 1916.

26. Ibid., Santo Domingo, 1915.

27. Annual Report, 1922, Zuni Indian Agency, RG 75, entry 64.

28. RG 75, entry 40, Santo Domingo, 1901.

29. Qoyawayma, *No Turning Back*, 24–25, 59, 106.

30. Ibid., 105–6, 93; Andrew Becenti, Navajo Oral History, roll 3, tape 371, p. 12, CSWR; Jesse Green, ed., *Cushing at Zuni: The Correspondence and Journals of Frank Hamilton Cushing, 1879–1884* (Albuquerque: University of New Mexico Press, 1990), 345.

31. RG 75, entry 40, Taos, 1902.

32. RG 75, entry 40, Santa Fe, 1902.

33. Anonymous, Navajo Oral History, reel 11, tape 26, p. 10, CSWR; Qoyawayma, *No Turning Back*, 56; K. Tsianina Lomawaima, *They Called It Prairie Light: The Story of Chiloco Indian School* (Lincoln: University of Nebraska Press, 1994), 91.

34. "An Interview with Petra Chavez Romero of Jemez Pueblo, May 20, 1986," *Santa Fe Indian School: The First 100 Years Project*, MSS 595, box 1, folder 1, p. 7, CSWR, University of New Mexico, Albuquerque, New Mexico. For an excellent discussion of the link between clear gender boundaries and "civilization" in broader America, see Bederman, *Manliness and Civilization*.

35. Jacobs, *Engendered Encounters*, 6.

36. RG 75, entry 42, folder H.

37. Ibid., folder F.

38. Ibid., folder M.

39. Ibid., folder L.

40. RG 75, entry 40, Santa Clara, 1916.

41. Stoler, *Race and the Education of Desire*, 190.

42. RG 75, entry 40, Cochiti, 1909.

43. Ibid., San Jose, 1900; Ibid., San Juan, 1901.

44. RG 75, entry 83, subheading 820.4.

45. RG 75, entry 40, Española, 1905.

46. RG 75, entry 42, folder H.

47. Ibid., folder L.

48. Bonnie Duran astutely notes that "the imagery of the stereotypical Drunken Indian—violent, lawless, impetuous—emerges clearly . . . as one of the instruments that attuned Western collective consciousness to the notion of a North America waiting the civilizing and rationalizing missions of European settlement." In other words, "alcohol was used . . . to define both the meaning and value of 'Indian' versus white identity and the moral grounding and guiding principles of colonization." Bonnie Duran, "Indigenous versus Colonial Discourse: Alcohol and American Indian Identity," in *Dressing in Feathers: The Construction of the Indian in American Popular Culture*, ed. S. Elizabeth Bird (New York: Westview Press, 1996), 113–14.

49. RG 75, entry 40, box 9, Santa Fe, 1914.

50. RG 75, entry 40, Picuris, 1905.

51. RG 75, entry 42, folder J.

52. Ibid., folder L.

53. Mrs. Walter K. Marmon, Laguna Pueblo, Pueblo Oral History Collection, roll 9, tape 514, p. 11, CSWR; RG 75, entry 42, folder N.

54. RG 75, entry 42, folder G.

55. RG 75, entry 40, Picuris, 1907.

56. Ibid., Taos, 1906.

57. Ibid., Taos, 1907.

58. McKinney, "History of the Albuquerque Indian School," 123.

59. Reports of the Charges against Supt. Creager, Albuquerque School, July 29, 1891.

60. Ibid.

61. Ibid.

62. RG 75, entry 83, subheading 830.

63. RG 75, entry 40, Santo Domingo, 1902.

64. Ibid.

65. Ibid.

66. Cabán, *Constructing a Colonial People*, 129.

CHAPTER THREE

1. Rudolfo Acuña, *Occupied America: A History of Chicanos* (New York: Harper & Row, 1981), 19; Menchaca, *Recovering History, Constructing Race*, 217.

2. See the work of Montoya, *Translating Property*; and Reichard, " 'Justice is God's law.' "

3. Duggan, *Sapphic Slashers*; Hodes, *White Women, Black Men*; Findlay, *Imposing Decency*.

4. U.S. Bureau of the Census, *Population, 1900* (Washington, DC: United States Printing Office, 1900), 549. Of the criminal indictments filed in the district courts of those four counties between 1880 and roughly the end of the territorial period in 1912, between .5 and 1 percent were rape charges, resulting in

TABLE 3.4. RAPE INDICTMENTS BY COUNTY

	Rape Indictments	Total Indictments	Percentage
Bernalillo (1883–1917)	33	5,177	0.6%
Doña Ana (1880–1911)	41	3,879	1.1%
San Miguel (1880–1908)	54	4,027	1.3%
Santa Fe (1883–1911)	18	3,447	0.5%
Total	146	16,530	0.8%

Source: New Mexico State Records Center and Archives, Santa Fe.

approximately one rape indictment per year in every county except San Miguel (see table 3.4). In San Miguel County, over a span of twenty-eight years, there were fifty-four rape charges, or about two a year. It should be remembered that the vast majority of cases that reached the county criminal dockets were made up of petty offenses—like violating Sunday liquor laws, permitting gambling, operating "bawdy houses," and the sale of liquor without a license or to minors—indictments that never reached the trial phase.

5. See D'Emilio and Freedman, *Intimate Matters*; and Hodes, *White Women, Black Men*.

6. The available transcripts of testimony during New Mexico rape trials, most transcribed upon appeal of the case to the territorial supreme court, focus on male physical violence inflicted upon women, on the terrifying, humiliating corporeal realities of sexual assault. Given the institutional and emotional barriers to reporting, let alone bringing charges of rape, I begin with the assumption that these women were all speaking courageously and truthfully about their experiences.

7. *Territory of New Mexico v. Prudencio Martinez and Felipe Garcia*, San Miguel County, District Court, Criminal Case # 4710, 1908, State Records Center and Archives, Santa Fe, NM (hereafter NMSRCA).

8. Like several towns in New Mexico, the arrival of the railroad created a "New" Las Vegas (also known as East Las Vegas) a short distance from "Old" Las Vegas. As occurred in Albuquerque, "Old Town" in Las Vegas contained mostly Hispano inhabitants.

9. *NM v. Martinez, Garcia.*

10. Leticia M. Garza-Falcón, *Gente Decente: A Borderlands Response to the Rhetoric of Dominance* (Austin: University of Texas Press, 1998).

11. *Territory of New Mexico v. Geronimo Pino*, Supreme Court Case #790, 1898, NMSRCA.

12. Ibid.

13. Ibid.

14. Ibid.
15. Ibid.
16. Ibid.
17. *NM v. Edie*, Bernalillo County Criminal Case #1457, 1891, NMSRCA.
18. Ibid.
19. Ibid.
20. Ibid.
21. Ibid.
22. Ibid.
23. Ibid.
24. See Lott, *Love and Theft*, 137; Roediger, *The Wages of Whiteness*, 108; Elliott West, *The Saloon on the Rocky Mountain Mining Frontier* (Lincoln: University of Nebraska Press, 1979), 133; John F. Kasson, *Rudeness and Civility: Manners in Nineteenth-Century Urban America* (New York: Hill and Wang, 1990), 78.
25. *NM v. Edie.*
26. *Territory of New Mexico v. Ricardo Alva*, Supreme Court Case #1571, 1913, 25, 32, 26, NMSRCA.
27. *State of New Mexico v. Ricardo Alva, Record of Cases, Supreme Court of New Mexico, 1913–1914* (Santa Fe: New Mexico Printing Co., 1915), 147.
28. The 1865 revised statutes for the territory of New Mexico prescribed a punishment of at least five years in prison for any individual who "shall ravish, and carnally know any female of the age of ten years or more by force and against her will." A life term in prison was the punishment for a convicted rapist of "any female under the age of ten years." The 1865 law against "ravishing" and "carnally knowing" a female over ten included an interesting provision. The statute ended with the clause, "provided, she is not a common prostitute." That is, no female over the age of ten could bring a charge of rape if she was a "common prostitute." Twenty years later, in 1884, the compiled laws of New Mexico repeated the same provision word for word, including the "common prostitute" provision that seemed to tolerate the sexual assault of prostitutes. By 1897, however, the "common prostitute" provision had disappeared from the books. Lawmakers raised the age of consent to fourteen and added several new clauses. The law now included "idiocy, imbecility, or any unsoundness of mind, either temporary or permanent" and "weakness produced by intoxicating, narcotic or anesthetic agent" as legitimate explanations for the absence of resistance or the victim's mistaken consent to sexual intercourse. Even if a drugged, intoxicated, anesthetized, or "mentally unsound" woman consented to intercourse, it was still rape. Lawmakers also prohibited rape charges against "any one who was under the age of fourteen years at the time of the act alleged," with the exception of those whose "physical ability to accomplish penetration is proved as an independent fact beyond a reasonable doubt." Though the 1897 statute focused on boys under fourteen, physical

ability to "accomplish penetration" in men often well over the age of fourteen would play an important role in many rape trials. See *Revised Statutes and Laws of the Territory of New Mexico* (St. Louis: RP Studley & Co., 1865), 326; *Compiled Laws of New Mexico, 1884* (Santa Fe: New Mexico Printing Co.,1885), 404; and *Compiled Laws of New Mexico, 1897* (Santa Fe: New Mexico Printing Co., 1897), 344. For rape in other historical contexts, see Bederman, *Manliness and Civilization*; Antonia Castañeda, "Sexual Violence in the Politics and Policies of Conquest: Amerindian Women and the Spanish Conquest of Alta California," in *Building with Our Hands: New Directions in Chicana Studies*, ed. Adela de le Torre and Beatriz Pesquera (Berkeley: University of California Press, 1993); D'Emilio and Freedman, *Intimate Matters*; Shani D'Cruze, *Crimes of Outrage: Sex, Violence, and Victorian Working Women* (DeKalb: Northern Illinois University Press, 1998); Karen Dubinsky, *Improper Advances: Rape and Heterosexual Conflict in Ontario, 1880–1929* (Chicago: University of Chicago Press, 1993); Leslie K. Dunlap, "The Reform of Rape Law and the Problem of White Men: Age-of-Consent Campaigns in the South, 1885–1910," in *Sex, Love, Race: Crossing Boundaries in North American History*, ed. Martha Hodes (New York: New York University Press, 1999), 294–312; Laura F. Edwards, "Sexual Violence, Gender, Reconstruction, and the Extension of Patriarchy in Granville County, North Carolina," *North Carolina Historical Review* 68 (July 1991): 237–60; Gutiérrez, *When Jesus Came*; Lisbeth Haas, *Conquests and Historical Identities in California, 1769–1936* (Berkeley: University of California Press, 1995); Jacquelyn Dowd Hall, " 'The Mind That Burns in Each Body': Women, Rape, and Racial Violence," in *Powers of Desire: The Politics of Sexuality*, ed. Ann Snitow, Christine Stansell, and Sharon Thompson (New York: Monthly Review Press, 1983); Hodes, *White Women, Black Men*; Mary E. Odem, *Delinquent Daughters: Protecting and Policing Adolescent Sexuality in the United States, 1885–1920* (Chapel Hill: University of North Carolina Press, 1995); and Rosaura Sánchez, *Telling Identities: The Californio Testimonios* (Minneapolis: University of Minnesota Press, 1995).

29. *Revised Statutes and Laws*, 326; *Compiled Laws of New Mexico, 1884*, 404; *Compiled Laws of New Mexico, 1897*, 344; *Session Laws of the State of New Mexico, 1915* (Denver: WH Courtwright, 1915), 59; *Territory of New Mexico v. Ricardo Alva*, 112. New Mexico was typical in respect to its age-of-consent legislation. See Odem, *Delinquent Daughters*, 14, for a list of age-of-consent laws in the United States.

30. *Territory of New Mexico v. Ricardo Alva*, 87, 88, 91.

31. Ibid.

32. Ibid.

33. See D'Emilio and Freedman, *Intimate Matters*; D'Cruze, *Crimes of Outrage*; and Dubinsky, *Improper Advances*.

34. *Territory of New Mexico v. Ricardo Alva*, 104, 60, 24, 36.

35. Bederman, *Manliness and Civilization*.

36. *Territory of New Mexico v. Ricardo Alva*, 104, 60, 24, 36.
37. Almaguer, *Racial Fault Lines*; Menchaca, *Recovering History, Constructing Race*.
38. Women and Native American men did not serve on juries in New Mexico.
39. See Bederman, *Manliness and Civilization*; D'Emilio and Freedman, *Intimate Matters*; Dunlap, "The Reform of Rape Law"; Edwards, "Sexual Violence"; Hall, " 'The Mind That Burns in Each Body' "; and Hodes, *White Women, Black Men*.
40. Garza-Falcón, *Gente Decente*; Meléndez, *So All Is Not Lost*.
41. *Territory of New Mexico v. Bonifacio Mares*, Supreme Court Case #875, 1901, NMSRCA.
42. Ibid.
43. *Territory of New Mexico v. Claudio Armijo*, Supreme Court Case #2242, 1920, NMSRCA.
44. Ibid.
45. Ibid.
46. Ibid.

CHAPTER FOUR

1. *Albuquerque Morning Journal*, May 8, 1909, 8.
2. Meléndez, *"So All Is Not Lost."*
3. Porter A. Stratton, *The Territorial Press of New Mexico, 1834–1912* (Albuquerque: University of New Mexico Press, 1969), 2, 24, 36, 41.
4. Ibid., 27–28, 36.
5. Ibid., 45.
6. *Albuquerque Morning Journal*, February 4, 1907, 8.
7. Ibid., March 10, 1918, 2.
8. *Santa Fe New Mexican*, November 3, 1910, 8; *Albuquerque Morning Journal*, February 11, 1907, 8.
9. *Albuquerque Democrat*, December 7, 1882, 4.
10. Following Mary Douglas's suggestion that images of a society as disordered and chaotic or well ordered and hierarchical inevitably draw much of their symbolic resonance from images of the human body, Peter Stallybrass and Allon White have noted that images of large female bodies often signified an inversion from "normal" bourgeois social ordering. An excessive fondness for food and drink, for instance, or images of a body whose orifices are poorly guarded could function as "a synecdoche for sexual desire, the longings of the flesh" and could signal, for some, a disturbing loosening of societal bonds. Douglas, *Natural Symbols*, 74; and Stallybrass and White, *The Politics and Poetics of Transgression*, 63.
11. *Albuquerque Morning Democrat*, July 2, 1898, 3.
12. For information on the Penitentes, see Martha Weigle, *Brothers of Light, Brothers of Blood: The Penitentes of the Southwest* (Albuquerque: University of New Mexico Press, 1976); White, *"It's Your Misfortune,"* 41.

13. *Albuquerque Morning Journal*, April 11, 1907, 7.

14. *Santa Fe Daily New Mexican*, March 11, 1892, 2.

15. *Santa Fe New Mexican*, December 17, 1898, 1.

16. RG 75, entry 40, Picuris, 1901.

17. *Albuquerque Morning Democrat*, May 30, 1890, 4.

18. Ibid., May 30, 1895, 4.

19. *Santa Fe New Mexican*, May 30, 1905, 1.

20. *Albuquerque Morning Journal*, May 27, 1910, 5.

21. John Bodnar, *Remaking America: Public Memory, Commemoration, and Patriotism in the Twentieth Century* (Princeton: Princeton University Press, 1992), 16; Benedict Anderson, *Imagined Communities: Reflections on the Origin and Spread of Nationalism*, rev. ed. (London: Verso, 1991); Mary Ryan, *Civic Wars: Democracy and Public Life in the American City during the Nineteenth Century* (Berkeley: University of California Press, 1997). See also Mary P. Ryan, "The American Parade: Representations of the Nineteenth-Century Social Order," in *The New Cultural History*, ed. Lynn Hunt (Berkeley: University of California Press, 1989), 131–53; Kirk Savage, *Standing Soldiers, Kneeling Slaves: Race, War, and Monument in Nineteenth-Century America* (Princeton: Princeton University Press, 1997); and David Waldstreicher, "Rites of Rebellion, Rites of Assent: Celebrations, Print Culture, and the Origins of American Nationalism," *Journal of American History* 82 (June 1995): 37–61.

22. Joseph Roach, *Cities of the Dead: Circum-Atlantic Performance* (New York: Columbia University Press, 1996), 2–3, 38–39.

23. Meléndez, *"So All Is Not Lost"*; Ramón A. Gutiérrez, "Aztlán, Montezuma, and New Mexico: The Political Uses of American Indian Mythology," in *Aztlán: Essays on the Chicano Homeland*, ed. Rudolfo A. Anaya and Francisco Lomeli (Albuquerque: University of New Mexico Press, 1989), 172–90.

24. Gutiérrez, "Aztlán, Montezuma, and New Mexico," 178.

25. *Albuquerque Morning Journal*, January 1, 1920, 2.

26. *Santa Fe New Mexican*, November 3, 1910, 8; Earl Lewis and Heidi Ardizzone, *Love on Trial: An American Scandal in Black and White* (New York: W. W. Norton, 2001).

27. *Santa Fe New Mexican*, June 1, 1910, 8.

28. Ibid., May 30, 1905, 5.

29. Ibid., May 1, 1905, 1.

30. *Albuquerque Morning Democrat*, June 3, 1890, 4.

31. *Albuquerque Morning Journal*, May 30, 1909, 2.

32. Ibid., May 27, 1910, 5.

33. Ibid., May 30, 1909, 2.

34. Ibid., July 5, 1911, 1.

35. *Albuquerque Morning Democrat*, October 17, 1896, 1. For a more full description of this event and the life of Margarita/Margaret Otero Harrison, see Pablo

R. Mitchell, "Queen for a Day: Margaret/Margarita Otero Harrison and Intermarriage in Turn-of-the-Century Albuquerque," in *Explorations in American History*, ed. Sandra McMahon and Louis Tanner (Albuquerque: Center for the American West Press, 1995), 51–80.

36. *Albuquerque Morning Journal*, March 15, 1918, 2.

37. For information on the tendency of white Americans to dress as "Indians," see Philip J. Deloria, *Playing Indian* (New Haven: Yale University Press, 1998). For minstrelsy, see Roediger, *The Wages of Whiteness*, 118; and Lott, *Love and Theft*.

38. *Albuquerque Morning Democrat*, September 2, 1894, 4.

CHAPTER FIVE

1. *Albuquerque Democrat*, December 7, 1882, 4.

2. Duggan, *Sapphic Slashers*.

3. *Santa Fe New Mexican*, June 20, 1910, 6.

4. *Albuquerque Morning Journal*, January 4, 1920, 2.

5. *Santa Fe New Mexican*, May 10, 1905, 1.

6. *Albuquerque Morning Democrat*, February 5, 1895, 1.

7. Thanks to María E. Montoya for this valuable idea. See Montoya, *Translating Property*, for a particularly nuanced discussion of the role of racialization and gender in land displacement.

8. See Reva B. Siegel, "The Modernization of Marital Status Law: Adjudicating Wives' Rights to Earnings, 1860–1930," *Georgetown Law Journal* 82 (September 1994), 2127–211; and Richard H. Chused, "Late Nineteenth Century Married Women's Property Law: Reception of the Early Married Women's Property Acts by Courts and Legislatures," *American Journal of Legal History* 29 (January 1985): 3–35.

9. Thanks to Carroll Smith-Rosenberg for this observation.

10. Duggan, *Sapphic Slashers*.

11. Cynthia Secor-Welsh, "Governor Miguel Antonio Otero, 1897–1906: Agent for Change" (Master's thesis, University of New Mexico, 1984), 14; *Santa Fe Daily New Mexican*, December 22, 1888, 4. For more information on Miguel Otero, see María E. Montoya, "The Dual World of Governor Miguel A. Otero: Myth and Reality in Turn-of-the-Century New Mexico," *New Mexico Historical Review* 67 (January 1992), 13–31; Miguel Antonio Otero, *My Life on the Frontier, 1864–1882* (Albuquerque: University of New Mexico Press, 1987); and Miguel Antonio Otero, *My Nine Years as Governor, 1897–1906* (Albuquerque: University of New Mexico Press, 1940).

12. Robert M. Utley, *Billy the Kid: A Short and Violent Life* (Lincoln: University of Nebraska Press, 1989), 15, 193–95.

13. See Pablo R. Mitchell, " 'You Just Don't Know Mrs. Baca': Intermarriage, Mixed Heritage, and Identity in New Mexico" (unpublished manuscript). For discussions of intermarriage in the Southwest, see Jane Dysart, "Mexican

Women in San Antonio, 1830–1860: The Assimilation Process," *Western Historical Quarterly* (October 1976), 365–75; González, "The Spanish-Mexican Women of Santa Fé"; Deutsch, *No Separate Refuge*, 35; George J. Sánchez, *Becoming Mexican American: Ethnicity, Culture, and Identity in Chicano Los Angeles, 1900–1945* (New York: Oxford University Press, 1993); and Paul R. Spickard, *Mixed Blood: Intermarriage and Ethnic Identity in Twentieth-Century America* (Madison: University of Wisconsin Press, 1989). For examples of the relationship between intermarriage and unbalanced gender ratios in the American West, see Susan L. Johnson, "Sharing Bed and Board: Cohabitation and Cultural Difference in Central Arizona Mining Towns, 1863–1873," in *The Women's West*, ed. Susan Armitage and Elizabeth Jameson (Norman: University of Oklahoma Press, 1987), 77–92; Karen Isaksen Leonard, *Making Ethnic Choices: California's Punjabi Mexican Americans* (Philadelphia: Temple University Press, 1992); and Sylvia Van Kirk, *Many Tender Ties: Women in the Fur Trade Society, 1670–1870* (Norman: University of Oklahoma Press, 1980).

14. For some recent examples, see Gutiérrez, *When Jesus Came*; Hodes, *White Women, Black Men*; Montoya, *Translating Property*; Gary B. Nash, "The Hidden History of Mestizo America," *Journal of American History* 82 (December 1995): 941–62; Peggy Pascoe, "Miscegenation Law, Court Cases, and Ideologies of 'Race' in Twentieth-Century America," *Journal of American History* 83 (June 1996): 44–69; Peggy Pascoe, "Race, Gender, and Intercultural Relations: The Case of Interracial Marriage," *Frontiers* 1 (1991): 5–18; Glenda Riley, *Building and Breaking Families in the American West* (Albuquerque: University of New Mexico Press, 1996); David D. Smits, " 'Squaw Men,' 'Half-Breeds,' and Amalgamators: Late Nineteenth-Century Anglo-American Attitudes toward Indian-White Race-Mixing," *American Indian Culture and Research Journal* 15 (Fall 1991): 29–61; and Spickard, *Mixed Blood*.

15. Lewis and Ardizzone, *Love on Trial*, 28; Pascoe, "Miscegenation Law."

16. *Albuquerque Morning Journal*, July 6, 1911, 1.

17. Limón, *Dancing with the Devil*, 25–26.

18. *Albuquerque Morning Journal*, March 29, 1918, 4.

19. RG 75, entry 40, Cochiti, 1905.

20. Ibid., Española, 1906.

21. Record of Birth, Deaths, and Illnesses, 1900–1910, Zuni Indian Agency, RG 75, entry 69.

22. *Santa Fe New Mexican*, May 8, 1905, 5.

23. *Daily New Mexican*, June 28, 1890, 4.

24. *Albuquerque Morning Democrat*, March 2, 1895, 2.

25. Ibid., April 4, 1895, 1.

26. *Albuquerque Morning Journal*, May 29, 1909, 2.

27. *Daily New Mexican*, April 24, 1905, 1.

28. *Albuquerque Morning Democrat*, February 24, 1895, 1.

29. Ibid.

30. Gary Hoppenstand, "Ambrose Bierce and the Transformation of the Gothic Tale in the Nineteenth-Century American Periodical," in *Periodical Literature in Nineteenth-Century America*, ed. Kenneth M. Price and Susan Belasco Smith (Charlottesville: University Press of Virginia, 1995), 226. See also Martha Banta, "Periodicals Back (Advertisers) to Front (Editors): Whose National Values Market Best?" in *Reciprocal Influences: Literary Production, Distribution, and Consumption in America*, ed. Steven Fink and Susan S. Williams (Columbus: Ohio State University Press, 1999), 173–98.

31. According to Judith Walkowitz, the tale(s) of Jack the Ripper swirled with more general societal concerns ranging from fears of working-class rebellion to increasing sexual license among middle-class women to London's changing social geography. See Walkowitz, *City of Dreadful Delight*, 2–3.

32. D'Emilio and Freedman, *Intimate Matters*, 216.

33. As Gail Bederman reminds readers, the great scandal for white Americans, especially white male Americans, of turn-of-the-century African American boxing champion Jack Johnson stemmed as much from his longtime white female companions as it did from his ability to beat white men to a pulp. Bederman, *Manliness and Civilization*, 3. Martha Hodes notes more generally that in the years following Reconstruction in the South, fears about African American male sexuality run rampant came to "[bear] more equal weight" with the threat posed by the "sexual depravity and agency of poor white women." Martha Hodes, "The Sexualization of Reconstruction Politics: White Women and Black Men in the South after the Civil War," *Journal of the History of Sexuality* 3 (1993): 417.

34. Duggan, *Sapphic Slashers*, 3.

35. *Santa Fe New Mexican*, July 25, 1911, 3.

36. *U.S. Bureau of the Census, 1900*, Bernalillo County, New Mexico. Byron A. Johnson and Sharon P. Johnson, *Gilded Palaces of Shame: Albuquerque's Red-light Districts, 1880–1914* (Albuquerque: Gilded Age Press, 1983), 80.

37. *U.S. Census, 1910*, Bernalillo County, New Mexico; *U.S. Census, 1920*, Bernalillo County, New Mexico.

38. *NM v. Lizzie McGrath*, 1911, Supreme Court Case #1364, State Records Center and Archives, Santa Fe, NM.

39. Ibid.

40. Editorial, "Sex Education-Sex Hygiene," *New Mexico Medical Journal* 5 (March 1910): 140.

41. *Albuquerque Morning Democrat*, March 10, 1895, 1.

42. Marion S. Goldman, *Gold Diggers and Silver Miners: Prostitution and Social Life on the Comstock Lode* (Ann Arbor: University of Michigan Press, 1981), 134–35.

43. See Foley, *The White Scourge*, 6; Bederman, *Manliness and Civilization*; and Duggan, *Sapphic Slashers*.

44. Duggan, *Sapphic Slashers*, 158.

CHAPTER SIX

1. Marc Simmons, *Spanish Pathways: Readings in the History of Hispanic New Mexico* (Albuquerque: University of New Mexico Press, 2001), 60. See also Jake W. Spidle Jr., *Doctors of Medicine in New Mexico: A History of Health and Medical Practice, 1886–1986* (Albuquerque: University of New Mexico Press, 1986), for an excellent overview of the history of medicine in New Mexico; and Regina Morantz-Sanchez, *Sympathy and Science: Women Physicians in American Medicine* (New York: Oxford University Press, 1985), for a discussion of orthodox and sectarian medicine, the water-cure treatment, and the role of gender difference in the rise of modern medicine.

2. Record of Births, Deaths, and Illnesses, 1900–1910, Zuni Indian Agency, RG 75, entry 69.

3. Ibid.

4. RG 75, entry 40, box 9, Taos, 1902.

5. Spidle, *Doctors of Medicine in New Mexico*, 31, 67.

6. Ibid., 33, 52–58, 68.

7. Leslie J. Reagan, *When Abortion Was a Crime: Women, Medicine, and Law in the United States, 1867–1973* (Berkeley: University of California Press, 1997); Smith-Rosenberg, *Disorderly Conduct*; Trachtenberg, *The Incorporation of America*; Wiebe, *The Search for Order*.

8. Stoler, *Race and the Education of Desire*, 106.

9. Stern, "Buildings, Boundaries, and Blood."

10. Troy C. Sexton, "Mxyomatous Degeneration of the Chorionic Villi," *New Mexico Medical Journal* (*NMMJ* hereafter) 5 (July 1910): 246–49; C. M. Yates, "Status of Tuberculosis in the City of Roswell," *NMMJ* 5 (August 1910): 270–72; James Vance, "The Post Operative Treatment of Abdominal Section," *NMMJ* 4 (March 1909): 9–14; Louis J. Lautenbach, "Nose and Throat Disease: A Contributory Cause of Pulmonary Tuberculosis," *NMMJ* 5 (September 1910): 298–300. For other examples of the racial marking of patients, see George K. Angle, "Clinical Report of Five Cases of Milk Sickness," *NMMJ* 4 (July 1909): 4–7; and E. L. Ward, "The Neglected Prostate," *NMMJ* 17 (November 1916): 53–58.

11. Elliott C. Prentiss, "Observations on Amoebic Dysentery," *NMMJ* 10 (August 1913): 116.

12. G. F. Brooks, "Many Years Professional Experience in the Aztec Land—The Mexican Republic," *NMMJ* 13 (March 1915): 214–16. See also Gutiérrez, "Aztlán, Montezuma, and New Mexico."

13. M. K. Wylder, "Artificial Feeding of Infants," *NMMJ* 5 (August 1910): 276; Editorial, "Health of the American Indian," *NMMJ* 10 (April 1913): 8.

14. Editorial, "The Race Question Overdone," *NMMJ* 5 (May 1910): 189.

15. Untitled, *NMMJ* 4 (September 1908): 28.

16. Howard D. King, "Some Race Observations from an Epidemiological Viewpoint," *NMMJ* 11 (October 1913): 31–35.

17. Editorial, *NMMJ* 5 (July 1910): 231; Francis T. B. Fest, "Sex Education-Social Hygiene," *NMMJ* 5 (March 1910): 139, 140.

18. C. M. Mayes, "Municipal Hygiene," *NMMJ* 9 (March 1913): 139; "Do You Know That," *NMMJ* 16 (May 1916): 34; Editorial, "Disinfection and Contagion Carriers," *NMMJ* 10 (June 1913): 62.

19. R. E. McBride, "The New Mexico Medical Society: Some Duties and Opportunities," *NMMJ* 4 (September 1908): 10–15; Stern, "Buildings, Boundaries, and Blood"; Shah, *Contagious Divides*.

20. Editorial, "Sex Education—Sex Hygiene," *NMMJ* 5 (March 1910): 140.

21. Historians have noted that medical discourses concerning syphilis frequently offered physicians and public health advocates flexible rhetorical props for the elaboration of difference and identity. See D'Emilio and Freedman, *Intimate Matters*; Janet Lynne Golden, ed., *Framing Disease: Studies in Cultural History* (New Brunswick: Rutgers University Press, 1992); and Charles E. Rosenberg, *Explaining Epidemics and Other Studies in the History of Medicine* (Cambridge: Harvard University Press, 1992).

22. Editorial, "Innocent Victims of the Black Plague," *NMMJ* 10 (August 1913): 114–15.

23. "Syphilis and the Nervous System," *NMMJ* 11 (October 1913): 37.

24. William Allen Pusey, "Syphilis as a Modern Problem," *NMMJ* 15 (October 1915): 38.

25. "The Cause and Control of Cancer," *NMMJ* 12 (May 1914): 44; Book review, *NMMJ* 10 (September 1913): 168.

26. Harriet Randall Flanders, "A Plea for General Instruction in Practical Hygiene," *NMMJ* 14 (July 1915): 116–20.

27. Editorial, "Temperance versus Prohibition," *NMMJ* 5 (July 1910): 232–33.

28. Editorial, "Cure for Criminal Tendencies," *NMMJ* 9 (February 1913): 108. Left unclear in the article was whether the relapsed thief continued to act bright and cheerful and hold his head erect as he committed his crimes.

29. Book review, *NMMJ* 10 (September 1913): 167–68.

30. Ibid.

31. Bederman, *Manliness and Civilization*, 25.

32. Cynthia E. Russett, *Sexual Science: The Victorian Construction of Womanhood* (Cambridge: Harvard University Press, 1989), 11; J. A. Reidy, "Headaches," *NMMJ* 5 (September 1909): 11–12; F. W. Noble, "A New Method of Treatment for Tubercular or Mixed Infection of the Lymph Nodes of the Neck," *NMMJ* 11 (December 1913), 96–98. In terms of distinctions between women and men, Russett has noted that, in the same way that "primitive people" supposedly "lagged behind Europeans," the "overwhelming consensus" of nineteenth-century sexual science held that "women were inherently different from men in their anatomy, physiology, temperament, and intellect."

33. R. L. Bradley, "Diagnosis and Surgical Treatment of the More Common Gall

Bladder Diseases," *NMMJ* 4 (May 1909): 4; "Women Motorists," *NMMJ* 9 (March 1913): 135–36.

34. As Iris Young nicely summarizes, in American society "women are essentially identified with sexuality," while Cynthia Russett describes the "biological imperative that insisted that women be breeders first and foremost." Iris Young, *Justice and the Politics of Difference* (Princeton: Princeton University Press, 1990), 129; Russett, *Sexual Science*, 124. See also Thomas Laqueur, who writes, "This radical naturalization, the reduction of women to the organ [the ovary] that now, for the first time, marked an incommensurable difference between the sexes and produced behavior of a kind not found in men," in *Making Sex: Body and Gender from the Greeks to Freud* (Cambridge: Harvard University Press, 1990), 216.

35. W. T. Joyner, "Salpingitis," *NMMJ* 9 (January 1913): 102.

36. William Howe, "Conduct of Normal Labor through Parturition," *NMMJ* 11 (December 1913): 101; J. W. C., "Is the Pregnant Woman Receiving the Care and Attention She Demands," *NMMJ* 5 (March 1910): 142–43.

37. C. M. Yater, "Operative Treatment of Uterine Retro-Displacements," *NMMJ* 11 (February 1914): 161–62; W. T. Joyner, "Salpingitis," *NMMJ* 9 (January 1913): 103.

38. Harriet R. Flanders, "A Plea for General Instruction in Practical Hygiene," *NMMJ* 14 (July 1915): 115; Editorial, "Where There Are Children," *NMMJ* 16 (July 1916): 108; M. K. Wylder, "Artificial Feeding of Infants," *NMMJ* 5 (August 1910): 277; W. W. McCormick, "Alcoholism: Acute and Chronic," *NMMJ* 4 (July 1909): 8.

39. C. E. Lukens, "Human Waste, and the Children of the Needy," *NMMJ* 14 (April 1915): 12–22.

40. S. D. Swope, "Carcinoma of the Mamma," *NMMJ* 10 (May 1913): 53–59. See also B. L. Sulzbacher, "Perineal Repair, with Report of a Case," *NMMJ* 15 (November 1915): 207–18.

41. F. F. Fadely, "Impotence," *NMMJ* 15 (November 1915): 149–53.

42. Evelyn Fisher-Frisbie, "Gonorrhea in the Female," *NMMJ* 7 (January 1912): 128.

43. Smith-Rosenberg, *Disorderly Conduct.*

44. Stoler, *Race and the Education of Desire.*

45. "Memorial," *NMMJ* 4 (May 1909): 26

46. William Howe, "A Plea for the Preservation and Restoration of the Perineum," *NMMJ* 14 (April 1915): 22–26.

47. McBride, "New Mexico Medical Society," 10–15.

48. Ibid.

49. Editorial, "Carelessness and Diphtheria," *NMMJ* 11 (December 1913): 86; James A. Rolls, "The Sanitary Needs of Santa Fe," *NMMJ* 5 (May 1910): 202–6.

50. S.D. Swope, "A Visit to Rochester and the Mayo Clinic," *NMMJ* 10 (August 1913): 121–26.

51. Ibid.

52. See Lott, *Love and Theft*, 143; Bederman, *Manliness and Civilization*, chap. 1; and Deloria, *Playing Indian*. See also Alan M. Kraut, *Silent Travelers: Germs, Genes, and the "Immigrant Menace"* (New York: Basic Books, 1994); Stoler, *Race and the Education of Desire*; and Young, *Justice and the Politics of Difference*, 182.

53. Deeply imbedded in the rise of modern medicine was the use of impoverished patients as, often unsuspecting, test subjects in the trials of new operative techniques and treatment regimens. Edward Shorter puts it concisely. "Younger women," he says, "became the keystone of modern medical practice." Edward Shorter, *Doctors and Their Patients: A Social History* (New York: Simon and Schuster, 1985), 110. Carroll Smith-Rosenberg has noted the central role in the late nineteenth century of gender conflicts and anti-abortion politics in the "struggle for professional hegemony" of the "regular" (i.e., AMA-certified, university-educated) physicians. Smith-Rosenberg, *Disorderly Conduct*, 233. See also Barbara Bates, *Bargaining for Life: A Social History of Tuberculosis, 1876–1938* (Philadelphia: University of Pennsylvania Press, 1992); Linda Gordon, *Woman's Body, Woman's Right: Birth Control in America* (New York: Penguin Books, 1990); Joel D. Howell, *Technology in the Hospital: Transforming Patient Care in the Early Twentieth Century* (Baltimore: Johns Hopkins University Press, 1995); Ludmilla Jordanova, *Sexual Visions: Images of Gender in Science and Medicine between the Eighteenth and Twentieth Centuries* (Madison: University of Wisconsin Press, 1989); Laqueur, *Making Sex*; Emily Martin, *The Woman in the Body: A Cultural Analysis of Reproduction* (Boston: Beacon Press, 1992); Morantz-Sanchez, *Sympathy and Science*; and Mary Poovey, " 'Scenes of an Indelicate Character': The Medical 'Treatment' of Victorian Women," *Representations* 14 (Spring 1986): 137–68.

54. Leila Peabody, "The Hypochondriac," *NMMJ* 10 (September 1913): 142–43. That the poet, Leila Peabody, is a woman accentuates the ambiguous role of bourgeois female patients in medical discourse. For a discussion of the New Woman, see Smith-Rosenberg, *Disorderly Conduct*, 245–96.

55. Judith Walzer Leavitt, "Birthing and Anesthesia: The Debate over Twilight Sleep," in *Women and Health in America*, ed. Judith Walzer Leavitt (Madison: University of Wisconsin Press, 1984), 175–84.

56. Editorial, " 'Twilight Sleep' in the Light of Day," *NMMJ* 13 (February 1915): 158–59.

57. S. G. Sewell, "Diet and Rest in the Treatment of Pulmonary Tuberculosis," *NMMJ* 4 (March 1909): 8; John H. Bradshaw, "The Meddlesome Doctor," *NMMJ* 4 (July 1909): 15; S. G. Von Almen, "Constipation," *NMMJ* 10 (May 1913): 39; Editorial, *NMMJ* 9 (March 1913): 136–37.

58. "Tuberculosis and Patent Medicine," *NMMJ* 1 (March 1906): 25.

59. Stallybrass and White, *The Politics and Poetics of Transgression*.

CHAPTER SEVEN

1. *Albuquerque Daily Citizen*, June 10, 1889, 3, 4; *Albuquerque Morning Democrat*, March 1, 1895, 1; *La Opinión Pública* (Albuquerque), March 25, 1893, 1, 2.

2. By the 1890s, according to William Leach and others, the threat of "overproduction, glut, panic, and depression" led to new forms of merchandising. New enticements such as "display and decoration, advertising, fashion, style, [and] service" emerged to attract consumers to purchase the products rapidly pouring from America's factories and warehouses. William Leach, *Land of Desire: Merchants, Power, and the Rise of a New American Culture* (New York: Vintage Books, 1993), 16. See also Elaine S. Abelson, *When Ladies Go A-Thieving: Middle-Class Shoplifters in the Victorian Department Store* (New York: Oxford University Press, 1989); Susan Porter Benson, *Counter Cultures: Saleswomen, Managers, and Customers in American Department Stores, 1890–1940* (Urbana: University of Illinois Press, 1986); Rita Felski, *Gender of Modernity* (Cambridge: Harvard University Press, 1995); Jackson Lears, *Fables of Abundance: A Cultural History of Advertising in America* (New York: Basic Books, 1994); Kathy Peiss, *Cheap Amusements: Working Women and Leisure in Turn-of-the-Century New York* (Philadelphia: Temple University Press, 1986); Ryan, *Civic Wars*; David Scobey, "Anatomy of a Promenade: The Politics of Bourgeois Sociability in Nineteenth-Century New York," *Social History* 17 (May 1992): 203–27; and Don Slater, *Consumer Culture and Modernity* (Cambridge: Polity Press, 1997).

3. McClintock, *Imperial Leather*, 209, 223.

4. *Albuquerque Daily Citizen*, June 10, 1889, 4.

5. Smith-Rosenberg, *Disorderly Conduct*, 181.

6. *Albuquerque Morning Democrat*, September 2, 1894, 4.

7. Ibid., September 4, 1894, 1.

8. *Santa Fe Weekly Democrat*, November 5, 1880, 3.

9. *Albuquerque Democrat*, June 14, 1883, 4.

10. *Albuquerque City Directory* (Albuquerque: Hughes and McCreight, 1901), 50.

11. *Albuquerque Journal-Democrat*, August 3, 1901, 8.

12. *Albuquerque Morning Journal*, May 12, 1909, 6.

13. Ibid.

14. *La Opinión Pública* (Albuquerque), March 25, 1893, 1 (translation mine).

15. *La Bandera Americana* (The American Flag) (Albuquerque), February 13, 1903, 4 (translation mine).

16. Ibid., August 10, 1901, 1.

17. Cited in Meyer, *Speaking for Themselves*, 125.

18. *Albuquerque Morning Democrat*, September 1, 1894, 3.

19. *Albuquerque Daily Citizen*, March 23, 1895, 3.

20. *Tribune Citizen* (Albuquerque), June 7, 1910, 4.

21. Ibid., 6.

22. *Santa Fe Weekly Democrat*, November 19, 1880, 4 (emphasis mine).

23. Albuquerque Morning Democrat, September 6, 1894, 4.

24. Ibid., September 5, 1894, 1.

25. *Albuquerque Daily Citizen*, March 21, 1895, 3.

26. *Las Vegas Daily Optic*, April 29, 1908, 2.

27. *Albuquerque Morning Democrat*, July 3, 1894, 2; *Albuquerque Daily Citizen*, January 4, 1898, 2.

28. *Albuquerque Daily Citizen*, January 7, 1898, 3.

29. *Santa Fe Weekly Democrat*, November 5, 1880, 4.

30. Ibid., 3.

31. *Albuquerque Democrat*, June 14, 1883, 4.

32. *Albuquerque Morning Democrat*, September 2, 1894, 2.

33. Reagan, *When Abortion Was a Crime*.

34. Thanks to David Scobey and Virginia Scharff for their observations on the importance of questions of "transit" and mobility.

35. *Revised Statutes and Laws of the Territory of New Mexico* (St. Louis: R. P. Studley & Co., 1865), chap. 51, sec. 11, p. 320; *1884 Compiled Laws of New Mexico* (Santa Fe: New Mexico Printing Company, 1885), chap. 2, sec. 698, p. 398; *1897 Compiled Laws of New Mexico* (Santa Fe: New Mexico Printing Company, 1897), sec. 1074, p. 342; *1919 Session Laws of New Mexico* (Albuquerque: Albright & Anderson, 1919), chap. 4, secs. 1–3, p. 6. According to the 1865 criminal code for the territory of New Mexico, any person who "administer[ed] to any woman pregnant with a quick child any medicine, drug, or substance whatever, or use[d] or employ[ed] any instrument or other means" with the intent of "destroy[ing]" such child was guilty of third-degree murder. Only when a physician advised that the procedure was "necessary to preserve the life" of the mother was it legal to terminate a pregnancy after quickening, that is, after a mother perceived movement in the fetus. The compiled laws of 1885 and 1897 contained precisely the same wording. In 1907 New Mexico legislators made one important change, increasing the severity of the crime from third-degree murder to a second-degree offense, but left the remainder of the statute the same. Only in 1919 did abortion laws in the state change dramatically. According to the new legislation, inducing an abortion in "any pregnant woman," regardless of before or after the point of quickening, was a felony punishable by fine and/or imprisonment. "Pregnancy" the bill designated as "that condition of a woman from the date of conception to the birth of the child." Finally, the law required not one, but two physicians, both licensed by the state, to approve an abortion to "preserve the life of the woman, or to prevent serious and bodily injury." Like most of the country, New Mexico law between 1865 and 1919 protected the right of physicians to perform abortions when necessary to save a woman's life. Unlike many states and territories, however, New Mexico only abandoned the quickening doctrine in 1919. In this sense, New Mexico differed consider-

ably from the general trend in the country. Janet Farrell Brodie, following the lead of Carroll Smith-Rosenberg, James Mohr, and others, argues that between the 1860s and the 1880s state after state passed new and more stringent regulations governing reproductive control. Under pressure from the American Medical Association and "social purity" reformers, lawmakers tightened existing loopholes and helped "drive abortion underground, making it far more difficult, expensive, and dangerous to obtain," in effect criminalizing abortion. Although some states, such as New York, prohibited abortion at any stage of pregnancy, most states prior to the late nineteenth century followed a common law tradition that held that abortions performed before quickening were not punishable offenses. Most states even permitted abortions after quickening if the mother's life was endangered. By the turn of the century, however, many states had followed the lead of New York and abandoned the quickening doctrine, criminalizing all abortions except those necessary to save a woman's life. Furthermore, under the 1873 Comstock Law, and smaller state laws like it, it became a felony to "mail any products or information about contraception or abortion." This anti-abortion legislation passed in the late nineteenth century would last until the 1960s. Janet Farrell Brodie, *Contraception and Abortion in Nineteenth-Century America* (Ithaca: Cornell University Press, 1994), 255. See also Smith-Rosenberg, *Disorderly Conduct*, 217–44; Reagan, *When Abortion Was a Crime*; and James Mohr, *Abortion in America: The Origins and Evolution of National Policy, 1800–1900* (New York: Oxford University Press, 1978).

36. *Albuquerque Daily Citizen*, March 18, 1895, 2.
37. Ibid., January 4, 1899, 4.
38. *Albuquerque Morning Journal*, January 4, 1920, 2.
39. *Albuquerque Daily Citizen*, March 21, 1895, 1.
40. *Santa Fe Weekly Democrat*, October 21, 1880, 1.
41. *Albuquerque Democrat*, December 7, 1882, 4.
42. McClintock, *Imperial Leather*, 229–30.
43. Judith DeMark notes that African Americans comprised 3 percent of Albuquerque's 1900 population. DeMark, "The Immigrant Experience," 61. Forty years later that percentage was 1.5 percent. Quintard Taylor, *In Search of the Racial Frontier: African Americans in the American West* (New York: W. W. Norton, 1998), 263.
44. *Santa Fe Weekly Democrat*, October 7, 1880, 3.
45. *Albuquerque Democrat Journal*, January 18, 1883, 1.
46. *Tribune Citizen* (Albuquerque), June 7, 1910, 3.
47. *Albuquerque Morning Journal*, March 9, 1918, 2.
48. *Santa Fe Weekly Democrat*, November 5, 1880, 4.
49. *Albuquerque Daily Democrat*, March 21, 1884; in Johnson and Johnson, *Gilded Palaces of Shame*, 37.
50. *Albuquerque Morning Journal*, August 1, 1882; in Johnson and Johnson, *Gilded Palaces of Shame*, 35 (emphasis in original).

51. *Albuquerque Morning Journal,* April 16, 1882; in Johnson and Johnson, *Gilded Palaces of Shame,* 35; *Albuquerque Daily Journal,* October 27, 1881; in Johnson and Johnson, *Gilded Palaces of Shame,* 15.
52. *La Opinión Pública* (Albuquerque), March 25, 1893, 3 (translation mine).
53. Nancy F. Cott, *Public Vows: A History of Marriage and the Nation* (Cambridge: Harvard University Press, 2000), 136.
54. *Santa Fe New Mexican,* July 28, 1911, 5.
55. *Albuquerque Morning Journal,* July 2, 1911, 8.
56. Kenneth Balcomb, *A Boy's Albuquerque, 1898–1912* (Albuquerque: University of New Mexico Press, 1980), 8, 37.
57. *NM v. Lizzie McGrath,* 1911, NMSRCA.
58. Felski, *Gender of Modernity,* 62; Smith-Rosenberg, *Disorderly Conduct,* 217–44.
59. *Albuquerque Morning Journal,* October 8, 1882, 2.
60. Ibid., March 8, 1918, 3.
61. Dana Frank, *Purchasing Power: Consumer Organizing, Gender, and the Seattle Labor Movement, 1919–1929* (New York: Cambridge University Press, 1994).
62. *Albuquerque Democrat,* May 24, 1883, 4.
63. *Albuquerque Daily Democrat,* May 7, 1883; in Johnson and Johnson, *Gilded Palaces of Shame,* 46.
64. *Albuquerque Democrat,* August 24, 1883, 1.
65. *Albuquerque Morning Journal,* May 12, 1909, 6.
66. Benson, *Counter Cultures.*
67. Findlay, *Imposing Decency.*
68. *Albuquerque Daily Journal,* February 2, 1882, 4
69. Ibid.

CHAPTER EIGHT

1. Smith-Rosenberg, *Disorderly Conduct*; Duggan, *Sapphic Slashers*; Reagan, *When Abortion Was a Crime*; Stern, "Buildings, Boundaries, and Blood."
2. D'Emilio and Freedman, *Intimate Matters.* Other writers have similarly addressed the relationship between sexuality and modernity. Michel Foucault makes sexuality absolutely central to modernity, arguing that "what is peculiar to modern societies, in fact, is not that they consigned sex to a shadow existence, but that they dedicated themselves to speaking of it *ad infinitum,* while exploiting it as *the* secret." Michel Foucault, *History of Sexuality.* Vol. 1: *An Introduction* (New York: Vintage Books, 1977), 35. Sharon Ullman argues that "modern sexuality . . . refers to the twentieth-century redefinition of sexuality as a means of self-realization rooted in pleasure and unconnected to reproduction." Sharon R. Ullman, *Sex Seen: The Emergence of Modern Sexuality in America* (Berkeley: University of California Press, 1993), 3. Judith Walkowitz nicely summarizes, "The discourse of sexuality was a privileged object of analysis, the essential place to grasp the workings of power in modern Western societies." Walkowitz, *City of Dreadful Delight,* 8. Finally, Rita Felski, in see-

ing the modern era as "predicated upon an individuated and self-conscious subjectivity," questions "the belief that modernity can be reduced to a single meaning and historical logic." Rather, she advocates a "multi-perspectival approach to the cultural politics of modernity," focusing on "women's complex and changing relationships to the diverse political, philosophical and cultural legacies of modernity." Felski, *Gender of Modernity*, 13, 8.

3. Duggan, *Sapphic Slashers*.

4. Rosaura Sánchez, "Dismantling the Colossus: Martí and Ruiz de Burton on the Formulation of Anglo América," in *José Martí's "Our America": From National to Hemispheric Cultural Studies*, ed. Jeffrey Belnap and Raúl Fernández (Durham, NC: Duke University Press, 1998), 115–28; José David Saldívar, "Nuestra América's Borders: Remapping American Cultural Studies," in Belnap and Fernández, eds., *José Martí's "Our America,"* 144–75; Limón, *Dancing with the Devil*.

5. Amy Kaplan, "Black and Blue on San Juan Hill," in *Cultures of United States Imperialism*, ed. Amy Kaplan and Donald E. Pease (Durham, NC: Duke University Press, 1993), 219–36; Kristin Hoganson, *Fighting for American Manhood: How Gender Politics Provoked the Spanish-American and Philippine-American Wars* (New Haven: Yale University Press, 2000).

6. Amy Kaplan, *The Anarchy of Empire in the Making of U.S. Culture* (Cambridge: Harvard University Press, 2003).

7. Stern, "Buildings, Boundaries, and Blood"; John Nieto-Phillips, "Citizenship and Empire: Race, Language, and Self-Government in New Mexico and Puerto Rico, 1898–1917," *Centro Journal* 11 (Fall 1999): 51–74; Richard Rodriguez, "True West: Relocating the Horizon of the American Frontier," *Harper's Magazine* 293 (September 1996): 43.

8. Clearly, much more work needs to be done along this question, with further comparative work juxtaposing dominant trends in the creation of the body politic in modern America to that of modern Latin America. For example, while historians have begun to document the history of American Spanish-language newspapers, few have investigated such newspapers for their links to more "modern" trends such as advertising, leisure pursuits, and crime reporting and spectacle. Scholars could also pay more attention to rituals and body practices relating to death and burial in both the United States and Mexico. Likewise, the development of modern, professionalized medicine in Mexico or Latin America and its links to developments in Europe and the United States deserves more sustained examination, particularly as such developments relate to emerging racial and sexual scientific classifications.

9. Roediger, *The Wages of Whiteness*; Bederman, *Manliness and Civilization*.

10. Lipsitz, *The Possessive Investment in Whiteness*, 3; Almaguer, *Racial Fault Lines*; Foley, *The White Scourge*; Jacobson, *Whiteness of a Different Color*; Duggan, *Sapphic Slashers*.

11. Stoler, *Race and the Education of Desire*. The final sentence adapts David Roediger's assertion regarding the intertwining of race and class in American history. Roediger, *The Wages of Whiteness*, 11.

12. Almaguer, *Racial Fault Lines*; Foley, *The White Scourge*; Menchaca, *Recovering History, Constructing Race*.

13. Vicki L. Ruiz, *From Out of the Shadows: Mexican Women in Twentieth-Century America* (New York: Oxford University Press, 1998).

14. Montoya, *Translating Property*; Deutsch, *No Separate Refuge*; González, "The Spanish-Mexican Women of Santa Fé"; Castañeda, "Sexual Violence."

15. Stallybrass and White, *The Politics and Poetics of Transgression*, 191.

16. Lott, *Love and Theft*, 163.

17. Stoler, *Race and the Education of Desire*, 177.

18. Walkowitz, *City of Dreadful Delight*.

BIBLIOGRAPHY

PRIMARY SOURCES

Bernalillo County Marriage Records, Bernalillo County Courthouse, Albuquerque, New Mexico.

Bernalillo County Marriage Register, 1890, Bernalillo County Courthouse, Albuquerque, New Mexico.

Compiled Laws of New Mexico, 1884. Santa Fe: New Mexico Printing Co., 1885.

Compiled Laws of New Mexico, 1897. Santa Fe: New Mexico Printing Co., 1897.

Laws of the State of New Mexico. Albuquerque: Albright & Anderson, 1912.

Laws of the State of New Mexico. Albuquerque: Central Printing, 1921.

Navajo Oral History Collection, Center for Southwest Research, University of New Mexico, Albuquerque, New Mexico.

1919 Session Laws of New Mexico. Albuquerque: Albright & Anderson, 1919.

Pueblo Oral History Collection, Center for Southwest Research, University of New Mexico, Albuquerque, New Mexico.

Pueblo Records, National Archives and Records Administration, Rocky Mountain Branch, Denver, Colorado.

Reports of the Charges against Supt. Creager, Albuquerque School, July 29, 1891.

Revised Statutes and Laws of the Territory of New Mexico. St. Louis: RP Studley & Co., 1865.

Santa Fe Indian School: The First 100 Years Project. MSS 595, Box 1, Folder 1, Center for Southwest Research, University of New Mexico, Albuquerque, New Mexico.

Session Laws of the State of New Mexico, 1915. Denver: W. H. Courtwright, 1915.

Strong Bros. Funeral Directors and Embalmers (pamphlet). Albuquerque: Albright & Anderson Printers, 1911.

U.S. Bureau of the Census. *Population, 1900*. Washington, DC: United States Printing Office, 1900.

———. *Tenth Census of the United States, 1880, Bernalillo County, New Mexico.* Washington, DC, 1880.

———. *Eleventh Census of the United States, 1890, Bernalillo County, New Mexico.* Washington, DC, 1890.

———. *Twelfth Census of the United States, 1900, Bernalillo County, New Mexico.* Washington, DC, 1900.

———. *Thirteenth Census of the United States, 1910, Bernalillo County, New Mexico.* Washington, DC, 1910.

———. *Fourteenth Census of the United States.* Washington, DC, 1920.

PERIODICALS

Albuquerque City Directory and Business Guide
Albuquerque Democrat
Albuquerque Democrat-Journal
Albuquerque Journal-Democrat
Albuquerque Morning Democrat
Albuquerque Morning Journal
Albuquerque Review
Daily Citizen (Albuquerque)
Daily New Mexican (Santa Fe)
La Bandera Americana (Albuquerque)
La Opinión Pública (Albuquerque)
Las Vegas Daily Optic
New Mexico Medical Journal
Raton Range
The Swastika (Des Moines, NM)
Santa Fe Daily New Mexican
Santa Fe New Mexican
Santa Fe Weekly Democrat
Tribune Citizen (Albuquerque)

COURT CASES

Elfego Baca v. Francisquita Pohmer de Baca, Civil Case #15069, Bernalillo County, New Mexico.

Probate Court Case #5393, Elfego Baca, Bernalillo County, New Mexico.

Probate Court Case #8496, Francisquita Pohmer de Baca, Bernalillo County, New Mexico.

State of New Mexico v. William G. Bassett, Supreme Court Case #2295, 1919, SRCA.

Territory of New Mexico v. Amado Ancheta, Supreme Court Case #1678, 1915, SRCA.

Territory of New Mexico v. Bonifacio Mares, Supreme Court Case #875, 1901, State Records Center and Archives, Santa Fe, New Mexico (SRCA).

Territory of New Mexico v. Charles Easter, Bernalillo County, New Mexico, #5152, 1913, SRCA.

Territory of New Mexico v. Florencio Pfeifer, Bernalillo County, New Mexico, #4557, 1909, SRCA.

Territory of New Mexico v. Geronimo Pino, Supreme Court Case #790, 1898, SRCA.

Territory of New Mexico v. Pablo Archuleta, Santa Fe County, New Mexico, #3854, 1911, SRCA.

Territory of New Mexico v. Prudencio Martinez and Felipe Garcia, San Miguel County, District Court, Criminal Case #4710, 1908, SRCA.

Territory of New Mexico v. Ricardo Alva, Supreme Court Case #1571, 1913, SRCA.

Territory of New Mexico v. Robert H. Pierce, Bernalillo County Criminal Case #4413, 1909, SRCA.

Territory of New Mexico v. VP Edie, Bernalillo County Criminal Case #1457, 1891, SRCA.

SECONDARY SOURCES

Abelson, Elaine S. *When Ladies Go A-Thieving: Middle-Class Shoplifters in the Victorian Department Store.* New York: Oxford University Press, 1989.

Acuña, Rudolfo. *Occupied America: A History of Chicanos.* New York: Harper & Row, 1981.

Adams, David Wallace. *Education for Extinction: American Indians and the Boarding School Experience, 1875–1928.* Lawrence: University of Kansas Press, 1995.

Adams, Henry. *The Education of Henry Adams.* Boston: Houghton Mifflin, 1973.

Almaguer, Tomás. *Racial Fault Lines: The Historical Origins of White Supremacy in California.* Berkeley: University of California Press, 1994.

Anderson, Benedict. *Imagined Communities: Reflections on the Origin and Spread of Nationalism.* Rev. ed. London: Verso, 1991.

Anzaldúa, Gloria. *Borderlands/*La Frontera: *The New Mestiza.* San Francisco: Spinsters/Aunt Lute, 1987.

Arellano, Anselmo. "The People's Movement: Las Gorras Blancas." In *The Contested Homeland: A Chicano History of New Mexico*, ed. Erlinda Gonzales-Berry and David Maciel, 59–82. Albuquerque: University of New Mexico Press, 2000.

Balcomb, Kenneth. *A Boy's Albuquerque, 1898–1912.* Albuquerque: University of New Mexico Press, 1980.

Banta, Martha. "Periodicals Back (Advertisers) to Front (Editors): Whose National Values Market Best?" In *Reciprocal Influences: Literary Production,*

Distribution, and Consumption in America, ed. Steven Fink and Susan S. Williams, 173–98. Columbus: Ohio State University Press, 1999.

Bates, Barbara. *Bargaining for Life: A Social History of Tuberculosis, 1876–1938.* Philadelphia: University of Pennsylvania Press, 1992.

Bederman, Gail. *Manliness and Civilization: A Cultural History of Gender and Race in the United States, 1880–1917.* Chicago: University of Chicago Press, 1995.

Beibel, Charles D. "Cultural Change on the Southwest Frontier: Albuquerque Schooling, 1870–1895." *New Mexico Historical Review* 55 (July 1980): 209–30.

Benson, Susan Porter. *Counter Cultures: Saleswomen, Managers, and Customers in American Department Stores, 1890–1940.* Urbana: University of Illinois Press, 1986.

Berman, Marshall. *All That Is Solid Melts into Air: The Experience of Modernity.* New York: Penguin Books, 1982.

Bodnar, John. *Remaking America: Public Memory, Commemoration, and Patriotism in the Twentieth Century.* Princeton: Princeton University Press, 1992.

Braidotti, Rosi. *Nomadic Subjects: Embodiment and Sexual Difference in Contemporary Feminist Theory.* New York: Columbia University Press, 1994.

Bray, Abigail, and Claire Colebrook. "The Haunted Flesh: Corporeal Feminism and the Politics of (Dis)Embodiment." *Signs* 24 (Autumn 1998): 35–67.

Brodie, Janet Farrell. *Contraception and Abortion in Nineteenth-Century America.* Ithaca: Cornell University Press, 1994.

Brown, Jennifer S. H. *Strangers in the Blood: Fur Trade Company Families in Indian Country.* Vancouver: University of British Columbia Press, 1980.

Butler, Anne. *Daughters of Joy, Sisters of Misery: Prostitutes in the American West, 1865–90.* Urbana: University of Illinois Press, 1985.

Butler, Judith. *Bodies that Matter: On the Discursive Limits of 'Sex.'* New York: Routledge, 1993.

———. "For a Careful Reading." In *Feminist Contentions: A Philosophical Exchange*, ed. Seyla Benhabib, Judith Butler, Drucilla Cornell, and Nancy Fraser. New York: Routledge, 1995.

———. *Gender Trouble: Feminism and the Subversion of Identity.* New York: Routledge, 1990.

Cabán, Pedro A. *Constructing a Colonial People: Puerto Rico and the United States, 1898–1932.* New York: Westview Press, 1999.

Cantú, Norma E. "Los Matachines de la Santa Cruz de la Ladrillera: Notes toward a Socio-literary Analysis." In *Feasts and Celebrations in North American Ethnic Communities*, ed. Ramón A. Gutiérrez and Genevieve Fabre, 57–70. Albuquerque: University of New Mexico Press, 1995.

Castañeda, Antonia. "Sexual Violence in the Politics and Policies of Conquest: Amerindian Women and the Spanish Conquest of Alta California." In

Building with Our Hands: New Directions in Chicana Studies, ed. Adela de le Torre and Beatriz Pesquera, 15–33. Berkeley: University of California Press, 1993.

Chused, Richard H. "Late Nineteenth Century Married Women's Property Law: Reception of the Early Married Women's Property Acts by Courts and Legislatures." *American Journal of Legal History* 29 (January 1985): 3–35.

Connell-Szasz, Margaret. "Albuquerque Congregationalists and Southwestern Social Reform: 1900–1917." *New Mexico Historical Review* 55 (July 1980): 231–52.

Cott, Nancy F. *Public Vows: A History of Marriage and the Nation.* Cambridge: Harvard University Press, 2000.

Craver, Rebecca McDowell. *Impact of Intimacy: Mexican-Anglo Intermarriage in New Mexico, 1821–1846.* El Paso: Texas Western Press, 1982.

D'Cruze, Shani. *Crimes of Outrage: Sex, Violence, and Victorian Working Women.* DeKalb: Northern Illinois University Press, 1998.

Deloria, Philip J. *Playing Indian.* New Haven: Yale University Press, 1998.

DeMark, Judith B. "The Immigrant Experience in Albuquerque, 1880–1920." Ph.D. diss., University of New Mexico, 1984.

D'Emilio, John, and Estelle B. Freedman. *Intimate Matters: A History of Sexuality in America.* New York: Harper & Row, 1988.

Deutsch, Sarah. *No Separate Refuge: Culture, Class, and Gender on an Anglo-Hispanic Frontier in the American Southwest, 1880–1940.* New York: Oxford University Press, 1987.

Dominguez, Virginia R. *White by Definition: Social Classification in Creole Louisiana.* New Brunswick, NJ: Rutgers University Press, 1986.

Douglas, Mary. *Natural Symbols: Explorations in Cosmology.* New York: Routledge, 1970.

Dubinsky, Karen. *Improper Advances: Rape and Heterosexual Conflict in Ontario, 1880–1929.* Chicago: University of Chicago Press, 1993.

Duggan, Lisa. *Sapphic Slashers: Sex, Violence, and American Modernity.* Durham, NC: Duke University Press, 2000.

Dunlap, Leslie K. "The Reform of Rape Law and the Problem of White Men: Age-of-Consent Campaigns in the South, 1885–1910." In *Sex, Love, Race: Crossing Boundaries in North American History*, ed. Martha Hodes, 294–312. New York: New York University Press, 1999.

Duran, Bonnie. "Indigenous versus Colonial Discourse: Alcohol and American Indian Identity." In *Dressing in Feathers: The Construction of the Indian in American Popular Culture*, ed. S. Elizabeth Bird, 111–28. New York: Westview Press, 1996.

Dysart, Jane. "Mexican Women in San Antonio, 1830–1860: The Assimilation Process." *Western Historical Quarterly* (October 1976): 365–75.

Edwards, Laura F. "Sexual Violence, Gender, Reconstruction, and the Extension of Patriarchy in Granville County, North Carolina." *North Carolina Historical Review* 68 (July 1991): 237–60.

Faragher, John Mack, et al., eds. *Out of Many, Volume One, Brief 4th Edition*. New York: Prentice Hall, 2003.

Felski, Rita. *Gender of Modernity*. Cambridge: Harvard University Press, 1995.

Findlay, Eileen J. Suárez. *Imposing Decency: The Politics of Sexuality and Race in Puerto Rico, 1870–1920*. Durham, NC: Duke University Press, 2000.

Foley, Neil. *The White Scourge: Mexicans, Blacks, and Poor Whites in Texas Cotton Culture*. Berkeley: University of California Press, 1997.

Foner, Eric, and John A. Garraty, eds. *The Reader's Companion to American History*. Boston: Houghton Mifflin, 1991.

Foster, Susan Leigh. "Choreographies of Gender." *Signs* 24 (Autumn 1998): 1–33.

Foucault, Michel. *The History of Sexuality*. Vol. 1: *An Introduction*. New York: Vintage Books, 1977.

Frank, Dana. *Purchasing Power: Consumer Organizing, Gender, and the Seattle Labor Movement, 1919–1929*. New York: Cambridge University Press, 1994.

Frankenberg, Ruth. *White Women, Race Matters: The Social Construction of Whiteness*. Minneapolis: University of Minnesota Press, 1993.

Garza-Falcón, Leticia M. Gente Decente: *A Borderlands Response to the Rhetoric of Dominance*. Austin: University of Texas Press, 1998.

Gilfolye, Timothy J. *City of Eros: New York City, Prostitution, and the Commercialization of Sex, 1790–1920*. New York: Norton, 1992.

Gilmore, Glenda. *Gender and Jim Crow: Women and the Politics of White Supremacy in North Carolina, 1896–1920*. Chapel Hill: University of North Carolina Press, 1996.

Golden, Janet Lynne, ed. *Framing Disease: Studies in Cultural History*. New Brunswick: Rutgers University Press, 1992.

Goldman, Marion S. *Gold Diggers and Silver Miners: Prostitution and Social Life on the Comstock Lode*. Ann Arbor: University of Michigan Press, 1981.

Gómez-Pena, Guillermo. *The New World Border*. San Francisco: City Lights, 1996.

González, Deena J. "The Spanish-Mexican Women of Santa Fé: Patterns of Their Resistance and Accommodation, 1820–1880." Ph.D. diss., University of California, Berkeley, 1985.

Gordon, Linda. *Woman's Body, Woman's Right: Birth Control in America*. New York: Penguin Books, 1990.

Green, Jesse, ed. *Cushing at Zuni: The Correspondence and Journals of Frank Hamilton Cushing, 1879–1884*. Albuquerque: University of New Mexico Press, 1990.

Gutiérrez, David G. "Migration, Emergent Ethnicity, and the 'Third Space': The Shifting Politics of Nationalism in Greater Mexico." *Journal of American History* 86 (September 1999): 481–517.

Gutiérrez, Ramón A. "Aztlán, Montezuma, and New Mexico: The Political Uses of American Indian Mythology." in *Aztlán: Essays on the Chicano Homeland*, ed. Rudolfo A. Anaya and Francisco Lomeli, 172–90. Albuquerque: University of New Mexico Press, 1989.

———. "Decolonizing the Body: Kinship and the Nation." *American Archivist* 57 (Winter 1994): 86–99.

———. "El Santuario de Chimayó: A Synthetic Shrine in New Mexico." In *Feasts and Celebrations in North American Ethnic Communities*, ed. Ramón A. Gutiérrez and Genevieve Fabre, 71–86. Albuquerque: University of New Mexico Press, 1995.

———. *When Jesus Came, the Corn Mothers Went Away: Marriage, Sexuality, and Power in New Mexico, 1500–1846*. Stanford: Stanford University Press, 1991.

Gutiérrez-Jones, Carl. *Rethinking the Borderlands: Between Chicano Culture and Legal Discourse*. Berkeley: University of California Press, 1995.

Gutmann, Myron P., et al. "The Demographic Impact of the Mexican Revolution in the United States." (Translation of "Los efectos demográficos de la revolución Mexicana en Estados Unidos," *Historica Mexicana* 50 [2000]: 145–65).

Haas, Lisbeth. *Conquests and Historical Identities in California, 1769–1936*. Berkeley: University of California Press, 1995.

Hale, Grace Elizabeth. *Making Whiteness: The Culture of Segregation in the South*. New York: Pantheon Press, 1998.

Hall, Jacquelyn Dowd. " 'The Mind That Burns in Each Body': Women, Rape, and Racial Violence." In *Powers of Desire: The Politics of Sexuality*, ed. Ann Snitow, Christine Stansell, and Sharon Thompson. New York: Monthly Review Press, 1983.

Higham, John. "The Re-Orientation of American Culture in the 1890's." In *Writing American History: Essays on Modern Scholarship*, ed. John Higham, 73–102. Bloomington: Indiana University Press, 1970.

Hinsley, Curtis M. "Zunis and Brahmins: Cultural Ambivalence in the Gilded Age." In *Romantic Motives: Essays on Anthropological Sensibility*, ed. George W. Stocking Jr. Madison: University of Wisconsin Press, 1989.

Hodes, Martha. "The Sexualization of Reconstruction Politics: White Women and Black Men in the South after the Civil War." *Journal of the History of Sexuality* 3 (1993): 402–17.

———. *White Women, Black Men: Illicit Sex in the Nineteenth-Century South*. New Haven: Yale University Press, 1997.

Hoganson, Kristin. *Fighting for American Manhood: How Gender Politics Provoked the Spanish-American and Philippine-American Wars*. New Haven: Yale University Press, 2000.

Hoppenstand, Gary. "Ambrose Bierce and the Transformation of the Gothic Tale in the Nineteenth-Century American Periodical." In *Periodical Literature in Nineteenth-Century America*, ed. Kenneth M. Price and Susan Belasco Smith, 220–38. Charlottesville: University Press of Virginia, 1995.

Howell, Joel D. *Technology in the Hospital: Transforming Patient Care in the Early Twentieth Century.* Baltimore: Johns Hopkins University Press, 1995.

Huning, Franz. *Trader on the Santa Fe Trail.* Albuquerque: University of Albuquerque Press, 1973.

Hyde, Alan. *Bodies of Law.* Princeton: Princeton University Press, 1997.

Jacobs, Margaret D. *Engendered Encounters: Feminism and Pueblo Cultures, 1879–1934.* Lincoln: University of Nebraska Press, 1999.

Jacobson, Matthew Frye. *Whiteness of a Different Color: European Immigrants and the Alchemy of Race.* Cambridge: Harvard University Press, 1998.

Johnson, Byron A. *Old Town Albuquerque, New Mexico: A Guide to Its History and Architecture.* Albuquerque: Albuquerque Museum, n.d.

Johnson, Byron A., and Sharon P. Johnson. *Gilded Palaces of Shame: Albuquerque's Redlight Districts, 1880–1914.* Albuquerque: Gilded Age Press, 1983.

Johnson, Judith R. "John Weinzirl: A Personal Search for the Conquest of Tuberculosis." *New Mexico Historical Review* 63 (August 1988): 141–55.

Johnson, Susan L. "Sharing Bed and Board: Cohabitation and Cultural Difference in Central Arizona Mining Towns, 1863–1873." In *The Women's West*, ed. Susan Armitage and Elizabeth Jameson, 77–92. Norman: University of Oklahoma Press, 1987.

Jordanova, Ludmilla. *Sexual Visions: Images of Gender in Science and Medicine between the Eighteenth and Twentieth Centuries.* Madison: University of Wisconsin Press, 1989.

Kaplan, Amy. *The Anarchy of Empire in the Making of U.S. Culture.* Cambridge: Harvard University Press, 2003.

———. "Black and Blue on San Juan Hill." In *Cultures of United States Imperialism*, ed. Amy Kaplan and Donald E. Pease, 219–36. Durham, NC: Duke University Press, 1993.

Kaplan, Amy, and Donald E. Pease, eds. *Cultures of United States Imperialism.* Durham, NC: Duke University Press, 1993.

Kasson, John F. *Rudeness and Civility: Manners in Nineteenth-Century Urban America.* New York: Hill and Wang, 1990.

Keleher, William A. *New Mexicans I Knew: Memoirs 1892–1969.* Albuquerque: University of New Mexico Press, 1983.

Kraut, Alan M. *Silent Travelers: Germs, Genes, and the "Immigrant Menace."* New York: Basic Books, 1994.

Lamar, Howard R. *The Far Southwest, 1846–1912.* New York: W. W. Norton, 1970.

———, ed., *The New Encyclopedia of the American West.* New Haven: Yale University Press, 1998.

Lange, Charles H., Carroll L. Riley, and Elizabeth M. Lange, eds. *The*

Southwestern Journals of Adolph F. Bandelier, 1889–1892, Volume Four.
Albuquerque: University of New Mexico Press, 1984.

Laqueur, Thomas. *Making Sex: Body and Gender from the Greeks to Freud.*
Cambridge: Harvard University Press, 1990.

Larson, Robert W. *New Mexico's Quest for Statehood, 1846–1912.* Albuquerque:
University of New Mexico Press, 1968.

Leach, William. *Land of Desire: Merchants, Power, and the Rise of a New American
Culture.* New York: Vintage Books, 1993.

Lears, Jackson. *Fables of Abundance: A Cultural History of Advertising in America.*
New York: Basic Books, 1994.

Leavitt, Judith Walzer. "Birthing and Anesthesia: The Debate over Twilight
Sleep." In *Women and Health in America,* ed. Judith Walzer Leavitt, 175–84.
Madison: University of Wisconsin Press, 1984.

Lehman, Terry Jon. "Santa Fé and Albuquerque 1870–1900: Contrast and
Conflict in the Development of Two Southwestern Towns." Ph.D. diss.,
Indiana University, 1974.

Leonard, Karen Isaksen. *Making Ethnic Choices: California's Punjabi Mexican
Americans.* Philadelphia: Temple University Press, 1992.

"Letters of William Forrest Howard to Minnie F. Hayden." *New Mexico Historical
Review* 56 (January 1981): 41–69.

Lewis, Earl, and Heidi Ardizzone. *Love on Trial: An American Scandal in Black
and White.* New York: W. W. Norton, 2001.

Limón, José. *Dancing with the Devil: Society and Cultural Poetics in Mexican-
American South Texas.* Madison: University of Wisconsin Press, 1994.

Lipsitz, George. *The Possessive Investment in Whiteness: How White People Profit
from Identity Politics.* Philadelphia: Temple University Press, 1998.

Lomawaima, K. Tsianina. *They Called It Prairie Light: The Story of Chiloco Indian
School.* Lincoln: University of Nebraska Press, 1994.

Lott, Eric. *Love and Theft: Blackface Minstrelsy and the American Working Class.*
New York: Oxford University Press, 1995.

Lowe, Lisa. *Immigrant Acts: On Asian American Cultural Politics.* Durham: Duke
University Press, 1996.

Martin, Emily. *The Woman in the Body: A Cultural Analysis of Reproduction.*
Boston: Beacon Press, 1992.

McClaren, Angus. *The Trials of Masculinity: Policing Sexual Boundaries,
1870–1930.* Chicago: University of Chicago Press, 1997.

McClintock, Anne. *Imperial Leather: Race, Gender, and Sexuality in the Colonial
Contest.* London: Routledge, 1995.

McKinney, Lillie G. "History of the Albuquerque Indian School." *New Mexico
Historical Review* 20 (April 1945): 109–38, 207–26.

Meléndez, A. Gabriel. *"So All Is Not Lost": The Poetics of Print in Nuevomexicano
Communities, 1834–1958.* Albuquerque: University of New Mexico Press, 1997.

Melzer, Richard. "A Dark and Terrible Moment: The Spanish Flu Epidemic of 1918 in New Mexico." *New Mexico Historical Review* 57 (July 1982): 213–36.

Menchaca, Martha. *Recovering History, Constructing Race: The Indian, Black, and White Roots of Mexican Americans.* Austin: University of Texas Press, 2001.

Meyer, Doris. *Speaking for Themselves: Neomexicano Cultural Identity and the Spanish-Language Press, 1880–1920.* Albuquerque: University of New Mexico Press, 1996.

Miller, Darlis A. "Intercultural Marriages in the American Southwest." In *New Mexico Women,* ed. Joan M. Jenson and Darlis A. Miller, 95–119. Albuquerque: University of New Mexico Press, 1983.

Miller, William Ian. *The Anatomy of Disgust.* Cambridge: Harvard University Press, 1997.

Mitchell, Pablo R. "Accomplished Ladies and *Coyotes*: Marriage, Power, and Straying from the Flock in Territorial New Mexico, 1880–1920." In *Sex, Love, Race: Crossing Boundaries in North American History,* ed. Martha Hodes, 331–51. New York: New York University Press, 1999.

———. "Queen for a Day: Margaret/Margarita Otero Harrison and Intermarriage in Turn-of-the-Century Albuquerque." In *Explorations in American History,* ed. Sandra. McMahon and Louis Tanner, 51–80. Albuquerque: Center for the American West Press, 1995.

———. " 'You Just Don't Know Mrs. Baca': Intermarriage, Mixed Heritage, and Identity in New Mexico." Unpublished manuscript.

Mohr, James. *Abortion in America: The Origins and Evolution of National Policy, 1800–1900.* New York Oxford University Press, 1978.

Montgomery, Charles H. *The Spanish Redemption: Heritage, Power, and Loss on New Mexico's Upper Rio Grande.* Berkeley: University of California Press, 2002.

———. "The Trap of Race and Memory: The Language of Spanish Civility on the Upper Rio Grande." *American Quarterly* 52 (September 2000): 478–513.

Montoya, María E. "The Dual World of Governor Miguel A. Otero: Myth and Reality in Turn-of-the-Century New Mexico." *New Mexico Historical Review* 67 (January 1992): 13–31.

———. *Translating Property: The Maxwell Land Grant and the Conflict over Land in the American West, 1840–1900.* Berkeley: University of California Press, 2002.

Moran, Jeffrey P. " 'Modernism Gone Mad': Sex Education Comes to Chicago, 1913." *Journal of American History* 83 (September 1996): 481–513.

Morantz-Sanchez, Regina. *Sympathy and Science: Women Physicians in American Medicine.* New York: Oxford University Press, 1985.

Nash, Gary B. "The Hidden History of Mestizo America." *Journal of American History* 82 (December 1995): 941–62.

"Necrology: Elfego Baca." *New Mexico Historical Review* 21 (1946): 74–76.

Nieto-Phillips, John M. "Citizenship and Empire: Race, Language, and Self-

Government in New Mexico and Puerto Rico, 1898–1917." *Centro Journal* 11 (Fall 1999): 51–74.

———. " 'No Other Blood': History, Language, and 'Spanish American' Ethnic Identity in New Mexico, 1880s–1920s." Ph.D. diss., University of California, Los Angeles, 1997.

———. "Spanish American Ethnic Identity and New Mexico's Statehood Struggle." In *Contested Homeland: A Chicano History of New Mexico*, Erlinda Gonzales-Berry and David R. Maciel, 97–142. Albuquerque: University of New Mexico Press, 2000.

Nostrand, Richard L. *The Hispano Homeland.* Norman: University of Oklahoma Press, 1992.

Odem, Mary E. *Delinquent Daughters: Protecting and Policing Adolescent Sexuality in the United States, 1885–1920.* Chapel Hill: University of North Carolina Press, 1995.

Omi, Michael, and Howard Winant. *Racial Formation in the United States: From the 1960's to the 1990's.* New York: Routledge, 1994.

Otero, Miguel Antonio. *My Life on the Frontier, 1864–1882.* Albuquerque: University of New Mexico Press, 1987.

———. *My Nine Years as Governor, 1897–1906.* Albuquerque: University of New Mexico Press, 1940.

Panunzio, Constantine. "Intermarriage in Los Angeles, 1924–1933." *American Journal of Sociology* 47 (1942): 690–701.

Parish, William J. *The Charles Ilfeld Company: A Study of the Rise and Decline of Mercantile Capitalism in New Mexico.* Cambridge: Harvard University Press, 1961.

Pascoe, Peggy. "Miscegenation Law, Court Cases, and Ideologies of 'Race' in Twentieth-Century America." *Journal of American History* 83 (June 1996): 44–69.

———. "Race, Gender, and Intercultural Relations: The Case of Interracial Marriage." *Frontiers* 1 (1991): 5–18.

Peiss, Kathy. *Cheap Amusements: Working Women and Leisure in Turn-of-the-Century New York.* Philadelphia: Temple University Press, 1986.

Peixotto, Ernest. *Our Hispanic Southwest.* New York: Charles Scribner's Sons, 1916.

Poovey, Mary. " 'Scenes of an Indelicate Character': The Medical 'Treatment' of Victorian Women." *Representations* 14 (Spring 1986): 137–68.

Qoyawayma, Polingaysi. *No Turning Back: A True Account of a Hopi Indian Girl's Struggle to Bridge the Gap between the World of Her People and the World of the White Man.* Albuquerque: University of New Mexico Press, 1964.

Rael-Gálvez, Estévan. "Identifying Captivity and Capturing Identity: Narratives of American Indian Slavery, Colorado and New Mexico, 1776–1934." Ph.D. diss., University of Michigan, 2002.

Rafael, Vicente L. "White Love: Surveillance and Nationalist Resistance in the

U.S. Colonization of the Philippines." In *Cultures of United States Imperialism*, ed. Amy Kaplan and Donald E. Pease, 185–218. Durham, NC: Duke University Press, 1993.

Reagan, Leslie J. *When Abortion Was a Crime: Women, Medicine, and Law in the United States, 1867–1973*. Berkeley: University of California Press, 1997.

Reichard, David A. " 'Justice is God's law': The Struggle to Control Social Conflict and United States Colonization of New Mexico, 1846–1912." Ph.D. diss., Temple University, 1996.

Riley, Glenda. *Building and Breaking Families in the American West*. Albuquerque: University of New Mexico Press, 1996.

Roach, Joseph. *Cities of the Dead: Circum-Atlantic Performance*. New York: Columbia University Press, 1996.

Rodriguez, Richard. "True West: Relocating the Horizon of the American Frontier." *Harper's Magazine* 293 (September 1996): 37–46.

Rodríguez, Sylvia. *The Matachines Dance: Ritual Symbolism and Interethnic Relations in the Upper Rio Grande Valley*. Albuquerque: University of New Mexico Press, 1996.

Roediger, David R. *The Wages of Whiteness: Race and the Making of the American Working Class*. London: Verso, 1991.

Rosaldo, Renato. *Culture and Truth: The Remaking of Social Analysis*. Boston: Beacon Press, 1989.

Rosen, Ruth. *The Lost Sisterhood: Prostitution in America, 1900–1918*. Baltimore: Johns Hopkins University Press, 1982.

Rosenberg, Charles E. *Explaining Epidemics and Other Studies in the History of Medicine*. Cambridge: Harvard University Press, 1992.

Ruiz, Vicki L. *From Out of the Shadows: Mexican Women in Twentieth-Century America*. New York: Oxford University Press, 1998.

Russett, Cynthia E. *Sexual Science: The Victorian Construction of Womanhood*. Cambridge: Harvard University Press, 1989.

Ryan, Mary P. "The American Parade: Representations of the Nineteenth-Century Social Order." In *The New Cultural History*, ed. Lynn Hunt, 131–53. Berkeley: University of California Press, 1989.

———. *Civic Wars: Democracy and Public Life in the American City during the Nineteenth Century*. Berkeley: University of California Press, 1997.

Saldívar, José David. *Border Matters: Remapping American Cultural Studies*. Berkeley: University of California Press, 1997.

———. "Nuestra América's Borders: Remapping American Cultural Studies." In *José Martí's "Our America": From National to Hemispheric Cultural Studies*, ed. Jeffrey Belnap and Raúl Fernández, 144–75. Durham, NC: Duke University Press, 1998.

Sánchez, George J. *Becoming Mexican American: Ethnicity, Culture, and Identity in Chicano Los Angeles, 1900–1945*. New York: Oxford University Press, 1993.

Sánchez, Rosaura. "Dismantling the Colossus: Martí and Ruiz de Burton on the Formulation of Anglo América." In *José Martí's "Our America": From National to Hemispheric Cultural Studies.* ed. Jeffrey Belnap and Raúl Fernández, 115–28. Durham, NC: Duke University Press, 1998.

———. *Telling Identities: The Californio Testimonios.* Minneapolis: University of Minnesota Press, 1995.

Sando, Joe S. *Pueblo Nations: Eight Centuries of Pueblo Indian History.* Santa Fe: Clear Light Publishers, 1998.

Santiago-Valles, Kelvin A. *"Subject People" and Colonial Discourses: Economic Transformation and Social Disorder in Puerto Rico, 1898–1947.* Albany: State University of New York Press, 1994.

Savage, Kirk. *Standing Soldiers, Kneeling Slaves: Race, War, and Monument in Nineteenth-Century America.* Princeton: Princeton University Press, 1997.

Schackel, Sandra. *Social Housekeepers: Women Shaping Public Policy in New Mexico, 1920–1940.* Albuquerque: University of New Mexico Press, 1992.

———. " 'The Tales Those Nurses Told!': Public Health Nurses among the Pueblo and Navajo Indians." *New Mexico Historical Review* 65 (April 1990): 225–49.

Schlissel, Lillian, Byrd Gibbons, and Elizabeth Hampsten, eds. *Far from Home: Families of the Westward Journey.* New York: Schocken Books, 1989.

Schmidt, Leigh Eric. "The Commercialization of the Calendar: American Holidays and the Culture of Consumption, 1870–1930." *Journal of American History* 78 (December 1991): 887–916.

Scobey, David. "Anatomy of a Promenade: The Politics of Bourgeois Sociability in Nineteenth-Century New York." *Social History* 17 (May 1992): 203–27.

Scott, Joan W. "The Evidence of Experience." *Critical Inquiry* 17 (Summer 1991): 773–97.

Secor-Welsh, Cynthia. "Governor Miguel Antonio Otero, 1897–1906: Agent for Change." Master's thesis, University of New Mexico, 1984.

Shah, Nayan. *Contagious Divides: Epidemics and Race in San Francisco's Chinatown.* Berkeley: University of California Press, 2001.

Shorter, Edward. *Doctors and Their Patients: A Social History.* New York: Simon and Schuster, 1985.

Siegel, Reva B. "The Modernization of Marital Status Law: Adjudicating Wives' Rights to Earnings, 1860–1930." *Georgetown Law Journal* 82 (September 1994), 2127–211.

Silber, Nina. *The Romance of Reunion: Northerners and the South, 1865–1900.* Chapel Hill: University of North Carolina Press, 1994.

Simmons, Marc. *New Mexico: An Interpretive History.* Albuquerque: University of New Mexico Press, 1977.

———. *Spanish Pathways: Readings in the History of Hispanic New Mexico.* Albuquerque: University of New Mexico Press, 2001.

Slater, Don. *Consumer Culture and Modernity*. Cambridge: Polity Press, 1997.

Sloane, David Charles. *The Last Great Necessity: Cemeteries in American History*. Baltimore: Johns Hopkins University Press, 1995.

Smith-Rosenberg, Carroll. "The Body Politic." In *Coming to Terms: Feminism, Theory, Politics*, ed. Elizabeth Weed, 101–21. New York: Routledge, 1989.

———. "Dis-Covering the Subject of the 'Great Constitutional Debate,' 1786–1789." *Journal of American History* (December 1992): 841–73.

———. *Disorderly Conduct: Visions of Gender in Victorian America*. New York: Oxford University Press, 1985.

Smits, David D. " 'Squaw Men,' 'Half-Breeds,' and Amalgamators: Late Nineteenth-Century Anglo-American Attitudes toward Indian-White Race-Mixing." *American Indian Culture and Research Journal* 15 (Fall 1991): 29–61.

Spicer, Edward H. *Cycles of Conquest: The Impact of Spain, Mexico, and the United States on the Indians of the Southwest, 1533–1960*. Tucson: University of Arizona Press, 1962.

Spickard, Paul R. *Mixed Blood: Intermarriage and Ethnic Identity in Twentieth-Century America*. Madison: University of Wisconsin Press, 1989.

Spidle, Jake W., Jr. " 'An Army of Invalids': New Mexico and the Birth of a Tuberculosis Industry." *New Mexico Historical Review* 61 (July 1986): 179–201.

———. *Doctors of Medicine in New Mexico: A History of Health and Medical Practice, 1886–1986*. Albuquerque: University of New Mexico Press, 1986.

Stallybrass, Peter, and Allon White. *The Politics and Poetics of Transgression*. Ithaca: Cornell University Press, 1986.

Stepan, Nancy Leys. "Race, Gender, Science, and Citizenship." *Gender and History* 10 (April 1998): 26–52.

Spicer, Edward H. *Cycles of Conquest: The Impact of Spain, Mexico, and the United States on the Indians of the Southwest, 1533–1960*. Tucson: University of Arizona Press, 1962.

Stern, Alexandra Minna. "Buildings, Boundaries, and Blood: Medicalization and Nation-Building on the US-Mexico Border, 1910–1930." *Hispanic American Historical Review* 79, no. 1 (February 1999): 41–81.

Stoler, Ann L. *Race and the Education of Desire: Foucault's History of Sexuality and the Colonial Order of Things*. Durham, NC: Duke University Press, 1996.

Stratton, Porter A. *The Territorial Press of New Mexico, 1834–1912*. Albuquerque: University of New Mexico Press, 1969.

Szasz, Margaret. *Education and the American Indian: The Road to Self-Determination, 1928–1973*. Albuquerque: University of New Mexico Press, 1974.

Taylor, Quintard. *In Search of the Racial Frontier: African Americans in the American West*. New York: W. W. Norton, 1998.

Tobias, Henry J., and Charles E. Woodhouse. "New York Investment Bankers and

New Mexico Merchants: Group Formation and Elite Status among German Jewish Businessmen." *New Mexico Historical Review* 65 (January 1990): 21–47.

Trachtenberg, Alan. *The Incorporation of America: Culture and Society in the Gilded Age.* New York: Hill and Wang, 1982.

Trennart, Robert A. "Fairs, Expositions, and the Changing Image of Southwestern Indians, 1876–1904." *New Mexico Historical Review* 62 (April 1987): 127–50.

———. *The Phoenix Indian School: Forced Assimilation in Arizona, 1891–1935.* Norman: University of Oklahoma Press, 1988.

Ullman, Sharon R. *Sex Seen: The Emergence of Modern Sexuality in America.* Berkeley: University of California Press, 1993.

Utley, Robert M. *Billy the Kid: A Short and Violent Life.* Lincoln: University of Nebraska Press, 1989.

Van Kirk, Sylvia. *Many Tender Ties: Women in the Fur Trade Society, 1670–1870.* Norman: University of Oklahoma Press, 1980.

Waldstreicher, David. "Rites of Rebellion, Rites of Assent: Celebrations, Print Culture, and the Origins of American Nationalism." *Journal of American History* 82 (June 1995): 37–61.

Walkowitz, Judith R. *City of Dreadful Delight: Narratives of Sexual Danger in Late-Victorian London.* Chicago: University of Chicago Press, 1991.

Weigle, Martha. *Brothers of Light, Brothers of Blood: The Penitentes of the Southwest.* Albuquerque: University of New Mexico Press, 1976.

West, Elliott. *The Saloon on the Rocky Mountain Mining Frontier.* Lincoln: University of Nebraska Press, 1979.

White, Richard. *"It's Your Misfortune and None of My Own": A New History of the American West.* Norman: University of Oklahoma Press, 1991.

Wiebe, Robert H. *The Search for Order, 1877–1920.* New York: Hill and Wang, 1967.

Wilson, Chris. *The Myth of Santa Fe: Creating a Modern Regional Tradition.* Albuquerque: University of New Mexico Press, 1997.

Woodward, C. Vann. *Origins of the New South, 1877–1913.* Baton Rouge: Louisiana State University Press, 1951.

Young, Iris M. *Justice and the Politics of Difference.* Princeton: Princeton University Press, 1990.

Zelinsky, Wilbur. *Nation into State: The Shifting Symbolic Foundations of American Nationalism.* Chapel Hill: University of North Carolina Press, 1988.

INDEX

abortion, 112, 123–25, 138, 158, 207n35
Adams, David Wallace, 28
adultery, 16
advertisements: for alcohol, 156; for clothes, 152–55; about constipation, 157–59; for food and beverages, 156, 163; for patent medicine, 156–59; about sexual dysfunction, 159; for skin care, 155
advertising: and colonialism, 150; gender distinctions in, 159–60
African Americans, 6–7; and bodily comportment, 99–100; demographics of, 15, 101; and domesticity, 112–15, 120–21; and medicine, 127–30; newspaper depictions of, 97–100, 162–63; and racialization, 177; and sexuality, 53, 72–73, 101, 103, 107–8, 114–15
African ancestry, 10
age-of-consent laws, 68–69, 71–72

agriculture, 13–14
Albuquerque Indian School, 11–13, 29, 47–49
Albuquerque, NM: alcohol consumption in, 67; consumer culture in, 163, 168–69; demographics of, 10, 13, 150–51; marriages in, 104, 108–10; medicine in, 138; newspaper articles about, 85, 101, 111; prostitution in, 116–17, 165, 167, 170; public events in, 88–90, 93, 95, 97–99; rape trials in, 63–64
alcohol: advertisements for, 156; and Anglos, 134–35; consumption of, 165–66; and Hispanos, 59, 67–68; and Indians, 44–45, 128; and rape, 63–64, 66–68
Almaguer, Tomás, 72, 179, 181
American Indians. See Indians
American Medical Association, 125, 208n35
Anderson, Benedict, 91